Pregnancy Childbirth and the Newborn

A Complete Guide For Expectant Parents

by Penny Simkin, R.P.T.;
Janet Whalley, R.N., B.S.N.; and Ann Keppler, R.N., M.N.,
of the Childbirth Education Association of Seattle

Illustrations and Photographs
by Childbirth Graphics, Ltd.

Meadowbrook Books
18318 Minnetonka Boulevard
Deephaven, Minnesota 55391

Library of Congress Cataloging in Publication Data

Simkin, Penny, 1938-
  Pregnancy, childbirth, and the newborn.

  Bibliography: p.
  Includes index.
  1. Pregnancy.   2. Childbirth.   3. Infants (Newborn)—Care
and hygiene.   I. Whalley, Janet, 1945-
II. Keppler, Ann, 1946-   . III. Title.
RG525.S585   1984   618.2   83-21941
  ISBN 0-88166-004-3

The illustrations and photographs in this book were developed
by Childbirth Graphics, Ltd. Many of them are available as
full-size color posters or color slides. Contact Childbirth
Graphics, Ltd., P.O. Box 17025, Irondequoit Div. B., Rochester,
NY 14617.

Text design by Terry Dugan
Cover design by Anne Brownfield
Composition by Gloria Otremba
Keylining by Don Nicholes

The contents of this book have been reviewed and checked for
accuracy and appropriateness by medical doctors. However,
the authors, editors, reviewers, and publisher disclaim all
responsibility arising from any adverse effects or results that
occur or might occur as a result of the inappropriate application of any of the information contained in this book. If you
have a question or concern about the appropriateness or application of the treatments described in this book, consult your
health care professional.

10 9 8 7 6 5 4 3

Printed in the United States of America

Table of Contents

Dedication

To our families: Peter, Andy, Bess, Linny, Mary, and Lizzy Simkin; Doug, Scott, and Mike Whalley; Jerry, Eric, and Heidi Keppler;

To the thousands of expectant parents whom we have taught and who have taught us so much;

And to the Childbirth Education Association of Seattle, which since 1950 has educated, supported, and represented expectant parents in their transition to parenthood.

Acknowledgements

Pregnancy, Childbirth, and the Newborn is an outgrowth of the popular class manual, *Becoming Parents,* published by the Childbirth Education Association of Seattle. The first two editions were edited by Gillian Mitchell, then Education Director. The third edition, published in 1979, was revised and edited by Janet Whalley, Penny Simkin, and Ann Keppler. When we began revising once again, the project grew far beyond the original scope, resulting in a completely new book.

In writing this book, we have benefitted from the expertise and assistance of our colleagues in the Childbirth Education Association of Seattle—fellow instructors, knowledgeable parents, and professional consultants to our organization. We are particularly grateful to the following for reading chapters for clarity and accuracy: Julie Blystad; Celeste Gates; Sandi Hall; Claudia Hoffman; Judy Hulse; Laurie Jury; Julie Kirschbaum; Charlotte Kibbie; Sue Lentz; Pam Russo; Linda Whiteside; Sally Avenson, R.N., C.N.M.; John Coppes, M.D.; Steven Dassel, M.D.; Douglas DerYuen, M.D.; Lawrence Donohue, M.D.; James Joki, M.D.; Helen Kennison, R.N.; Jack Lamey,

M.D.; Virginia Larsen, M.D.; Ken Main, R.Pharm.; Lynn Moen; Michael Mulroy, M.D.; Carla Reinke, R.N., B.S.N.; Richard Soderstrom, M.D.; Carol Verga, R.N., C.N.M.; Nancy White, M.D.; Bonnie Worthington-Roberts, Ph.D.; Peggy Allen, R.N., B.S.N.; Lynn Bingisser, R.N., B.S.N.; Terry Elsas, R.N., M.N.; Pam Gaddis, R.P.T.; Judy Herrigel, R.N., B.S.N.; Bernice Kegel, R.P.T.; Carol McManus, R.P.T.; Candice Mentele, R.N., M.N.; Jackie Pendergrass, R.N.; Janet Peterson, R.P.T.; Denise Reinke, R.N., B.S.N.; Sue Sasnett, O.T.R.; Eileen Schroeder, R.P.T.; Kathy Stedman, R.P.T.; Nancy Street, R.P.T.; Carole Willison, R.N., B.S.N.

We have appreciated the patient cooperation of our editor, Tom Grady. We thank Jamie Bolane for her creativity and willingness to develop new illustrations to meet our needs. We also want to express our gratitude to our typist, John Maillet; to Velma Davis and Lola Caldwell, for support provided in numerous ways; and to Virginia Larsen, M.D., the founder of the Childbirth Education Association of Seattle, who continues to provide inspiration.

Preface

T he birth of a baby is the birth of a family—a joyous event with long-lasting significance. As childbirth educators, we have found that knowledge, preparation, and teamwork greatly enrich this experience. This book is the result of our desire to provide a complete and practical guide to childbirth and early parenthood. But we wanted to do more than that. We wanted to provide a personal approach. We recognize and respect the differences among women, men, couples, and babies—in personalities, health status, priorities, needs, and wishes. We hope our approach will help each woman and her partner learn what they need to make good decisions, to adapt the labor techniques to suit themselves, and, generally, to begin parenthood with the self-confidence that comes with understanding and active participation.

Although there are many ways to have a baby and many choices to make throughout the childbearing period, we all have some wishes in common. All parents, doctors, midwives, and other health care providers want, first and foremost, a healthy mother and a healthy baby. Everyone also wants emotional fulfillment for the family. In fact, emotional satisfaction is not a separate goal unrelated to health and safety, because psychological well-being enhances the physical health of both mother and baby.

Parents and their professional caregivers can best achieve these goals by working together to discuss and clarify their questions, concerns, and plans for care. This book can enhance their relationship by helping parents gain the information, skills, and confidence necessary to be responsible, active participants in their own care. A look at the table of contents indicates the wide range of topics discussed and the emphasis on responsible self-care.

We have made a special effort to fully describe labor as the normal physiologic process that it is. We hope to take the surprises out of the experience by showing the wide range of variations possible in the normal process. In addition, we have not neglected to discuss difficulties and complications. Throughout the book, we have emphasized what the mother or couple can do using their own resources to keep comfortable and enhance the labor pattern. We have also discussed the medical methods that can help when there are problems.

The psychomotor skills, such as exercise, relaxation, breathing patterns, labor positions and comfort measures, are a vital part of preparation for childbirth. In our combined thirty-seven years' experience in childbirth education, we have found that by presenting these skills within a broad, flexible framework, parents can adapt and individualize them to suit themselves. Thus, this book will be useful to women with differing personalities, individual styles of learning and coping, and unique labor patterns. The role of the father or labor companion is fully explored to enable each childbearing couple to find the best ways to work together.

Recognizing that the need for preparation is not limited to the birth experience, we have included an extensive discussion of the early parenting period. We present a problem-solving approach to the challenges of early parenthood—breastfeeding, infant behavior, sibling preparation, and changing family relationships.

We have enjoyed our work in bringing this book into existence. We hope our readers also find it enjoyable as they use it to prepare for a safe and joyful birth and a confident family beginning. If you have any comments about this book, you may direct them to us at the Childbirth Education Association of Seattle, P.O. Box 31234, Seattle, WA 98103.

Chapter One Becoming Parents

Pregnancy is a state of becoming: an unborn baby is becoming a person capable of life outside the safe, protective, and totally sufficient environment of the mother's body, and a man and woman are becoming parents. This state lasts about nine months, and it allows parents-to-be the opportunity to learn, adjust, plan, and prepare for parenthood. For most people, becoming parents is a greater life change than any other they will experience. Parenthood is permanent, and the physical, emotional, and spiritual nurturing of a child is both a heavy responsibility and a delightful opportunity.

Most mothers- and fathers-to-be look forward to the rewards and joys of parenthood. They want to produce the healthiest baby possible and bring up a happy, secure person who reflects their hopes and dreams. In fact, expectant parents spend much time individually and together thinking and dreaming about their child. What kind of person will the child become? What kind of guidance, role models, examples, and discipline are best? As they begin examining themselves and each other, evaluating their strengths and weaknesses as parents, some people wonder if they have the essential qualities of the ideal parent. They use the time during pregnancy to develop the characteristics they believe are essential in fulfilling their new roles.

Pregnancy is a positive growth experience for most expectant parents. This is a time to draw on or develop a support system—to talk to other pregnant women or expectant fathers; to find prenatal care and get referrals for assistance, if needed; to strengthen bonds or "mend fences" with their own parents; to take childbirth preparation and parenting classes; and to read books. This is a time to assess one's lifestyle and make changes if necessary to ensure optimal health (good diet, exercise, avoiding harmful substances.)

Birth as Transition

The birth process—labor and delivery—provides the transition from pregnancy to parenthood. In a day or less, the nine-month-long state of pregnancy is over, and the permanent state of parenthood has begun. Despite the relative brevity of childbirth, however, all cultures see it as an event equal in significance to death. Birth is celebrated everywhere as a joyous event, and is surrounded by rituals associated with hope, promise, and new life.

For the individual parent, the birth experience has great and lasting significance. The anticipation of birth brings to the surface a woman's deep feelings about her sexuality, her mother, her parents' relationship, her childhood, and her expectations of herself both in labor and as a mother. A man also looks at these factors in himself and in his own background as he anticipates fatherhood.

Their need to complete this major life transition with as much safety and emotional satisfaction as possible leads prospective parents to seek advice, guidance, and help. They may turn to experienced parents, their own parents, doctors, midwives, psychologists, nurses, childbirth educators, and authors of books. They store all the suggestions and advice they receive, along with their own experience, knowledge, and common sense. From all these influences, parents choose the pattern they will follow in preparing for childbirth.

As expectant parents, you have probably experienced some of the feelings described here. You may have been struck by the vast amount of information available, the number of "experts" ready and willing to advise you, and the number of decisions left for you to make. Perhaps this reflects the fact that pregnancy is usually a normal healthy process that you can understand well enough to make these decisions. Because pregnancy and birth are stressful, you will benefit greatly from medical supervision and advice, but childbearing is also highly personal and emotionally significant, and your participation in your care is necessary for maximum safety and satisfaction.

Pregnancy is not a disease, although at this time of extra demand on your body, you are more vulnerable to medical complications than at other times in your life. Therefore, you benefit from prenatal care and regular checkups throughout pregnancy. By the same token, labor is not an acute illness that ends when the baby is born, although it is a time of stress for both you and your baby that sometimes exceeds the boundaries of normal and requires medical intervention.

As long as pregnancy and birth remain normal, parents can, if they wish, play a major role in decision making. If a complication develops, then the medical caregiver assumes a greater role in this process.

There is no universal agreement among medical professionals or among the general public on the single best—safest and most satisfying—way to give birth, especially for the healthy woman experiencing a normal pregnancy. Many types of care are offered, and you, the expectant parents, should investigate the choices available and decide what kind of care seems appropriate to you, depending on your needs, desires, and priorities. Your choice of a caregiver and a place of birth determine, to a great extent, the kind of birth experience you will have. The following discussion will help you make informed decisions regarding your care.

Choosing a Caregiver

Your options for a caregiver are many. Obstetricians, family practitioners, midwives, and others provide care to the child-bearing woman.

Obstetrician/gynecologists have graduated from medical school and have had three or more years of additional training in obstetrics and gynecology. Much of the focus of their education is on detection and treatment of obstetrical and gynecological problems. To qualify for board certification, they must pass an exam administered by the American College of Obstetricians and Gynecologists.

Family practice physicians have graduated from medical school and have completed two or more years of additional training in family medicine. The focus of their education is on the health care needs of the entire family. Referrals are made when the care of a specialist is needed. To qualify for board certification, they must pass an exam administered by the American Academy of Family Practice.

Certified nurse-midwives (CNM) have graduated from a school of nursing, passed an exam to become registered nurses, and completed one or more years of additional training in midwifery. The focus of their education is on normal health care during the childbearing year, parent education, prevention of and screening for possible problems, and newborn care, making them specialists in the care of uncomplicated, normal pregnancies and births. Referrals are made to a physician when needed. To become certified, they must pass an exam administered by the American College of Nurse-Midwives.

Licensed midwives have completed training according to their state's requirements. Requirements vary from state to state. The focus of their education is similar to that of certified nurse-midwives. Referrals are made to physicians when needed. To become licensed, they must pass an exam administered by their state government.

There are others who provide care for pregnant and childbearing women. These include naturopaths, chiropractors, and lay midwives. Their qualifications and standards of care vary—some are skilled and some are novices. Some practice within the law and others practice without legal sanction.

An important consideration in choosing your caregiver is how specialized your care should be. This depends on your health care needs. If you are healthy and are experiencing a normal pregnancy, you can choose from any of the specialities offering maternity care. If your pregnancy is complicated or problems are anticipated during labor and birth, your options are more limited and an obstetrician should be involved in your care, either as your sole caregiver or in consultation with your family practitioner or midwife. The latter possibility is most likely if you live far away from an obstetrician, or if you are being cared for in a group practice that provides both midwifery or family practice and obstetrics.

In the United States, obstetricians provide most of the care to childbearing women. Family practice physicians are often chosen because they provide maternity care as well as medical care for the entire family. Having a midwife as caregiver is becoming an increasingly popular option. Parents choose midwives because midwives offer maternity care and counseling to healthy women who would like minimal intervention in pregnancy and birth and maximal involvement in their own care. Midwives deliver babies in a variety of settings—homes, hospitals, and birthing centers.

Another important consideration when evaluating caregivers is their general philosophical approach to pregnancy and childbirth, which is influenced by their education, training, and personal experiences. Some caregivers see pregnancy and birth as a family-centered event, and leave much of the decision-making to the parents. Some prefer to assume most of the decision-making and leave few choices to the parents. Some rely heavily on technology and interventions, such as electronic fetal monitoring, medications, and episiotomy, in caring for the healthy, normal childbearing woman. Others believe pregnancy and birth usually do not require intervention, and rely more on the woman's ability to contribute to a healthy pregnancy and on her body's ability to give birth. Look for a caregiver whose philosophical approach appeals to you, and who is qualified to provide care appropriate to your health needs.

Initial Interview

As you consider your options, feel free to shop around. Interview more than one caregiver, if necessary, before choosing. Because you will probably be charged for an office visit, you may want to do some initial screening over the phone. Ask the office nurse about the qualifications and experience of the doctor or midwife. Ask about fees, who takes calls when the caregiver is off duty, and where he or she delivers. Many physicians and midwives have privileges at more than one hosptial. Some caregivers attend births at home or in birthing centers. Ask the local childbirth education group for suggestions and referrals.

Think of your first office visit as a chance to interview the caregiver; do not assume that it commits you. Try to have a general idea of what you are seeking in a caregiver. Once you decide to make an appointment with a doctor or midwife, be ready to ask questions that will give you an idea of the philosophy and type of care offered.

Since an initial interview will probably last only fifteen to thirty minutes, you will need to select only a few key questions. Choose from the following list or develop your own. Become as knowledgeable as possible about your questions before your initial appointment. This book will provide background for your questions. Your interview will help you decide if the caregiver is suitable for you.

Questions to Ask

• What do you see as my role and responsibilities during pregnancy and childbirth?

• May my partner attend prenatal appointments with me? Are there any restrictions on his being with me throughout labor and birth? During a cesarean birth?

• How do you feel about other family members (children, grandparents, and so on) or friends attending prenatal appointments or being present at birth?

• What recommendations do you make on nutrition during pregnancy (for example, foods to eat and to avoid, weight gain, and so on)? Do you provide nutritional counseling? Do you have specific recommendations on exercise, sex, and use of medicines and drugs (including over-the-counter drugs, tobacco, alcohol, and so on)?

• What are your feelings about prepared or natural childbirth? Approximately what proportion of your clients or patients are interested in unmedicated or natural childbirth?

• Do you have routine standing orders for your patients in labor? What are they? Can they be altered to conform to my needs and desires? Would you encourage and help me prepare a Birth Plan—a written list of my preferences for care during birth and post partum? (See pages 12 to 20.) Will you check my Birth Plan for safety and compatibility with your practices and hospital policies?

• Does your hospital have a birthing room? Would you deliver my baby in the birth room?

• What are the chances you will be present when I deliver? If you are not there, who covers for you? Will I have a chance to meet that person? Will that person respect the arrangements I have made with you? Will the hospital staff?

• If my labor is progressing normally, is it likely I will have intravenous fluids, artificial rupture of the membranes, electronic fetal monitoring, or episiotomy?

• How often do you find it necessary to use pitocin, forceps, vacuum extractor, or cesarean birth?

• If I were to develop complications during pregnancy or labor, would you manage my care? If not, to whom would you refer me?

• What are your policies regarding contact between parents and their baby immediately after the birth? May our newborn be cared for while she is with us or must she go to the nursery? Who will examine the baby after birth?

• How would you feel about my leaving the hospital within hours after the birth if I wish? Do you or the hospital have instructions for me to follow after an early discharge? Is there follow-up care available for me (home visits by nurse, midwife, or doctor, or phone follow-up)?

• How would you feel about my staying in the hospital longer than the usual stay to get more rest or to stay with my baby if she has to stay longer?

As you discuss these questions, listen as much to how the caregiver answers as to what he or she actually says. Is the caregiver impatient with you, defensive, or open to and comfortable with your questions? The responses will help you discover how the caregiver feels about prospective parents who take their responsibilities seriously. How do you feel this person will manage your care? Is this the person you would like to provide your care during labor and birth?

Choosing Your Childbirth Classes

Many institutions, nonprofit organizations, groups of doctors or midwives, and individuals offer childbirth preparation classes. Their programs vary in size, philosophy, cost, number of classes in the series, topics covered, and in the background and training of the teachers. They also vary in quality. If you have a choice in your area, you would be wise to compare the classes available before choosing.

Questions to Ask

• Who sponsors the classes? Your hospital, your physician or midwife, an independent childbirth education association, the Red Cross, your public health department, or a nonaffiliated individual?

• What is the background of the teacher: registered nurse, physical therapist, teacher, psychologist, social worker, college graduate, other? What is her training: national training and certification through such well-known childbirth education organizations as the International Childbirth Education Association (ICEA), the American Society for Psychoprophylaxis in Obstetrics (ASPO), or the American Academy of Husband-Coached Childbirth (AAHCC)? Has she been trained by a reputable local childbirth education association? Has she been trained through apprenticeship or observation of another teacher? Is she self-taught?

• What is the philosophy and approach of the teacher? Does she cover normal childbirth and variations from normal? Does she describe choices available and their pros and cons? Does she offer techniques for natural or prepared childbirth? Does she describe advantages and disadvantages, risks and benefits of various practices, procedures, and medications? Does she emphasize the parents' right and responsibility to be informed and to make decisions?

• Does the teacher cover topics other than childbirth: nutrition, fetal development, emotional aspects of pregnancy and parenthood, baby care and feeding? Are early pregnancy classes available?

• How long is the class series? How much time is spent in lecture and discussion; how much in practicing exercises, relaxation, and comfort measures?

• What is the cost of the series?

• Does she teach a particular method (such as Lamaze, Bradley, Read, Kitzinger, or others) or has she developed a method from many sources?

• What is the ratio of students to teachers? If classes are large, are there assistants or other teachers available to ensure individual attention?

After you investigate the classes available, you will find the one most suitable for you. If there is little or no choice in your community, it is still preferable to take whatever class is available and supplement any weak areas with reading. The suggested reading list at the end of this book will be helpful.

The Place of Birth

In the Hospital While most people in North America give birth in hospitals, hospitals vary widely in the services they offer, their staffs' attitudes toward patients, and their philosophies of care. You may have no choice in a rural area, but if there is a choice, you should try to learn about several hospitals, take their tours, and choose carefully the one that best meets your needs.

Hospitals committed to family-centered maternity care strive to be flexible and responsive to the mother's needs and family's wishes. Many family-centered hospitals, in an effort to provide a more homelike atmosphere, have introduced birthing rooms or birth centers that are available primarily to low-risk women (healthy women with normal pregnancies). These areas are more attractively decorated than the average labor room, and have comfortable furniture, television, and other amenities. Fewer medical interventions are used here.

If needed, emergency care is readily available. Some hospitals without birthing rooms provide individualized care to their patients. Other hospitals, even those claiming to provide family-centered maternity care, are rigid. Their staffs tend to operate by routine and protocol, treating all patients alike and allowing parents little or no say in their own and their baby's care.

If you have had a difficult pregnancy or if complications are anticipated for labor or birth, you will need a hospital that is capable of providing intensive care and that has complete obstetrical, anesthesia, blood bank, and laboratory services available twenty-four hours a day.

It helps to know the philosophy or attitude, procedures, and services of the hospitals in your area so you can choose wisely, work to make some changes, or, at least, know what to expect in advance. See the section on Birth Plans for ideas about specific features to check when comparing hospitals. You might ask about any routines while on a hospital tour, or ask your caregiver since the doctor's or midwife's orders determine your care while you are in the hospital.

Out of the Hospital

A small percentage of low-risk American women give birth outside the hospital—in clinics, birth centers, or at home with midwives or doctors in attendance. In these settings, there are few routines and few medical interventions. In addition, the cost of such care is usually far lower than the cost of hospital care.

With an out-of-hospital birth, you are likely to avoid routine interventions such as intravenous fluids, restriction to bed, electronic fetal monitoring, medications, and other procedures of questionable value in uncomplicated labors. By the same token, it is more difficult to get these same interventions if they become desirable or necessary. You should be screened carefully during pregnancy. If there are warning signs (such as a rise in blood pressure, bleeding, sugar or protein in the urine, anemia, or other signs), you will be transferred to in-hospital care. Even with careful pregnancy screening, between 15 and 27 percent of women who intend to give birth outside the hospital are transferred to the hospital during labor or post partum for problems judged to require obstetrical intervention.* Most transfers during labor are for nonemergencies, such as prolonged labor, prolonged ruptured membranes, or postpartum bleeding, where intervention or medication will help but is not an immediate necessity for the welfare of the baby or mother.

Emergency transfers are extremely rare in women who have been screened and who have uncomplicated, normal pregnancies. The principal unpredictable life-threatening conditions that can arise during labor and that require immediate medical action are cord prolapse, when the cord slips out before the birth; hemorrhage; the deprivation of the fetus' supply of oxygen during labor (due to bleeding, cord compression, and other factors).* All of these conditions are extremely serious and can occur in a hospital, too, but the odds for a good outcome are better in a hospital with alert and capable staff. Any transfer is a disappointment and an added expense for those planning an out-of-hospital birth. When deciding where to have the baby, you should take the possibility of transfer into account, along with the more obvious considerations of autonomy for the parents, which is usually greater outside the hospital, and safety in emergencies, which is greater in well-equipped and well-managed hospitals.

The best place for you is the place where you will feel most safe and comfortable, and where you can get the help you want and need as you make the transition to parenthood.

When Your Options Are Limited

For many expectant parents, neither their place of birth nor their caregiver is completely satisfying; either they live in an area where the choices are limited, they have very specific or strong wishes, or communication is poor. If you discover that your needs and wishes are unlikely to be met by your caregiver or place of birth, investigate your options:

1. *Find a more compatible caregiver or change the place of birth, or both.*
2. *Try to negotiate, with the goal of coming closer to meeting your needs.*
3. *Accept what they offer.*

The first option has already been discussed, and the third needs no discussion. The second option, however, may be the most likely one for you, especially if you are reasonably satisfied with your care but wish to be sure of particular points. Negotiation is a matter of communicating your wishes to your caregiver, getting feedback, and then compromising to reach agreement on your care. Using a Birth Plan can help ensure that your care is suitable.

The Birth Plan

A Birth Plan is essentially a list of the options you and your partner prefer for your birth experience. There are several advantages to having such a list:

Advantages to you. Preparing a Birth Plan requires you to think about, learn about, and discuss the available options. It helps you clarify your preferences in your own minds. It also serves as a review of your knowledge of labor and birth. The Birth Plan gives you a concrete vehicle for discussion with your caregiver. By enhancing communication and clarifying your expectations of each other, a Birth Plan can build trust and understanding among all members of the childbirth team. Because it is available to the people who will care for you during labor and birth, the Birth Plan spares you from having to explain your wishes and expectations throughout. The staff can consult your plan instead.

Advantages to your doctor or midwife. A Birth Plan helps your doctor or midwife understand your goals and expectations. By taking an interest in your Birth Plan, your caregiver can encourage and assist you in preparing a realistic plan that all of you find satisfactory. Prior discussion allows your caregiver to note and discuss any areas of misunderstanding or disagreement, allowing you to talk them over and work out a suitable compromise. If your caregiver signs or initials the Birth Plan, indicating that he or she approves it, the Birth Plan can become part of your total care plan. Of course, the Birth Plan is not a binding legal agreement, and a signature is neither a promise nor a guarantee that circumstances will not require a change in the plan.

Advantages to the nursing staff. When you enter the hospital in labor, you will probably be a stranger to the nurses. A Birth Plan is a communication tool through which the nurses can quickly become better acquainted with you. It acts as a guide, letting the staff know that you prepared the plan when you were calm and thoughtful and that the plan is what you really want. They can individualize your care, provide some input from their perspective, and inform you of other options. They then can help you even if, under the stress of labor, you forget your plan or become preoccupied, thus sparing you from later feelings of disappointment or regret.

Getting Started with a Birth Plan

Once you decide to prepare a Birth Plan, you should tell your caregiver that you want to make one, even before you know exactly what will go into it. This may be a new idea for your doctor or midwife, who may wonder about it at first, especially if he or she is accustomed to being solely responsible and to making most decisions on your behalf. You will want to explain why you are preparing a Birth Plan and how you want it used. You should emphasize that you want your Birth Plan to enhance cooperation and trust between you and your doctor or midwife and to help you to know what you can expect.

Reactions of doctors and midwives vary. If your caregiver is opposed to a Birth Plan, then you have gained valuable insight and can act on it. You can either give in and give up your Birth Plan, negotiate, or find another caregiver. At the very least, you have clarified your relationship and will not be confused or surprised in labor. When a doctor or midwife is supportive of a Birth Plan, it can be an excellent educational opportunity to discuss and plan how your labor and birth will be managed. The cooperation and trust that develop carry through the birth experience and add much to the satisfaction felt by all concerned. If problems arise during labor, the underlying understanding and trust are most reassuring as you have to adjust to changes in the plan.

Language of a Birth Plan

The wording you choose can have substantial impact on how your caregiver receives your Birth Plan. Language that clearly expresses your preferences and reflects a spirit of flexibility and cooperation on your part will be greeted by your caregiver in the same spirit. If your list of preferences reads more like a list of demands, it will be received defensively. Be polite and respectful. Phrases such as "would prefer," "if possible," and "unless medically necessary" indicate that you understand that it may be necessary to modify your plan. You can take this possibility into consideration and devote a section of your Birth Plan to the unexpected. There are still options, even if your labor becomes complicated and requires medical interventions you wanted to avoid, or if your baby has health problems.

Components of the Birth Plan

Your Birth Plan should contain a section on *normal labor and birth*, *care of the newborn*, and *the unexpected* (a cesarean birth, a premature or sick baby, the death of the baby). The section on care of the newborn should be on a separate sheet of paper, because it is placed in the baby's chart after birth.

The section on the unexpected will probably not be needed, but will be most helpful if something unforeseen does arise. An unexpected cesarean can be a disappointment, but if you have thought through the possibility and have developed a plan that retains some of your priorities, you will feel better about the experience.

The stress of having a baby who requires special care is enormous. If you have thought about this possibility and stated your preferences, it will not only help the staff in caring for you and your baby, but will also ease the process of making decisions at a time when you may be unable to think clearly.

There is one other possibility that haunts most parents to some degree—the possibility that their baby will not live. In the United States, between one and two babies per hundred die around the time of birth. Although those odds are quite favorable, a baby is vulnerable at birth, so it is wise not to ignore this possibility. You will need help in understanding and accepting the death, and you will need support through the grieving process. Who can provide you with that support? What options might help you? Many counselors recommend that parents see and hold their dead baby. Naming the baby, taking a photograph, footprint, or a lock of hair are all ways to acknowledge the baby's life and provide memories. A funeral or memorial service provides an opportunity for family and friends to come together to grieve, say good-bye to the baby, and indicate their caring for you. These options can help parents emotionally in a very difficult time. So, make a plan for this possibility and put it aside. You will probably not need it, but if you do, you will have your own plans to follow at a time when you might be unable to make them.

Options to Consider for Your Birth Plan

Much of what is done during labor and birth is routine. Some routines, such as the backlying position of birth, the use of stirrups, and changes of shifts of nurses and other staff, exist for the convenience of the staff or caregiver. Others, such as the use of silver nitrate or antibiotics for the baby's eyes, are required by law. Some practices, such as shaving the perineum, enemas, the wearing of surgical masks by all except mother, holding the baby upside down by the heels, and so on, became routine at a time when they were believed to be beneficial, but now are known to be of little or no benefit. Some routines, such as anesthesia and circumcision, may present an element of risk to mother or baby that may not be worth taking, depending on the circumstances and the benefits to be gained. Some routines, such as feeding sugar water to the baby, are simply habits, and no one seems to know exactly why they began. Some require your informed consent—that is, your caregiver explains the procedure, its benefits and risks, and the alternatives (including not doing it) and their benefits and risks. Your consent is recorded on your chart. Find out which routines you are likely to encounter, along with the reasoning behind them. Some routines may be unnecessary if you are having a normal childbirth. This book discusses most of the routine practices you may encounter. Use it as background for your Birth Plan and for discussion with your caregivers.

In addition, your childbirth classes and your childbirth educator can be helpful resources as you prepare your Birth Plan, especially if she or he is familiar with the options available in your community. Use your childbirth educator as a consultant on local practices, choices available, wording to use, or any aspect of the Birth Plan where you need help.

PROCEDURES OR PRACTICES TO CONSIDER FOR YOUR BIRTH

The following is a list of common practices in labor, birth, and postpartum, along with options for handling each. Use this book and others, discuss the options with your childbirth educator and caregiver, and take tours of local hospitals to discover what you want. Then make up a rough draft of your Birth Plan. Go over it with your caregiver and make a final draft. Make several copies—one to keep, one for your chart, and one for your baby's chart.

Procedure or Practice	Options
During Labor	
Enema	• No enema. • Self-administered at home. • Administered in hospital. • Oil retention or water enema.
Prep (shaving of pubic hair)	• No removal of pubic hair. • Clip hair around vagina. • Shave hair around vagina. • Shave all pubic hair.
Presence of partner(s)	• Mother's choice • One or more partners present throughout labor and birth. • At doctor's, nurse's, or anesthesiologist's discretion.
Position for labor	• Freedom to change position and walk around. • Confined to bed in various positions. • Confined to one position in bed.
Onset of labor	• Spontaneous (begins on its own). • Self-induced: nipple stimulation, enema, castor oil. • Induced after fetal maturity studies for medical reasons. • Medical or surgical induction: artificial rupture of the membranes, prostaglandin gel, intravenous pitocin. • Induced without fetal maturity studies.
Hydration/fluids	• Drinking water, juice. • Popsicles. • IV fluids. • Ice chips only. • No liquids.
Vaginal exams	• At mother's request. • Only when labor changes. • Occasionally. • Frequent.

Procedure or practice	Options
Monitoring fetal heart	• Auscultation with stethoscope. • Auscultation with Doptone. • Intermittent external electronic fetal monitoring. • Internal electronic fetal monitoring for medical reasons. • Routine continuous electronic monitoring—internal or external
Pain relief	• Relaxation, breathing, comfort measures. • Medications, anesthesia only at mother's request. • Medications routine.
Enhance or speed labor	• Walk, change position. • Nipple stimulation. • Enema. • Rupture of membranes. • Pitocin.
To empty bladder	• Walk to toilet. • Bedside commode. • Bed pan in bed. • Catheterization.

During Birth

Procedure or practice	Options
Position	• Choice of position. • Lithotomy and stirrups.
Expulsion techniques	• Spontaneous, short bearing-down • Directed pushing. • Prolonged pushing.
Speed up birth	• Gravity-enhancing positions. • Prolonged pushing on command. • Episiotomy. • Forceps or vacuum extractor.
Bed for birth	• Mother's choice of birth chair, bean bag, floor, or bed. • Birthing bed. • Labor bed. • Delivery table with stirrups.
Cleanliness of perineum	• Undraped, mother touches baby during birth. • Sterile, with drapes, masks, etc.
Care of perineum	• Try for intact perineum with massage, support, and hot compresses. • Anesthesia, episiotomy, and stitches. • Ice packs immediately after birth.

Procedure or practice	Options
After Birth	
Delivery of placenta	• Spontaneous. • Encouraged with breast stimulation, baby suckling. • Hastened with massage of the fundus, pitocin. • Manual extraction.
Cord cutting	• Clamp and cut after it stops pulsating. • Father cuts cord. • Clamp and cut immediately.
Baby Care	
Airway	• Baby coughs and expels own mucus. Suctioned if necessary. • Suction almost immediately. • Deep suctioning.
Warmth	• Baby skin-to-skin with mother, with blanket covering both. • Wrapped in heated blanket. • Placed in Kreiselman unit—bassinet with radiant heater. • Placed in thermostatically controlled, heated isolette.
Immediate care	• Baby held by parents and suckled by mother. Observed in parents' arms. • Kept near parents in bassinet or isolette. • Taken to nursery for observation, weighing, and feeding.
Eye care	• None. • Nonirritating agent, such as erythromycin or tetracycline, within 1 hour. • Silver nitrate, within 1 hour. • Silver nitrate immediately.
First feedings	• Breastfeeding on demand. • Scheduled breastfeeding. • Water, by medicine dropper or bottle, given by parents or nurse. • Glucose water. • Demand feedings with infant formula. • Scheduled formula feedings.
Contact with baby	• 24-hour rooming-in. • Daytime rooming-in. • For feedings only, in nursery at other times.
Circumcision	• None. • With parents present to comfort baby. • With no anesthesia. • With anesthesia. • Out-of-hospital circumcision.

Procedure or practice	Options
Discharge of mother and baby	• When desired. • Within 6 to 12 hours of birth. • 3 or more days after birth.

THE UNEXPECTED

If problems develop either during labor or afterwards, you may have to relinquish some of your desired options, and more interventions may be necessary for safety. The following are some options that are usually available even under such circumstances.

Cesarean Birth

Procedure or practice	Options
Timing (if cesarean is planned)	• After labor begins. • Scheduled before labor begins.
Partner's presence	• Father or partner present. • No partner present.
Anesthesia	• Regional anesthesia with little or no premedication. • Regional anesthesia with premedication. • General anesthesia.
Participation	• Screen lowered at time baby is delivered. • Anesthesiologist or obstetrician explains events. • No explanation to parents.
Contact with baby	• Held by father soon after birth, where mother can touch and see. • Breastfeeding as soon as possible. • Sent immediately to nursery or intensive care.
Discharge	• After 5 days. • After fewer than 5 days.

Premature or Sick Infant

Procedure or practice	Options
Contact with baby	• Parents visit and care for baby as much as possible. • If baby is in another hospital from mother, father goes with baby. • Baby separated from parents with little or no visiting.
Feeding when baby is able to digest food. Before this point, the baby will need to be fed intravenously.	• Mother nurses baby. • Mother's expressed milk to be given to baby by bottle, dropper, or tube. • Formula feeding by bottle, dropper, or tube. • Fed by parents or nurse.
Contact with support group	• Initiated by parents, nurses, or support group. • No contact.

As you can see, preparing a Birth Plan requires much time, thought, and information-gathering on your part. By the time you have finished, you should have a fairly complete picture of what you can expect in your birth experience and immediately afterwards. Not only will you and your caregivers have decided how your uncomplicated, normal labor and birth will be managed, but you will also know how unexpected variations and complications will be handled. The "homework" you do as you prepare your Birth Plan helps take away the surprises later when you need to rely on your caregivers to help you through labor and birth. The decisions you make in advance, when you are calm, nonstressed, and able to concentrate, will help carry you through and guide you and your caregivers at a time when you and your partner need to devote all your mental and physical energies to coping with childbirth.

Decisions to Make for the Postpartum Period

There are many other decisions to make during pregnancy that will affect you and the baby after birth. These also require information-gathering, discussion, and introspection.

• Who will provide health care for your baby? A pediatrician, family practice physician, nurse practitioner, or well-child clinic?

• Will your baby be breast- or bottlefed?

• Who will help at home after the birth?

• What preparations are needed for the baby (car seat, crib, room, clothes, and so on)?

• Will you work outside the home after the baby is born? If so, when? Who will provide child care? What are your options regarding working—part time, full time, long maternity leave? Will you continue to breastfeed while working?

While this list of questions is by no means complete, it gives you an idea of the kind of planning to begin now. Using the time during pregnancy to plan for post partum will ease the transition to parenthood.

Chapter Two **Pregnancy**

T he normal and healthy process of pregnancy brings profound physical and emotional growth for the expectant mother and similar psychological changes for the expectant father. This chapter explores the many changes you will experience during pregnancy and the dramatic fetal growth and development that take place from conception to birth. To help you understand pregnancy, information on reproductive anatomy, sexual function, and the process of conception will also be provided.

Reproductive Anatomy and Sexual Function

The Male   The *external genitalia* of the male consist of the *scrotum* and the *penis*. The scrotum contains two *testicles*, or male sex glands, which produce *sperm* or *spermatozoa*. Each testicle contains over 800 small, tightly coiled tubes, known as *seminiferous tubules*, which produce hundreds of millions of sperm in response to a hormone produced by the *pituitary gland*, located in the brain. Another hormone from the pituitary gland stimulates the testicle to produce the male sex hormone *testosterone*, which is not only responsible for the male's sexual characteristics (deep voice, facial and body hair, and others), but also ensures adequate development of sperm.

The seminiferous tubules join together to form the *epididymis*, a wider coiled tube that stores the sperm until they are mature and motile. As it leaves the scrotum and enters the pelvic cavity, the epididymis becomes the *vas deferens*, a duct that carries and stores the sperm. Into this duct the seminal vesicles, the prostate gland, and Cowper's glands also secrete fluids, and these secretions nourish the sperm and aid motility and fertility. Together with the sperm, these secretions make up the semen that is ejaculated into the vagina during sexual intercourse.

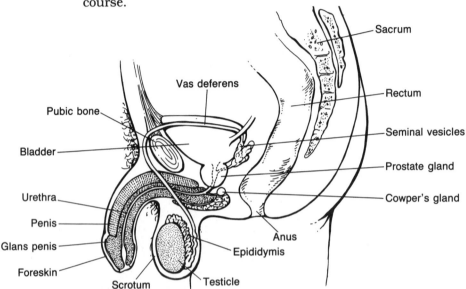

The male *urethra*, an extension of the vas deferens, leads from the bladder to the end of the penis. It serves the double function of transporting urine from the bladder and semen from the vas deferens. During urination and most other times, the penis is soft or flaccid. With sexual excitement, blood rapidly fills the tissues of the penis, causing it to expand and become firm and erect, facilitating insertion within the vagina during intercourse. With sexual excitement, muscles contract to close the duct to the bladder, keeping urine out of the semen. During orgasm, ejaculation triggers involuntary muscle contractions, which propel semen through the urethra. The penis normally ejaculates about three milliliters (less than a teaspoon) of semen, containing 150 million to 450 million sperm.

The Female

The following description and the accompanying illustrations of the female's reproductive anatomy and physiology provide the background for later discussion of conception, pregnancy, and birth. (They will also help you understand the exercises suggested in this book.)

A woman's *perineum* includes the pelvic floor muscles, external genitalia, urethra, anus, and perineal body (the area between the vagina and anus). The external *genitalia* include the vaginal opening, *clitoris*, *labia majora*, *labia minora*, and *mons pubis* (the fatty tissue over the pubic bone). The internal reproductive organs are the uterus (sometimes called the womb), the vagina, two fallopian tubes, and two ovaries. The *uterus* is a hollow, muscular, pear-shape organ situated in the pelvis—behind the bladder and in front of the rectum. Divided into two parts, the uterus has an upper part called the *body* and a lower part called the *cervix*, which protrudes into the *vagina*, the stretchy canal connecting the internal and external genitalia. Two *fallopian tubes* extend from the upper sides of the uterus toward the ovaries.

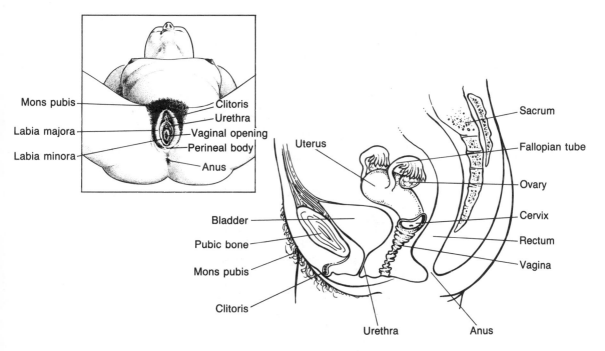

The two *ovaries*, located on each side of the uterus, are a woman's sex glands. One of their functions is to produce *estrogen* and *progesterone*, the female sex hormones. During adolescence, along with hormones from the pituitary and adrenal glands, estrogen stimulates the development of secondary sexual characteristics in the female, such as enlarged breasts, body hair, and others. The ovaries also ripen and expel *ova* (eggs). Of the hundreds of thousands of ova present in the ovaries, only about 400 to 450 actually are expelled (ovulated) in a woman's lifetime.

During a woman's reproductive years, except during pregnancy, the ovaries undergo cyclic changes, which occur monthly. The *menstrual cycle* is influenced by pituitary hormones, which cause an ovum to mature and its *follicle* (the sac surrounding the ovum) to enlarge and secrete estrogen. This process then stimulates the growth of the *endometrium* (the lining of the uterus).

Only one ovum is usually released from its follicle each month in a process called *ovulation*, which occurs about halfway through the menstrual cycle. After leaving the ovary, the ovum slowly drifts along the fallopian tube to the uterus. Under the influence of another pituitary hormone, the follicle begins producing progesterone, which stimulates further development of the lining of the uterus, enabling it to receive and nourish the fertilized ovum. If fertilization does not occur, the levels of estrogen and progesterone decrease, and the uterus sheds its unneeded lining along with the unfertilized ovum. This monthly shedding process is called menstruation.

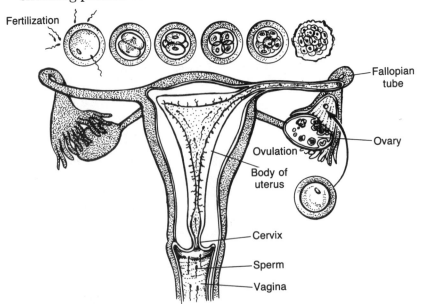

Becoming Pregnant—Conception

Becoming Pregnant—Conception

After sexual intercourse, sperm travel from your vagina through the cervix, into the cavity of the uterus, and along the fallopian tubes. Conception takes place when a single sperm penetrates or fertilizes an ovum, forming a single cell; at that moment you become pregnant and a new life begins. While many of the 150 million to 450 million sperm in the ejaculate reach the ovum, only one penetrates it, after many others have paved the way by dissolving the substances that surround the egg. Once an ovum is fertilized, a chemical reaction occurs, preventing other sperm from penetrating it. After fertilization, which usually takes place in the outer one-third of the fallopian tube, the ovum travels along the fallopian tube and several days later embeds within the lining of the uterus.

The inherited characteristics of your unborn child are determined at conception. Each ovum and sperm contains twenty-three chromosomes (which contain genetic material), half the number contained in all other human cells. The union of egg and sperm gives the fertilized ovum the full component of forty-six chromosomes—twenty-three from the mother and twenty-three from the father. These twenty-three pairs of chromosomes combine to give the baby unique inherited characteristics and traits such as skin, hair, and eye color; approximate height and body shape; blood type; sex; and many others.

One pair of chromosomes determines your new baby's sex. Women have a matching pair of X chromosomes (XX); all your ova carry X chromosomes, meaning that your baby will always get one X from you. Men have one X and one Y chromosome in their set of sex chromosomes, so some sperm carry X chromosomes and others carry Y chromosomes. Consequently, the sex of your unborn child is determined by the chromosome that the father contributes. For example, if a sperm carrying an X chromosome fertilizes the egg, the baby is a girl (XX); if the sperm carrying a Y chromosome fertilizes the egg, the baby is a boy (XY).

Confirming Your Pregnancy

Although pregnancy can be detected soon after you conceive, you might not suspect you are pregnant or test for pregnancy until you have missed a menstrual period. A pregnancy test checks your urine or blood for human chorionic gonadotropin (HCG), a hormone produced only during pregnancy. If you think you are pregnant, have your pregnancy confirmed early so you can get prenatal care, avoid environmental hazards, and pay special attention to your nutritional needs.

EARLY SIGNS AND SYMPTOMS OF PREGNANCY

- *Missed menstrual period.*
- *Breast changes (a heavy and full feeling, tenderness, tingling in the nipple area, and a darkened areola).*
- *Fullness or ache in the lower abdomen.*
- *Fatigue and drowsiness; faintness.*
- *Nausea or vomiting, or both.*
- *Frequent urination.*
- *Increased vaginal secretions.*
- *Positive pregnancy test.*

Calculating Your Due Date

Fetal life begins with the fertilization of the ovum, which occurs about two weeks after your last menstrual period. The length of the pregnancy, however, is calculated from the first day of your last menstrual period and lasts an average of 280 days or forty weeks. When the doctor or midwife says you are twelve weeks pregnant, it means that the fetus is ten weeks old. To calculate your due date, your caregiver subtracts three months from the first day of your last menstrual period and adds seven days. It might be more accurate to count ahead 266 days from the exact date of conception, but this may not be known. Normal pregnancies vary in length. It is best to think of your due date as approximate and expect the baby anytime within two weeks before or after that time. Two-thirds of all babies are born within ten days of their due dates.

Changes during Pregnancy for Mother, Father, and Baby

Pregnancy brings profound changes in your body, emotional adjustments for you and your partner, and dynamic growth and development of the fetus. Many of the physical changes that will occur are caused by changes in hormone production.

- *Human chorionic gonadotropin* (HCG), produced by the developing placenta, assures that the ovaries produce estrogen and progesterone until the placenta matures and takes over production of these hormones.

- *Estrogen* promotes the growth of the reproductive tissues by increasing the size of the uterine musculature, promoting growth of the uterine lining and its blood supply, increasing the amount of vaginal mucus, and stimulating the development of the duct system in the breasts. The high levels of estrogen in pregnancy probably influence water retention, subcutaneous fat buildup, and skin pigmentation.

- *Progesterone* inhibits smooth muscle contractions, so high levels of progesterone decrease the frequency of uterine contractions, helping to maintain your pregnancy. Progesterone also slows down or inhibits the contractions of the smooth muscles of other organs—such as the stomach and bowels, bladder and ureters, and walls of the blood vessels—and stimulates the secretion of the ovarian hormone *relaxin*, which relaxes and softens the ligaments, cartilage, and cervix, allowing these tissues to spread during the birth. Finally, progesterone raises your body temperature.

- Besides estrogen and progesterone, *other hormones* that influence growth, mineral balance, metabolism, and corticosteroid levels are produced in greater quantities and cause many physical changes during pregnancy.

Pregnancy is divided into three trimesters, each lasting approximately three months.

The First Trimester

The first trimester (the first three calendar months of pregnancy) is the "developmental period" for the fetus, since by the end of this period, all the fetal organ systems are formed and functioning. For you, the first trimester is a time of physical and emotional adjustment to the pregnant state.

The First Four Weeks of Pregnancy (conception to two weeks of fetal life)

Implantation in uterine wall

Fetus

After it has been fertilized, the ovum quickly changes from one cell to many. Within thirty minutes it begins dividing into two cells, then four, eight, sixteen, and so on. By the end of two days the cluster of cells is known as the *morula*. It takes about five days for the waving movements of tiny hairs (the cilia) and the contractions of the fallopian tube to propel this rapidly developing life along the tube to the uterus.

The fertilized ovum (now called a *blastocyst*) comes to rest on the uterine lining and implants usually in the upper part of the uterus. The blastocyst then develops tiny, rootlike projections (*chorionic villi*) that penetrate and extract nourishment from the uterine lining.

During the early weeks of pregnancy, the fertilized ovum receives its nourishment from the uterine lining (the endometrium), which becomes thicker and more vascular during your pregnancy. At the end of the first month of development, the chorionic villi extend well into the uterine lining and become an early placenta. Fetal blood circulates through this rootlike formation while your blood circulates into the spaces (intervillous spaces) surrounding the villi. A thin membrane separates the two blood streams and normally they do not mix.

Through a complex process of cell division and differentiation, the fetus, placenta, and amniotic sac and fluid are formed. The amniotic sac surrounds the blastocyst; later the fluid within the sac protects the fetus by acting as a buffer, maintaining an even temperature, and allowing for easy movement.

Expectant Mother

While all these events are occurring in and around the baby, you may have noticed only some breast swelling or tenderness, or an ache in your lower abdomen. And you have missed a menstrual period. The remarkable changes that you will experience have just begun.

The Fifth to Fourteenth Weeks of Pregnancy
(third to twelfth weeks of fetal life)

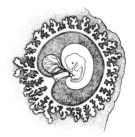

Five weeks

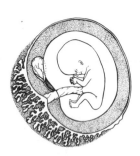

Eight weeks

Fetus

During the fifth to fourteenth weeks of pregnancy, the baby, now called an *embryo*, develops rapidly. A primitive nervous system, with a brain and a spinal column, begins to form. The circulatory system also develops, with the heart beating by the twenty-fifth day after conception. Although the embryo is only half the size of a pea, the body has a head, with eyes, ears, and a mouth forming. There are simple kidneys, liver, and digestive tract and a primitive umbilical cord. On the twenty-sixth day, arm buds appear and two days later, leg buds.

Although your baby's sex is determined at conception, the anatomy of the male and female baby appears the same until the fetus is about seven weeks old. Between the developing leg buds is a slit with a knob of tissue, the *genital tubercle*. Within the abdomen of the embryo are two embryonic sex glands. During the seventh week, if the embryo is male, the Y chromosome stimulates these sex glands to begin producing androgens, male hormones that cause the two sides of the slit to join, forming the scrotum. They also cause the genital tubercle to develop into a penis. In late pregnancy, the testicles descend from the abdomen into the scrotum. In the female, the embryonic structures take the female form—the slit becoming the vulva (or external genitalia), the genital tubercle becoming the clitoris, and the sex glands remaining within the baby as ovaries.

By the eighth week of fetal life, the embryo is complete. The face has eyes, nose, ears, and a mouth with lips, a tongue, and tooth buds in the gums. The arms have hands with fingers and fingerprints. The legs have knees, ankles, and toes. The new body also functions: the brain sends out impulses that coordinate the functions of other organs, the heart beats strongly, the stomach produces digestive juices, the liver manufactures red blood cells, and the arms move. The embryo grows about one millimeter a day, with different parts developing on different days. Between forty-six and forty-eight days the first true bone cells replace cartilage in the skeleton. Embryologists have determined that when these first bone cells appear in the upper arms, the embryonic period is complete. The developing baby is now called a *fetus.*

By the end of the third month of fetal life, the fetus is considerably active, although you probably do not yet detect any movements. Legs kick and arms move. The fetus can frown or smile, swallow amniotic fluid, and urinate. Drops of sterile urine mix with the amniotic fluid, which is exchanged and replaced about every three hours. Vocal cords are complete and shallow respiratory movements occur, but no sounds are produced nor actual breathing done because the fetus is in a watery environment. Eyelids cover the eyes and remain closed until the sixth

First trimester

month of fetal life. The sex can also be detected by now. By this time the baby is about three inches long and weighs about one ounce.

Placenta

By the third month of pregnancy, the placenta is completely formed and serves as an organ for producing hormones and exchanging nutrients and waste products. It is through the placenta that oxygen and nutrients such as dextrose, protein, fat, water, vitamins, and minerals are passed from you to the fetus. The placenta also provides protection against most bacteria, although most viruses and drugs cross from your bloodstream to the fetal system. Waste products from the fetus are exchanged through the placenta and are carried by your blood to your kidneys and lungs for excretion.

Expectant Mother

During this period, you may feel extraordinarily tired and require more sleep because of the new demands on your energy and because of the subsequent shift in your rate of metabolism. You may also experience nausea and vomiting during the early months of your pregnancy. Although this is usually called "morning sickness," it can occur at any time of the day and is thought to be caused by human chorionic gonadotropin (HCG), produced by the developing placenta. (See page 26 for more on HCG.) Ways to cope with the nausea and vomiting are discussed in chapter 4.

Although your breasts develop in puberty, the glandular tissue that produces milk does not fully develop until you become pregnant. As the levels of estrogen, progesterone, and other hormones increase during pregnancy, your breasts change. They will enlarge, and you may notice more prominent veins and feel a tingling sensation in your nipples. The area around each nipple (the *areola*) also enlarges and becomes darker. Little bumps, called *Montgomery glands*, become more prominent in this area and enlarge to produce more lubricant for the areola.

You may need to urinate frequently because of pressure of the enlarging uterus on your bladder. In addition, your vagina and cervix become bluish in color (*Chadwick's sign*), the cervix becomes softer, and vaginal secretions increase. Because the changes, although dramatic in nature, have been miniscule in size—the top of the uterus reaches barely above your pubic bone—you *feel* more different than you look.

Along with the physical changes, the early months of pregnancy are often filled with emotional ups and downs. The thought of motherhood may at times be pleasing to you, at other times not. You may cry easily. Mood swings seem more pronounced and may be difficult for you and your partner to understand.

Expectant Couple

Finding out that you are actually pregnant may bring about a mixture of emotions in you and your partner: pride in your ability to produce a child; fear of losing your independence; apprehension about changes in your relationship; doubts about your ability to parent; and happiness about becoming parents. Sharing your thoughts and feelings with each other can help you work through this time of transition.

Your sexual relationship may change during the first trimester. You may experience an increased interest in spontaneous sexual activity in pregnancy because you no longer have to worry about trying to get pregnant or trying to avoid pregnancy. Or your interest in sexual intercourse may decline because of fatigue, nausea, breast changes, or fear of miscarriage. If you have miscarried before or have bled vaginally during the pregnancy, there is good reason to avoid intercourse in the early months of pregnancy. Otherwise you and your partner should discuss your feelings about intercourse and do what is mutually desired.

The Second Trimester

The Fifteenth to Twenty-seventh Weeks of Pregnancy (thirteenth to twenty-fifth weeks of fetal life)

Fetus

The thirteenth week of fetal life marks the beginning of the "growth period," when the already formed organs and structures of the fetus enlarge and mature. Head hair, eyelashes, and eyebrows appear. Fine, downy hair (called *lanugo*) develops on the arms, legs, and back of the fetus. Fingernails and toenails appear. The heartbeat is stronger and can be heard by the seventeenth or eighteenth week with a stethoscope placed on your abdomen (or as early as the tenth week if an ultrasound fetal stethoscope is used).

By the end of the twenty-fourth week, the fetus is about twelve inches long and weighs about one and a half pounds. The skin is wrinkled and covered with a creamy protective coating called *vernix caseosa*. At some point during this period, you will probably feel the fetus move (called *quickening*). At first, you may feel a light tapping or fluttering sensation that reminds you of gas bubbles, or the gentle movements of the small fetus may go unnoticed until activity becomes more vigorous.

Expectant Mother

During these middle months of pregnancy, you will probably feel physically well, and your nausea and fatigue will lessen or disappear. The growth of your baby will continue, and your uterus will expand into your abdominal cavity in response to the enlarging fetus, placenta, and increased amniotic fluid. By

Second trimester

the end of the fifth month of pregnancy, the top of your uterus (called the *fundus*) reaches your navel. During monthly visits, your caregiver will measure the height of your fundus to make sure that the fetus is growing adequately and to estimate the length of your pregnancy. Although there are differences in fetal size and amount of amniotic fluid, the length of your pregnancy can be approximated by measuring the distance in centimeters between your pubic bone and the top of your uterus.

Your breasts will not increase much in size during the second trimester, but *colostrum* (a yellowish fluid produced before breastmilk) is usually present in the milk glands by the middle of pregnancy. Now is the time to begin preparing your breasts for breastfeeding. See chapter 12, page 238.

Just as your nipples and areola get darker during pregnancy due to hormonal changes, other skin areas also become more pigmented. If you are dark-haired, a line (called the *linea nigra*) between the pubic bone and the navel will darken. *Chloasma*, the mask of pregnancy, may appear as brown, irregularly shaped blotches around your eyes and nose. These areas of darker skin usually disappear after the birth of your baby.

Along with the physical changes, psychological changes occur in response to the advancing pregnancy and to the changes in your shape and size. Some women enjoy how they look, while others consider themselves unattractive, inconvenienced, and restricted. A heightened sense of growth and creativity may make you more aware of and moved by everyday experiences—a kind word, a beautiful sunset, a touching photograph, a needy child. In the middle months, you may want to start preparing for parenthood by reading books about child care or preparing the nursery and layette. You may recall more of your dreams than you did before pregnancy.

Expectant Couple

During the second trimester, pregnancy becomes more real for your partner. He can feel the baby move when he places his hand on your abdomen or when you are in close physical contact. This contact with the developing baby enhances his feelings of closeness and his interest in the pregnancy and the baby. He may or may not like your changing appearance.

During a normal pregnancy, you and your partner may continue sexual intercourse without harm to the fetus, who is thought to be adequately protected from penetration and the strong contractions that sometimes accompany orgasm by the structures of the pelvis, the cushioning effect of amniotic fluid, and the seal provided by the amniotic sac and mucous plug. Another concern has recently been raised about the safety of intercourse—a possible association between intercourse and infection of the amniotic membranes. Further research is needed to confirm this link and to examine risk factors.*

Your sexual interest may change during the last half of pregnancy. Intercourse in the traditional position with you on your back and your partner above can become awkward and uncomfortable as your abdomen enlarges. You may want to experiment with different positions and alternative methods of satisfaction. Stroking, caressing, or massaging are pleasurable ways to express a loving relationship without intercourse. Talking to each other about your physical and emotional needs can help you satisfy each other and enjoy the pregnancy.

The Third Trimester

The Twenty-eighth to Thirty-eighth Weeks of Pregnancy

(twenty-sixth to thirty-sixth weeks of fetal life)

Fetus

The third trimester is the "finishing period" for the fetus. Babies born during this period are able to survive, although their chances for both survival and easier transition to independent life improve as they near their due date. In late pregnancy, antibodies pass through the placenta to the fetus, providing your baby with short-term immunity to the diseases to which you are immune. Consequently, a premature infant receives less protection than a baby who is born at term.

During the last three months, the fetal features are refined: the fingernails reach the fingertips and may even need cutting at birth, the hair on the head grows, the lanugo almost disappears, fat is deposited under the skin, and buds for the permanent teeth are laid down behind the milk teeth buds.

You can learn much about your baby at this time. The fetus has periods of sleep and wakefulness and responds to bright light. Loud external noises may elicit a reaction and stir him into action. The baby can hear your voice and may respond to it after birth; and, of course, he hears other sounds as well: your digestion and heartbeat, the circulation of blood within your uterus, and other external sounds, such as music, your partner's voice, and so on.

At some point during the last trimester your baby assumes a favorite position or lie, usually head down. During prenatal visits your doctor or midwife will examine your abdomen to determine which position the fetus has adopted. The procedure used is known as *Leopold's maneuvers.*

As your baby grows and gains weight, his activity diminishes since there is less room to move. You may feel arm and leg movements rather than whole body shifts. If you feel a series of rhythmic jolts, your baby probably has the hiccups. Your baby may start sucking his thumb while still in the womb. The fetus gains about three and a half pounds and grows about five and a half inches during this part of your pregnancy.

Expectant Mother

During the third trimester, your uterus expands to a level just below your breast bone. Crowding by the uterus, in addition to high levels of progesterone, may give you indigestion and heartburn. You may also experience shortness of breath as your uterus presses upward on your diaphragm and ribs. Varicose veins in the legs, hemorrhoids, and swollen ankles sometimes develop due to the increased pressure within your abdomen, the decreased blood return from your lower limbs, and the effect of progesterone, which relaxes the walls of the blood vessels.

During the final months of pregnancy, you may develop small red elevations on the skin, called *vascular spiders*. These vascular changes may appear on your upper body and be accompanied by reddened palms. Also during this time, you may develop stretch marks on your abdomen, thighs, or breasts. These marks, called *striae gravidarum*, are reddish during pregnancy and become glistening white lines after the birth. Many women attempt to prevent these stretch marks by applying various lotions or oils to their skin, but there is no evidence that they are effective.

By the ninth month, you will probably start looking forward to the end of the pregnancy, relief from the physical discomforts, and the long-awaited joy of having the baby. You may become more introspective and find yourself thinking more and perhaps worrying about labor, birth, and the baby. Through childbirth education classes, you and your partner can learn more about labor, birth, and how to cope with the stresses of late pregnancy.

Expectant Couple

You and your partner may feel protective of the developing baby. You may find yourself more dependent on others. As you anticipate the responsibilities of parenthood, you may think more of your own parents and of the role models they provided. Adjustments in your sexual relationship continue as your abdomen enlarges. The lines of communication should remain open between you and your partner as your feelings, needs, and desires change.

Third trimester

The Thirty-ninth and Fortieth Weeks of Pregnancy (thirty-seventh and thirty-eighth weeks of fetal life)

Fetus

During the last two weeks, the fetal organs continue to mature to prepare your baby for life outside your uterus. The fetus also adds fat and gains about a pound. At birth, the average baby weighs about seven pounds, although the weight of a full-term baby can vary from five and a half to ten pounds. They average twenty inches in length, but a range of eighteen to twenty-two inches is normal. During pregnancy, the weight of the fertilized egg has increased six billion times! In the next twenty years, weight will only increase twenty times.

Placenta

The mature placenta is flat and round, about six to eight inches in diameter, and one inch thick; it weighs about one-seventh of the fetus' weight. The size and weight vary in proportion to the size of the baby.

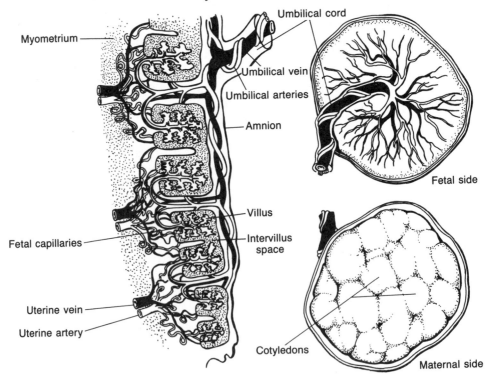

The side of the placenta that implants in the uterine wall (the maternal side) is rough and bloody, and it is divided into lobes called *cotyledons*. As the placenta ages, hard gritty areas (calcium deposits) begin to appear in this side. The fetal side of the placenta is smooth, pale, and shiny and is covered by the amniotic membrane. The amniotic and chorionic membranes extend from the edge of the placenta to form the sac (or bag of waters) that contains the amniotic fluid and fetus. Branches of the umbilical vein and arteries can be seen on the fetal side of the placenta spreading out from the umbilical cord.

Umbilical Cord

The umbilical cord links the placenta to your unborn baby. It extends from the fetus' navel to the approximate center of the placenta. The average cord length is twenty inches, but twelve to thirty-nine inches is considered normal. The moist, white cord has a spiral appearance; two arteries and one vein twist within it. Fetal blood flows at about four miles an hour, keeping the cord stiff like a garden hose full of water. At birth, as your baby breathes, her circulation pattern begins to change, sealing off the blood flow to her navel and rerouting more blood to her lungs.

Expectant Mother

About two weeks before the birth, your profile may change as the fetus descends into the pelvic cavity. This noticeable descent is called *engagement* or lightening. You will feel less pressure on your diaphragm and may find it easier to breathe and eat as the fetus becomes engaged in the pelvis. However, since the fetal head now presses on your bladder, you will need to urinate more frequently.

Toward the end of your pregnancy, noticeable contractions of the uterus increase in frequency. These *Braxton-Hicks contractions*, which have occurred intermittently throughout your pregnancy, help increase the efficiency of the uterine circulation. Though usually not directly associated with labor, these contractions ripen the cervix and prepare the uterine muscles for labor. As your pregnancy draws to a close and the fetal head presses into your pelvis, your cervix will become softer and thinner. This thinning is called *effacement* and is a sign of readiness for labor and birth.

Awkwardness and fatigue may add to your desire for the pregnancy to end. You may feel as though you have been and will be pregnant forever. At the same time, you may also experience a "nesting urge" in the form of a spurt of energy often resulting in preparations for your new baby. You will visit your physician or midwife more frequently as these physical changes indicate that your body is preparing for labor and birth. Soon the pregnancy will be over and another stage in your life cycle—parenthood—will begin.

Calendar of Pregnancy

The following Calendar of Pregnancy summarizes the changes commonly experienced during pregnancy. As you can see, pregnancy profoundly affects at least three people—the mother, the father, and the fetus. Use the calendar to help you anticipate and understand the changes.

CALENDAR OF PREGNANCY

First Trimester (First Three Months)

Fetal age	Conception to Four Weeks	Eight Weeks	Twelve Weeks
Fetal growth	• Is 1/4 inch long. • Rudimentary eyes, ears, mouth, and brain are forming. • Spine and spinal cord are forming. • Simple digestive system is developing. • Umbilical cord is forming. • Heart is beating by the 25th day. • Is called "ovum" until 2 weeks.	• Is 1-1/8 inches long and weighs 1/30 ounce. • Face is forming, eyes are shut. • Arms and legs are forming. • Long bones, internal organs, and brain are forming. • Tooth buds are forming. • Is now called an "embryo."	• Is 3 inches long and weighs 1 ounce. • Arms and legs can move. • Fingers and toes are formed. • Fingerprints are present. • Can smile and frown. • Sex is distinguishable. • Can urinate. • Is called a "fetus."
Placental and uterine changes	• Uterine lining is thick with increased blood supply, uterus is enlarging. • Cervix becomes softer. • Implantation of ovum is usually in upper back portion of uterus. • Placenta and umbilical cord are forming. • Chorionic gonadotropin is produced by chorionic villi (which become the placenta) and present in mother's blood and urine (used for pregnancy test).	• Uterus is size of a tennis ball. • Umbilical cord has definite shape. • Amniotic fluid cushions fetus, maintains even temperature, and allows easy movement.	• Uterus is size of a grapefruit. • Fundus is just above pubic bone. • Amniotic fluid fills uterine cavity and is continually replaced. • Placenta is small but complete; there is full exchange of nutrients and waste products. • Placenta is now the major source of estrogen and progesterone.
Common physical changes in mother	• Is not menstruating. • Has fullness or ache in pelvis. • May be nauseated, may vomit. • Is tired. • Has increased vaginal secretions. • May feel faint.	• Has to urinate more frequently. • Breasts are fuller, nipples may tingle, areola is darker. • May lose or gain up to 5 pounds.	
Common emotional changes in mother	• Focus is on body changes. • Moods widely vary. • "Motherhood" feelings are being sorted out. • Time seems long.		
Common emotions of father	• Is concerned with partner's mood swings and fatigue. • Pregnancy seems unreal.		
Common changes for both	• Parenting roles and priorities are questioned. • Sexual relationship may change. • May feel ambivalent toward pregnancy: joy and excitement vs. resentment and panic. • Feelings toward own parents are examined. • Finances may affect attitudes about approaching parenthood. • Well-being of baby may be a concern.		

CALENDAR OF PREGNANCY

Second Trimester (Middle Three Months)

Fetal age	Sixteen Weeks	Twenty Weeks	Twenty-four Weeks
Fetal growth	• Is 6 inches long and weighs 4 ounces. • Heartbeat is strong. • Muscles are active. • Skin is thin, transparent. • Downy hair (lanugo) covers body. • Fingernails and toenails are forming. • Swallows amniotic fluid.	• Is 10 to 12 inches and weighs 1/2 to 1 pound. • Heartbeat is audible. • Sucks thumb. • Hiccups. • Hair, eyelashes, eyebrows are present.	• Is 11 to 14 inches and weighs 1 to 1-1/2 pounds. • Skin is wrinkled and covered with protective coating (vernix caseosa). • Eyes are open. • Meconium is collecting in bowel. • Has strong grip.
Placental and uterine changes	• Uterus is 3 inches above pubic bone. • Placenta performs nutritional, respiratory, excretory, and most endocrine functions. • Amniotic fluid increases in amount.	• Uterus is at level of navel. • There are 2 to 3 pints of amniotic fluid. • Placenta is full size and covers about half the inner surface of uterus.	• Uterus is above level of navel. • Placenta is covering less of inner surface of uterus as uterus grows.
Common physical changes in mother	• Fetal movement is noticeable. • Nausea is usually gone. • Linea nigra may appear. • Mask of pregnancy (chloasma) may appear. • May become constipated. • May have food cravings (Pica). • May develop vaginitis. • May have nasal congestion.		• Pelvic joints are relaxing. • May have leg cramps. • Gums or nose may bleed. • Side or groin may be painful from round ligament contractions. • Voice may change. • Weight gain is from 13 1/2 to 15 1/2 pounds (0.8 to 1 pound per week).
Common emotional changes in mother	• Pregnancy is accepted and there is more interest in baby and parenting. • Daydreaming and dreaming at night increase. • Sense of growth and creativity develops. • Changing appearance brings varying feelings. • Time seems short.		
Common emotions of father	• Has varying feelings about partner's changing appearance. • Is evaluating readiness and ability to be a father.		
Common changes for both	• Sexual desires may change. • Pregnancy becomes more enjoyable. • Awareness of parenting styles increases.		

CALENDAR OF PREGNANCY

Third Trimester (Last Three and a Half Months)

Fetal age	Twenty-eight Weeks	Thirty-two Weeks	Thirty-six Weeks
Fetal growth	• Is 14 to 17 inches long and weighs 2-1/2 to 3 pounds. • Is adding body fat. • Is very active. • Rudimentary breathing movements are present.	• Is 16-1/2 to 18 inches and weighs 4 to 5 pounds. • Has periods of sleep and wakefulness. • Responds to sounds. • May assume birth position. • Bones of head are soft and flexible. • Iron is stored in liver.	• Is 19 inches and weighs 6 pounds. • Skin is less wrinkled. • Vernix caseosa is thick. • Lanugo is mostly gone. • Is less active. • Is gaining immunities from mother.
Placental and uterine changes	• Uterus is 3 finger-breadths above navel. • Amniotic fluid diminishes.	• Uterus is 6 finger-breadths above navel. • Braxton-Hicks contractions are more noticeable.	• Uterus is just below breast bone. • There are about 3 pints of amniotic fluid. • Efficiency of placenta is decreasing. • Hormone production is decreasing.
Common physical changes in mother	• May have backache. • May have heartburn. • May have shortness of breath. • May have hemorrhoids. • May have varicose veins. • May have anemia. • May have insomnia.	• Ankles may be swollen. • Stretch marks may appear. • Perspiration may increase. • Vascular spiders may appear. • Metabolism increases. • Urination usually increases. • Total weight gain is usually 24 to 30 pounds.	
Common emotional changes in mother	• Is focused on birth, possibly apprehensive of labor, delivery, the unknown. • Dependency on others increases. • Desires protection. • Time is a burden.		
Common emotions of father	• Is protective of family. • Questions fathering role. • May long for independence. • May question ability to provide support in labor.		
Common changes for both	• Changes in sexual relationship are still occurring. • Fears and concerns about pain of labor and birth, health of mother and baby, and responsibilities of parenting are felt.		

CALENDAR OF PREGNANCY

	Third Trimester	Birth	Post Partum
Fetal age	*Thirty-eight Weeks*		*Post Partum-The First Weeks*
Fetal growth	• Is about 20 inches; average weight is about 7 pounds. • Fingernails protrude beyond fingers. • Head is large compared to body; arms and legs are in flexed position. • Body fat is ample. • Lungs are mature.		• Newborn needs: sleep (10 to 20 hours/day), food and sucking, warmth, comfort—touching, cuddling, skin contact.
Placental and uterine changes	• Uterus is back to height at 34 weeks. • Placenta is 6 to 8 inches in diameter, 1 inch thick, and about 1 pound. • Umbilical cord is 12 to 39 inches (usually 20 to 22 inches), moist, white, twisted or spiral in appearance.		• Uterus is at height of navel right after birth and almost back to prepregnant size by 10 days postpartum.
Common physical changes in mother	• Braxton-Hicks contractions, lightening—engagement, increased energy, effacement are prelude to labor. • Contractions, bloody show, progressive effacement and dilatation, backache, ruptured membranes, and loose bowel movements may be signs of labor.		• Afterpains in uterus are common. • Urination and perspiration often increase. • Lochia (vaginal flow) is present. • Breasts enlarge if breastfeeding. • May be fatigued or excited and then fatigued. • Weight loss may be 10 to 15 pounds in early post partum. • If breastfeeding, menstruation will not return for several months; if not breastfeeding, should return in 4 to 8 weeks. • Ovulation may be delayed, but is possible within weeks.
Common emotional changes in mother			• Mood swings. • May have anxiety that increases with fatigue. • May be ambivalent toward the baby. • Time seems nonexistent.
Common emotions of father			• Is protective of family. • May feel left out at this time.
Common changes for both	• Are mentally prepared for birth. • Are excited and apprehensive, or both.		• Trial and error period; need sense of humor. • Sexual relationship is readjusted; contraception is needed. • Busy time; keep lines of communication open. • Parenting responsibilities are realized.

Chapter Three Prenatal Care

T horough prenatal care helps assure the birth of a healthy baby. Shortly after you become pregnant, you will start seeing your physician or midwife on a regular basis. During these prenatal visits, you will undergo certain routine examinations, and you will have an opportunity to ask questions and discuss your pregnancy with your caregiver. This is also the best time to discuss the idea of a Birth Plan and begin to work with your physician or midwife in the planning of your birth experience. At some time during your pregnancy, the father or your birth companion should accompany you to meet your caregiver and discuss his or her role at the birth. You should also try to meet your doctor's or midwife's partners or colleagues, since they might be on call at the time of birth.

Prenatal Exams

The following tests and examinations are performed at the first or second prenatal visit:

1. *A complete medical history and physical examination*

2. *A pelvic (vaginal) examination*
  - To estimate the size and shape of your pelvis
  - To confirm your pregnancy
  - To do a Pap smear to detect cervical cancer
  - To test for gonorrhea

3. *Blood tests*
  - To determine your blood type, Rh factor

- To test for anemia
- To test for infection
- To test for syphilis
- To test for German measles immunity
- To confirm your pregnancy

4. *Urine tests*
  - To check for protein, sugar, etc. (urinalysis)
  - To check for infection
  - To confirm your pregnancy

As your pregnancy progresses, you will visit your doctor or midwife each month; then every two weeks; then, toward the end of pregnancy, every week. At each prenatal visit, your caregiver will assess your health and the health of the developing baby. The procedures carried out at each visit include:

1. *A weight check*

2. *A blood pressure test*
  - To detect high blood pressure (hypertension or preeclampsia)

3. *Urine tests*
  - To detect excess protein, which may indicate preeclampsia
  - To detect high sugar levels, which may indicate diabetes

4. *Abdominal exams*
  - To measure the growth of the uterus (fundal height), which indicates the growth of the fetus and the length of the pregnancy
  - To estimate the size and position of the fetus (through Leopold's maneuvers)

Besides having these procedures, part of each prenatal visit is spent discussing your questions and concerns and your caregiver's recommendations about nutrition, exercise, employment, and the progress of your pregnancy.

Complications during Pregnancy

Early recognition and treatment of the complications that can develop during pregnancy are more likely if you are knowledgeable and observant. Since your doctor or midwife sees you only periodically during your pregnancy, keep him or her informed of any problems or adverse changes arising between visits. Optimal prenatal care depends on cooperation between the expectant parents and their caregiver.

Miscarriage

A *miscarriage*, or spontaneous abortion, is the unexpected and involuntary expulsion of the embryo or fetus before the twentieth week of pregnancy. Most of the time, doctors cannot determine what causes a miscarriage. Occasionally, a miscarriage occurs because of an acute infection, a severe physical shock, or an imbalance of hormones; more often it is caused by a defective ovum or sperm or by a faulty intrauterine environment.

The signs of a possible miscarriage are vaginal bleeding and intermittent pain. The pain often begins in the lower back and is later felt as abdominal cramping. Only rarely can a miscarriage be stopped. However, if you suspect you are having a miscarriage, call your caregiver for advice on what to do, for confirmation of the miscarriage, and to help ensure healing afterwards.

The majority of expectant parents who lose a baby from miscarriage feel shocked, grief-stricken, and depressed, even when the pregnancy has not been visible to others. A number of support groups and books are available to help you cope with this difficult time. (See Recommended Reading.)

Hyperemesis Gravidarum

Although rare, a condition called *hyperemesis gravidarum*, characterized by persistent nausea and vomiting, may begin in the first trimester. The condition is also accompanied by severe weight loss, dehydration, and changes in blood chemistry. Treatment, which is highly successful, includes medication to relieve nausea and vomiting or hospitalization to restore the balance of body fluids, or both. (For more information on hyperemesis gravidarum, see pages 63 to 64.)

Ectopic Pregnancy

Ectopic (or extrauterine) pregnancy is a rare condition in which the fertilized ovum implants itself outside the uterus, most commonly in the wall of a fallopian tube. The condition is frequently called a tubal pregnancy. The most common symptom of an ectopic pregnancy is abdominal pain. Because of the danger of a ruptured fallopian tube, treatment usually involves surgery—and termination of the pregnancy.

High Body Temperature (Fever)

A *high body temperature* for a prolonged period, especially in early pregnancy, may harm your baby. To lower a fever, drink plenty of liquids or take a lukewarm bath, sponge bath, or shower. Consult your doctor or midwife if your fever is over 100 degrees F. and certainly before taking any medication, even aspirin. Also be aware that hot tubs and saunas may raise your body temperature to a dangerously high level. (See chapter 4 for further discussion.)

Placenta Previa

In *placenta previa*, a condition that occurs about once in 200 pregnancies, the placenta is implanted over (or partially over) the cervix. The most characteristic symptom is vaginal bleeding after the seventh month of pregnancy; the bleeding is usually intermittent and is not usually accompanied by pain. As with any bleeding from the vagina, you should notify your physician or midwife immediately. An ultrasound or X-ray is often ordered to determine the location of the placenta and the cause of bleeding. Treatment might involve bed rest and close medical observation or, depending on your due date, a cesarean birth.

Abruptio Placentae

Abruptio placentae, the premature separation of the placenta from the uterus, occurs about once in 200 pregnancies, most often in the third trimester or during labor. Any or all of the following symptoms might appear: abdominal pain, tenderness and rigidity of the uterus, and vaginal bleeding.

Besides the danger of hemorrhage to the mother, extensive separation of the placenta deprives the baby of adequate oxygen, causing serious fetal distress. Treatment of abruptio placentae depends on how much bleeding has occurred and how far the labor has progressed. It commonly involves a cesarean birth.

Sexually Transmitted Diseases

Venereal disease or a *sexually transmitted disease* (STD) can also complicate and endanger your pregnancy. If you have (or have had) an STD, you must tell your physician or midwife, because your baby risks disease, death, or both. In the past, the infections commonly associated with sexual intercourse were syphilis and gonorrhea. Today other highly contagious infections, such as genital herpes and chlamydia, can also cause serious problems for the baby.

If you or your partner has (or has had) genital sores, discharge from the vagina or penis, difficulties with urination, or other genital discomforts, tell your physician or midwife so you can be tested and possibly treated. Treatment during pregnancy may include antibiotics or treatment of symptoms. Cesarean birth is the treatment of choice if you have a herpes sore in or around the vagina when labor begins, since the baby can become seriously infected during passage through the vagina.

Diabetes

Diabetes mellitus affects the body's ability to use sugar because of diminished insulin production and presents special problems for the pregnant woman. During pregnancy, diabetes becomes more difficult to control and can affect the unborn baby. If you are pregnant and diabetic, you need the care of a specialist.

Occasionally, a woman will exhibit signs of diabetes *after* she becomes pregnant. The discovery of sugar in the urine of a pregnant woman who is not diabetic indicates *gestational diabetes*. Detecting and treating this temporary condition is important if the pregnancy is to have a healthy outcome. Treatment usually involves a special diet and, in some cases, insulin injections. The mother and unborn baby must be observed closely, since the functioning of the placenta may be impaired near the due date and labor may need to be induced.

Preeclampsia (Toxemia)

One serious illness that occurs only during pregnancy is *preeclampsia*, also called toxemia. Preeclampsia is characterized by a sudden and excessive retention of fluid, rapid weight gain, an elevation of the blood pressure, and the presence of protein in the urine. Sometimes headaches, disturbances of vision, and dizziness also occur. If you have any of these symptoms, report them to your caregiver immediately.

Although its cause is not yet understood, statistics show that preeclampsia occurs in about 5 percent of pregnancies. It is more common in first-time mothers, especially teenagers and women over thirty. Women with chronic diabetes or high blood pressure, twin pregnancies, or poor diets are also more likely to develop preeclampsia. Undiagnosed and untreated, preeclampsia can progress to the severe stage—*eclampsia*—characterized by convulsions, coma, and, sometimes, fetal and maternal death.

The treatment for preeclampsia includes bed rest, close medical supervision, reduction of blood pressure, and sometimes delivery of the baby by induction of labor or cesarean section. Medications may be used to relax the mother, lower her blood pressure, and decrease the risk of convulsions. Recovery usually takes place soon after the birth of the baby.

Pregnancy in Women Over 35 Years Old

Advanced age is considered to increase the likelihood of pregnancy and labor complications, especially in the first-time mother. The chances of a number of complications, such as Down's syndrome in the baby, preeclampsia, and poor labor pattern, increase with age. If she has had thirty-five or more years of good health, the odds for a healthy pregnancy are better than if she is in less than optimal health. Aside from the recommendation that she have amniocentesis in early pregnancy to detect any of a number of inherited disorders or fetal defects, the pregnant woman over thirty-five is usually advised to do the same as any pregnant woman—take good care of herself, get good prenatal care, and enjoy the pregnancy.

Multiple Pregnancy

Any pregnancy in which the woman carries more than one baby is called a multiple pregnancy. Twins are relatively common, occurring about once in every eighty pregnancies. *Fraternal* twins are produced by the fertilization of two eggs by two sperm. *Identical* twins occur when one sperm fertilizes one egg, which later divides into two developing babies. One out of every three sets of twins is identical. Triplets occur about once in every 6,400 pregnancies, and quadruplets or quintuplets are even more rare.

A multiple birth may be suspected if two or more fetal heartbeats are heard or if you have a family history of twins, gain weight rapidly, or exceed normal uterine growth. Although ultrasound can usually confirm a multiple pregnancy, some remain undetected until birth.

Expecting twins can be both exciting and stressful. The experience will place extra demands on your body. You may be encouraged to increase the number of calories in your diet and you may need to rest more, because of fatigue and the possibility of premature labor. Since the birth of twins is complicated, you will probably be cared for by an obstetrician rather than a midwife or a family practitioner, and you will be at greater risk for prenatal complications. In addition to increased medical attention, you can also expect more attention from your friends and relatives.

Helpful books and support groups are available to help parents of twins cope with their unique emotional and practical problems. The National Organization of Mothers of Twins Club (5402 Amberwood Lane, Rockville, MD 20853) provides information, support, and the names of local twin groups.

Rh Incompatibility

Special care will be given to the pregnant woman with Rh (Rhesus) negative blood. About 85 percent of the population is Rh positive, which means they have the Rh factor (antigen) in their blood. You will be tested for the presence of Rh factor early in your pregnancy. If you are Rh negative (that is, if you have no Rh factor) and the baby is Rh positive, it is possible for the Rh factor from the baby to pass into your bloodstream. If this is your first pregnancy, the baby will probably be unaffected. However, if the condition is untreated, you will probably produce antibodies against the Rh factor. The next Rh positive baby you have may be harmed when your antibodies cross the placenta and actually destroy some of your unborn baby's red blood cells.

To avoid problems with subsequent pregnancies, the Rh negative mother is given an injection of Rh immune globulin (RhoGAM) after the birth of each Rh positive baby. This medication usually controls the problem of Rh incompatibility. An Rh negative mother who has a miscarriage or abortion should also receive this drug, in case the fetus was Rh positive.

If you are Rh negative, the number of antibodies in your blood will be assessed throughout your pregnancy. If you have become sensitized to the Rh factor, the number of antibodies increases, warranting further studies. Amniocentesis, the removal of amniotic fluid from the uterus, provides information on the effects of this sensitization on the fetus, who can suffer from mild to severe jaundice and anemia. Treatment possibilities include early delivery of the baby or, in selected cases, intrauterine blood transfusion. Newborn infants may be given blood transfusions if they have been severely affected by Rh incompatibility.

WARNING SIGNS DURING PREGNANCY

During your pregnancy, report any of the following warning signs to your doctor or midwife. In addition, your caregiver may ask you to report other pertinent signs and symptoms.

Warning Signs	Possible Problems
Vaginal bleeding	• Miscarriage • Placenta previa • Abruptio placentae • Premature labor
Abdominal pain	• Ectopic pregnancy • Abruptio placentae • Premature labor contractions
Leaking or gushing of fluid from the vagina	• Rupture of the membranes
Sudden puffiness or swelling of the hands, feet, or face.	• Preeclampsia (toxemia)
Severe, persistent headache	• Preeclampsia (toxemia)
Disturbance of vision— spots, flashes, or blind spots	• Preeclampsia (toxemia)
Dizziness, light-headedness	• Preeclampsia or supine hypotension (page 78)
Pain or burning sensation on urination	• Urinary tract infection • Sexually transmitted disease
Irritating vaginal discharge, genital sores, or itching	• Vaginal infection • Sexually transmitted disease
Fever—oral temperature over 100 degrees F.	• Infection
Persistent nausea or vomiting	• Hyperemesis gravidarum • Infection
Noticeable reduction in fetal activity	• Fetal distress

Tests for Fetal Well-Being and Maturity

If your physician or midwife suspects a pregnancy complication or if more information is needed on the size, age, or condition of the unborn baby, he or she will schedule additional tests. One test, Fetal Movement Counts, can be performed by the expectant mother at home. Others are performed in the clinic or hospital and require the expertise of the medical staff and the use of medical technology. Because many of the diagnostic examinations involve risks as well as benefits, carefully weigh the risks against the benefits before taking these tests. Before deciding on any prenatal test, it is also helpful to know whether and how the test results will affect your care.

In addition to the physician's or midwife's explanation, the chart on pages 49 to 50 provides basic information on the usual diagnostic tests. Ask questions before and during the examinations to reduce your anxiety, help you make decisions, and make you feel more comfortable.

Fetal Movement Count

The sample fetal-movement-count chart below* shows how to record daily fetal movements. You can make one out of squared paper. During the last few weeks of your pregnancy, keep track of your baby's movements. Even though babies move less toward the end of pregnancy, most healthy babies move at least ten times in a twelve-hour period; some move ten times in a half-hour. Daily fetal movement counts can help you evaluate your baby's well-being.

Each day, count the number of times you feel your baby move and indicate with an "S" on the chart the time you start counting. (This will depend either on your daily schedule or on the time of day your baby is most active.) When you have counted ten fetal movements, stop counting, and fill in the box corresponding to the time period during which the tenth fetal movement occurred. For instance, if you start counting at 9 a.m., place an "S" at that time. If you feel the tenth movement at 12:20 p.m., fill in the box that corresponds to 12:30 p.m. If you do not feel ten movements in twelve hours, write down the number of movements you have felt, and call your doctor or midwife to report this information.

	S	M	T	W	Th	F	S
8:00			S		S		
8:30	S			S		S	
9:00		S					
9:30							S
10:00			■				
10:30					■		
11:00							
11:30	■		■				
12:00							
12:30		■					■
1:00							
1:30							
2:00							
2:30							

TESTS FOR FETAL WELL-BEING AND MATURITY

The following tests evaluate the condition of the fetus and are rarely used by themselves. For example, if there is a question about fetal well-being in early pregnancy, an ultrasound and an amniocentesis might be ordered. If a question arises in later pregnancy, the doctor or midwife might ask you to count fetal movements daily, collect urine for estriol studies, and come in once or twice a week for non-stress testing. Ultrasound might also be used. If fetal well-being is still in question, a contraction stress test might be performed.

Test	Benefits/Purposes	Risks/Disadvantages
Amniocentesis. After a local anesthetic is given to numb the skin, a needle is passed through the abdominal and uterine walls into the amniotic sac, and fluid is withdrawn and sent to a laboratory for the appropriate examinations. Amniocentesis is usually performed in conjunction with ultrasound so the placement of the fetus, placenta, and umbilical cord can be determined.	• Provides information on certain genetic characteristics or diseases, fetal lung maturity, the age of the fetus, and the fetal condition (specifically, Rh incompatibility). • Helps make a decision about continuing or terminating a pregnancy.	• Risks miscarriage. • Risks injury to the fetus, placenta, or cord (greatly reduced if ultrasound is used prior to "tap"). • Produces a small amount of discomfort. • Is invasive and costly. • Timing may be a problem, since genetic analysis is not done until the fourteenth to the sixteenth week of pregnancy, and results are not available for about four weeks.
Fetoscopy (Visualization). This procedure is still in the experimental stage. After a local anesthetic is given, a small incision is made near the woman's pubic bone and a needle and small tube are inserted through the uterus into the amniotic sac. Then the needle is removed and a tiny lighted fiberoptic scope is inserted through the tube, allowing the examiner to see the fetus.	• Helps determine whether the fetus has any visible defects. • Allows treatment of the fetus (for example, blood transfusion).	• May have side effects for mother and fetus that are unknown at this time. • Carries same risks as amniocentesis in late pregnancy. • Is invasive, costly, and not widely available.
Ultrasound. High frequency sound waves are beamed into the woman's abdomen. The "echoes" bounce back from the baby, the placenta, and the mother's internal organs and are transmitted onto a video screen. It takes fifteen to thirty minutes to get an outline of the fetus and other structures.	• Confirms whether the pregnancy is uterine or ectopic. • Helps estimate the age of the fetus (by measuring the length of the fetus in the first trimester or the size of the head in the second trimester). • Helps assess the position and the condition of the placenta. • Detects how the fetus is lying in the uterus. • May confirm a multiple pregnancy. • Gives immediate results.	• Not established as being safe to the fetus in the long term, though it is probably safer than X-ray. • Is costly. • Has an accuracy rate dependent on the skill of the person interpreting the results and on the gestational age of the fetus. • Requires that mother have a full bladder, which may be uncomfortable.
X-ray. Ionizing radiation is used to take an internal picture of the mother and the fetus. (X-rays are used much less frequently since ultrasound has been developed.)	• Helps determine the size and shape of the mother's pelvis. • Helps discover the size and position of the baby. • Helps determine the location of the placenta.	• Is dangerous, since prenatal exposure to radiation has been associated with cancer and genetic mutations in babies.

Test	Benefits/Purposes	Risks/Disadvantages
Fetal movement counts. During late pregnancy, the woman counts and records the number of fetal movements she feels each day. (Most healthy babies move at least ten times in twelve hours.) See page 48.	• Helps assess the well-being of the fetus. • Is relatively simple and inexpensive. • Is noninvasive. • Is readily available.	• Requires more work by expectant mother. • Is not fully established as a reliable procedure. • Is difficult for mother to determine exactly what constitutes a single fetal movement.
Non-stress test. The fetal heart rate (FHR) is measured for about thirty minutes with an external electronic fetal monitor, and fetal rest and movement are noted. If there is no spontaneous fetal movement, the examiner may push on the woman's abdomen to stimulate movement. An increase in heart rate during fetal movement is a sign of well-being—called a positive or reactive test.	• Helps predict fetal well-being. • Costs less than oxytocin challenge test (described below). • Does not require hospitalization. • Is noninvasive.	• Is limited by lack of standardization in conducting the test. • Produces occasional false results.
Contraction stress test (CST) or oxytocin challenge test (OCT). This test indicates how the FHR responds to uterine contractions. The woman is given a form of oxytocin or her nipples are stimulated (causing a natural release of oxytocin) until she has three contractions within a ten-minute period. An electronic fetal monitor measures the FHR. Test results are negative if the heart rate remains normal. Test is positive if FHR indicates fetal distress, which may call for induced labor or a cesarean.	• Helps indicate how well the fetus can withstand the stress of labor contractions. • Helps determine if a high-risk pregnancy can be continued or should be terminated.	• May possibly induce premature labor. • Could lead to unnecessary intervention if results are false positive. • Is costly, since it is usually performed in the hospital or clinic.
Estriol excretion studies. Estriol, made jointly by the fetus and placenta, is a form of estrogen. The estriol content of a woman's 24 hour urine collection or a single sample of her blood is measured in several consecutive studies (usually weekly). If estriol drops, it is a sign that the fetus is not tolerating the pregnancy well.	• Helps estimate the efficiency of the placenta and the status of the fetus. Used when deciding whether to end or continue a complicated pregnancy.	• Is not considered accurate enough to be the only test used before deciding to induce or perform a cesarean. • Is costly. • Produces variable results with multiple pregnancy, the presence of a kidney infection, or the use of certain drugs.
Biophysical profile. This test evaluates 5 components—non-stress test, fetal movement, muscle tone, fetal breathing movements, and amniotic fluid volume. (The last 4 are determined by ultrasound.) Each component is scored from 0-2, so the possible total is 10 points.	• Is rapidly performed in office or clinic. • Is relatively risk-free. • High (6-10) and low (0-2) scores are fairly good predictors.	• Reliability is uncertain at this time, since the test is new. • Intermediate scores (3-5) are difficult to interpret.

Chapter Four
Nutrition and Health during Pregnancy

Your eating habits before and during pregnancy affect your baby's health as much as or more than any other single factor. Since eating properly greatly influences the future health of your baby, you should have a clear understanding of what is involved in providing the best nourishment for yourself and your unborn child.

It is never too late in pregnancy to improve your eating habits, since your baby will benefit from any improvements you make, even in late pregnancy. In fact, your baby's greatest need for iron, protein, and calcium occurs in the last eight to twelve weeks of pregnancy. Improving your diet will have other long-term effects on your children since they will grow up with better eating habits and they will feed their own families better. Good nutrition has important and long-lasting effects.

Over the years there has been much misunderstanding of what constitutes good nutrition during pregnancy. Such matters as weight gain, calorie intake, the use of salt, what foods to eat and avoid, and vitamin supplementation were poorly understood, and as a result women were given erroneous information. Today, nutritional information is based on more solid research and a better understanding of the physiology of pregnancy. In addition, in recent years, the effects of various drugs and environmental agents on the unborn baby have been studied. The pregnant woman who is informed can do much to ensure good health for her infant.

Good Nutrition during Pregnancy

During your pregnancy, you supply all the nutrients to your developing baby, who will weigh an average of seven pounds at birth. The baby's life-support system, consisting of the placenta, uterus, membranes, fluid, and maternal blood volume, also grows during pregnancy, developing as necessary to meet the increasing needs of the fetus. Your body also prepares for birth and the subsequent nourishment of the baby through breastfeeding. All these added demands require that you nourish yourself adequately; otherwise your pregnancy may deplete you of important nutrients.

Which foods (and how much) should you eat to assure your baby and yourself of the best possible outcome of pregnancy? Why are these foods important? How much weight should you gain while pregnant? What about salt, fluid retention, special diets, heartburn, nausea, and vomiting? What about drugs, tobacco, marijuana, caffeine, herbs, and the other nonfoods we sometimes use? In this section, these questions are discussed, and practical advice is offered, along with an opportunity to evaluate your own diet.

During pregnancy, you need about 300 calories per day more than you did when you were not pregnant. This amounts to a total of about 2,100 to 2,400 calories per day. These additional calories should be in the form of high-protein, high-calcium, and iron-rich foods. Three hundred calories are really not all that much—two tall glasses of milk, a bowl of hearty soup, a serving of meat, or three tablespoons of salad dressing or peanut butter—so do not add lots of high calorie, nonnutritious foods, such as cake, cookies, candies, and soft drinks to your diet.

Basically a good daily pregnancy diet is a varied diet—plenty of fresh fruits and vegetables, whole grains, dairy products, protein foods (such as meat, fish, nuts, eggs, and legumes), some fat, and about two quarts of fluid a day.

Food Groups

Good nutrition has been explained by separating foods into four basic groups: 1) dairy products, 2) meat and protein foods, 3) fruits and vegetables, and 4) breads and cereals. However, it is possible to eat daily from these four food groups and not take in all the necessary nutrients. Therefore, foods should be further sorted into seven basic groups: 1) dairy products, 2) eggs and meat, 3) green and yellow vegetables, 4) citrus fruits and vitamin C-rich foods, 5) potatoes, other vegetables, and fruits, 6) grain products, and 7) fats.

Two other food categories are important to nutrition-conscious people: 8) liquids and 9) sugar foods. Pregnant women should drink about eight cups of liquid per day. As for sugar foods, the body has no requirement for them. If they are eaten in

Chart 4a

BASIC FOOD GROUPS AND DIET ANALYSIS

Photocopy this page and use it to record the food... Try checking yourself several times during your pregnancy, especially... opposite each food group, indicate how many servings you eat on each day... "; if at dinner, "D"; and if as a snack, "S". The lower number of servings... have smaller appetites.

Food Group	One Serving Equivalent	Day 1	Day 2	Day 3	Changes to Make
Dairy products *(calcium-rich foods)*	1 cup milk or yogurt 1-1/2 cup cottage cheese 2-3 scoops ice cream 1-inch cube cheese				
High protein	3 ounces meat, fish, poultry, 1 cup dried beans, lentils, or tablespoons peanut butter, cheese (if not included abov...				
Green and yellow vegetables	1/2 cup spinach, broccoli, gre... squash, carrots, and so on ' and deep yellow are best.)				
Citrus fruits and vitamin C foods	4 ounces citrus juice 1 orange 1/2 grapefruit 1 tomato or 8 ounces juice 2/3 cup strawberries 1/6 watermelon				
Potatoes and other vegetables and fruits	1 potato, ear of corn, apple, banana 1/2 cup peaches, pineapple, apricots, beets, cauliflower, lettuce	1 LDS			
Bread, flour, and cereals	1 slice bread 1 ounce cold cereal 1/2-3/4 cup cooked cereal, macaroni, rice 1 cookie, muffin, slice of cake, dough- nut, pancake	2 - 4 BLS			
Fats and oils	1 tablespoon butter, margarine, or oil	1 - 2 BLDD			
Fluids	1 cup	8 + BB, SSS L, DD			
Sugar foods	3 teaspoons sugar 1/2 ounce hard candy, marshmallow, chocolate 1 tablespoon honey, jam, syrup, molasses	0 B			

excess, they may become substitutes for more nourishing food, and they may cause excessive weight gain. It is important to control your intake of sugar foods.

Chart 4a on page 53 lists these nine categories and the number of servings recommended daily for the pregnant woman. While these foods are categorized by the particular benefits they offer, there is an overlap (for example, group 1 dairy foods are high in protein, as are the foods in group 2, but they are in a separate category because of their high-calcium and low-iron content). It is a good idea to eat foods from all groups regularly (except group 9!).

As for the number of servings of food in each group, you have a certain amount of leeway, depending on your appetite, your prepregnant weight, and how far along you are in your pregnancy. In early pregnancy, you may experience nausea and a reduced appetite. At this time, the growing embryo does not have the nutritional needs that the fetus will have later, as she grows larger. If your nutrition was good when you became pregnant, you can tolerate a temporary loss of appetite in early pregnancy.

If you are well nourished but normally eat rather lightly, you may choose to eat smaller or fewer servings from each food group; but make sure you get plenty of variety. If you find you are gaining weight very rapidly, check your diet for calorie intake and select the lower calorie foods in each group. If you were undernourished or overweight when you became pregnant, concentrate on food quality and variety. Your weight gain may be more or less than the average, reflecting your body's individual needs.

SAMPLE DAILY MENU DURING PREGNANCY

Breakfast	**Lunch**	**Dinner**
1 toast	1 whole wheat roll	Potatoes with butter, margarine, or sour cream
Butter or margarine	Butter or margarine	
2 eggs	Chef's salad (meat, cheese, carrot, tomato, lettuce, blue cheese dressing)	Fish
Citrus fruit or juice		Spinach salad (oil and vinegar dressing)
Milk or water	Milk	Melon slice
		Milk and water

Snack options (1 to 2 per day): milk shake, granola bar, bran muffin, apple with peanut butter, carrot sticks, water, and juice.

Nutrients

Chart 4b on pages 56 to 58 presents a brief summary of nutrients and vitamins, their functions, and sources. Some nutrients, however, deserve special mention for their particular importance in pregnancy.

Protein All cells are formed from protein. In this period of rapid growth—of baby, placenta, uterus, breasts, and the volume of blood and amniotic fluid—your protein requirements increase by about 60 percent over your normal requirements.

Calcium Calcium promotes the mineralization of the fetal skeleton and teeth. The fetus requires approximately 66 percent more calcium than normal during the last trimester, when the teeth are forming and skeletal growth is most rapid. Calcium is also stored in the mother's bones as a reserve for later milk production.

Iron Iron is a major element required for the manufacture of *hemoglobin*, the oxygen-carrying protein in the blood. Your blood volume increases by 50 percent during pregnancy, so your need to provide hemoglobin and the other constituents of blood increases accordingly. In addition, during the last six weeks of pregnancy, the fetus stores enough iron in her liver to supplement her needs for the first three to six months of life. This is necessary because the main food during that period—breast milk or formula—only partially fulfills an infant's iron requirements. Since a healthy person absorbs only 5 to 10 percent of the iron she ingests, the National Research Council's Committee on Maternal Nutrition recommends a daily supplement during pregnancy of thirty to sixty milligrams of iron to ensure absorption of the iron needed each day.*

Although it is necessary for good nutrition, iron upsets the digestive tract in many people. The side effects—nausea, heartburn, diarrhea, or constipation—are related to the amount of elemental iron given and individual reactions, not to the type of preparation. In other words, whether you are taking ferrous sulfate, ferrous fumerate, or ferrous gluconate is less important than how much iron you take at a time. To relieve the unpleasant side effects, you may be advised to decrease each dose of iron or take food along with the tablets. Vitamin C-rich foods (citrus fruits, potatoes, tomatoes) or calcium-rich nondairy foods (eggs, whole grains) enhance the absorption of iron.*

Also remember that the easiest and most effective way to "take" iron is to eat plenty of foods rich in iron: liver and other organ meats, red meats, egg yolks, dried fruits, prune and apple juices, dried peas, beans, lentils, oysters, almonds, walnuts, and blackstrap molasses.

Vitamins   Vitamins are essential to most life functions (see chart 4b). They are classified by their solubility: water-soluble—C and B complex vitamins; and fat-soluble—vitamins A, D, E, and K. The water-soluble vitamins can be lost in cooking. Foods high in these vitamins should be eaten raw or cooked briefly in small amounts of water, stir-fried, or steamed.

Folic acid is a water-soluble vitamin in the B-complex. Because it is essential for the normal growth of all cells and is involved in RNA and DNA synthesis, the requirement for folic acid doubles during pregnancy. Since long storage and overcooking destroy folic acid, the National Research Council's Committee on Maternal Nutrition recommends a daily supplement of 400 micrograms during pregnancy.*

The only way to make sure you get all the vitamins and minerals you need is to eat a varied, high-quality diet. It is not a good idea to depend exclusively on vitamin or mineral supplements as your main source, since vitamin preparations contain only some of the essential nutrients and there are undoubtedly some essential nutrients that have not yet been discovered or whose functions are not yet fully understood.

Chart 4b		NUTRIENTS AND VITAMIN CHART*		
Key Nutrient	RDA	Important Functions	Important Sources	Comments
Calories	N—1,800 - 2,100 P—2,100 - 2,400 L—2,300 - 2,600	• Provide energy for tissue building and increased metabolic requirements.	Carbohydrates, fats, and proteins.	Calorie requirements vary according to your size, activity level, and weight.
Water or liquids	N—4 cups P—8+ cups L—8+ cups	• Carries nutrients to cells. • Carries waste products away. • Provides fluid for increased blood and amniotic fluid volume. • Helps regulate body temperature. • Aids digestion.	Water, juices, and milk.	Often neglected, but is an important nutrient.
Protein	N—46 g P—76 - 100 g L—66 g	• Builds and repairs tissues. • Helps build blood, amniotic fluid, and placenta. • Helps form antibodies. • Supplies energy.	Meat, fish, poultry, eggs, milk, cheese, dried beans and peas, peanut butter, nuts, whole grains, and cereals.	Fetal requirements increase by about 1/3 in late pregnancy as the baby grows.

N—nonpregnant
P—pregnant
L—lactating

*The main source for information in this chart is *Nutrition in Pregnancy and Lactation*, eds. B. Worthington-Roberts, J. Vermeersch, and S. Williams (St. Louis: C.V. Mosby Co., 1981).

Chart 4b		NUTRIENTS AND VITAMIN CHART		
Key Nutrient	RDA	Important Functions	Important Sources	Comments
Minerals				
Calcium	N—800 mg P—1,200 mg L—1,200 mg	• Helps build bones and teeth. • Important in blood clotting. • Helps regulate use of other minerals in your body.	Milk, cheese, whole grains, vegetables, egg yolk, whole canned fish, and ice cream.	Fetal requirements increase in late pregnancy.
Phosphorus	N—800 P—1,200 mg L—1,200 mg	• Helps build bones and teeth.	Milk, cheese, and lean meats.	Calcium and phosphorus exist in a constant ratio in the blood. An excess of either limits use of calcium.
Iron	N—18 mg P—18+ mg L—18+ mg	• Combines with protein to make hemoglobin. • Provides iron for fetal storage.	Liver, red meats, egg yolk, whole grains, leafy vegetables, nuts, legumes, dried fruits, prunes, and prune and apple juice.	Fetal requirements increase tenfold in last 6 weeks of pregnancy. Supplement of 30 to 60 mg of iron daily is recommended by the National Research Council.
Zinc	N—15 P—20 mg L—25 mg	• Component of insulin. • Important in growth of skeleton and nervous system.	Meat, liver, eggs, and seafood—especially oysters.	Deficiency can cause fetal malformations of skeleton and nervous system.
Iodine	N—150 mcg P—175 mcg L—200 mcg	• Helps control the rate of body's energy use. • Important in thyroxine production.	Seafoods, iodized salt.	Deficiency may produce goiter in infant.
Magnesium	N—300 mg P—450 mg L—450 mg	• Coenzyme in energy and protein metabolism. • Enzyme activator. • Helps tissue growth, cell metabolism, and muscle action.	Nuts, cocoa, green vegetables, whole grains, and dried beans and peas.	Most is stored in bones. Deficiency may cause neuromuscular dysfunctions.
Fat Soluble Vitamins				
Vitamin A	N—4,000 IU P—5,000 IU L—6,000 IU	• Helps bone and tissue growth and cell development. • Essential in development of enamel-forming cells in gum tissue. • Helps maintain health of skin and mucus membranes.	Butter, fortified margarine, green and yellow vegetables, and liver.	In excessive amounts, it is toxic to the fetus. It can be lost with exposure to light.
Vitamin D	N—200 - 400 IU P—400 - 600 IU L—400 - 600 IU	• Needed for absorption of calcium and phosphorus, and mineralization of bones and teeth.	Fortified milk, fortified margarine, fish liver oils, and sunlight on your skin.	Toxic to fetus in excessive amounts. Is a stable vitamin.

Chart 4b		NUTRIENTS AND VITAMIN CHART		
Key Nutrient	**RDA**	**Important Functions**	**Important Sources**	**Comments**
Vitamin E	N—12 IU P—15 IU L—15 IU	• Needed for tissue growth, cell wall integrity, and red blood cell integrity.	Vegetable oils, cereals, meat, eggs, milk, nuts, and seeds.	Enhances absorption of vitamin A.
Water Soluble Vitamins				
Folic Acid	N—400 mcg P—800 mcg L—600 mcg	• Needed for hemoglobin synthesis. • Involved in DNA and RNA synthesis. • Coenzyme in synthesis of amino acids.	Liver, leafy green vegetables, and yeast.	Deficiency leads to anemia. Can be destroyed in cooking and storage. Supplement of 400 mcg per day is recommended by the National Research Council. Oral contraception use may reduce serum level of folic acid.
Niacin	N—13 mg P—15 mg L—17 - 20 mg	• Coenzyme in energy and protein metabolism.	Pork, organ meats, peanuts, beans, peas, and enriched grains.	Stable, only small amounts lost in food preparation.
Riboflavin (B$_2$)	N—1.2 mg P—1.5 mg L—1.7 - 1.8 mg	• Coenzyme in energy and protein metabolism.	Milk, lean meat, enriched grains, cheese, and leafy greens.	Severe deficiencies lead to reduced growth and congenital malformations. Oral contraception use may reduce serum concentration of riboflavin.
Thiamin (B$_1$)	N—1.1 mg P—1.5 mg L—1.6 mg	• Coenzyme for energy metabolism.	Pork, beef, liver, whole grains, and legumes.	Its availability limits the rate at which energy from glucose is produced.
Pyridoxine (B$_6$)	N—2.0 mg P—2.5 mg L—2.5 mg	• Important in amino acid metabolism and protein synthesis. • Fetus requires more for growth.	Unprocessed cereals, grains, wheat germ, bran, nuts, seeds, legumes, and corn.	Excessive amounts may reduce milk supply in lactating women. May help control nausea in early pregnancy.
Cobalamin (B$_{12}$)	N—3.0 mcg P—4.0 mcg L—4.0 mcg	• Coenzyme in protein metabolism. • Important in formation of red blood cells.	Milk, eggs, meat, liver, and cheese.	Deficiency leads to anemia and central nervous system damage. Is manufactured by micro-organisms in intestinal tract. Oral contraceptives may reduce serum concentrates.
Vitamin C	N—60 mg P—80 mg L—60 mg	• Helps tissue formation and integrity. • Is the "cement" substance in connective and vascular substances. • Increases iron absorption.	Citrus fruits, berries, melons, tomatoes, chili peppers, green vegetables, and potatoes.	Large doses in pregnancy may create a larger-than-normal need in infant. Benefits of large doses in preventing colds have not been confirmed.

Weight Gain

How much weight should you gain during pregnancy? No single amount would be appropriate for every pregnant woman. Proper weight gain depends on many variables: your prepregnancy weight and stature, the size of your baby and placenta, and the quality of your diet before and during pregnancy. Until the early 1970s, most North American obstetricians placed great emphasis on limiting weight gain to between fourteen and seventeen pounds, believing this range would result in easier labors and less postpartum obesity. It was assumed that the fetus always managed to extract the necessary nutrients. By 1970, however, research studies investigating the association between weight gain and the health of the baby began showing that a higher weight gain during pregnancy resulted in more full-term pregnancies and larger, healthier babies. This led the National Research Council's Committee on Maternal Nutrition, in 1970, to recommend higher weight gains, with some allowance for individual circumstances.*

- If your prepregnancy weight was below normal, it may be wise for you to gain more weight than women who are normal or overweight. If your baby is large—over eight pounds—chances are your placenta is also larger than average. It stands to reason that you will gain more weight than if your baby and placenta are of average or small size.

- If the quality of your diet is normally excellent and you and your baby are of average size, you will probably gain about twenty-five pounds.

- If, on the other hand, you are overweight or if you ate many high-calorie, low-quality foods before pregnancy, you may not gain twenty-five pounds after you improve the quality of your diet. In other words, by replacing the high-calorie, nonnutritious foods with better-quality foods, you may gain less weight while benefiting your baby.

The point to keep in mind is that your weight gain is of secondary importance to the quality of your diet. If you eat consistently well, as described in this section, you can trust that the amount of weight you gain is the right amount for you.

You will be weighed at each prenatal visit, and your weight will be recorded on a chart similar to the one on the next page. This chart indicates a slow weight gain early in the pregnancy, picking up speed as the baby grows and his support system grows to meet his requirements. A typical prenatal weight gain would show an increase of two to four pounds by the end of the first trimester and about one pound per week thereafter. The chart can show your doctor or midwife how consistent your

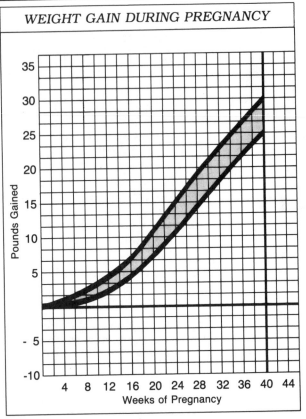

WEIGHT GAIN DURING PREGNANCY

weight gain is. A sudden, excessive gain or drop from one visit to the next can be a sign of illness or of problems in your pregnancy. It may also be a sign that you went on a food binge or starved yourself between visits!

If you gain twenty-five pounds and have a seven-and-a-half-pound baby, where does the rest of the weight go? The following list shows approximately how the weight is distributed during pregnancy:

WEIGHT DISTRIBUTION DURING PREGNANCY	
Baby	7 to 8 lbs.
Placenta	1 to 2 lbs.
Uterus	2 lbs.
Amniotic fluid	1 1/2 to 2 lbs.
Breasts	1 lb.
Blood volume	2 1/2 to 3 lbs.
Fat	5 lbs. or more
Tissue, fluid	4 to 7 lbs.
Total	**24 to 30 lbs.**

Most women accept the weight they put on during pregnancy, especially when they realize that it is lost either during birth or shortly thereafter. But what about that extra five pounds or more of fat? Since it may take weeks or months before that disappears, many weight-conscious women dislike putting on fat during pregnancy. Consider the following:

• It is not possible to gain only the weight necessary for the baby and the placenta and avoid adding the fat. The fat is not the last five pounds of weight you gain, so it cannot be avoided if you stop gaining weight at twenty pounds instead of twenty-five. In fact, fat is produced gradually along with the other components of the weight gain. Trying to avoid the fat may deprive you or your baby of essential nutrients.

• Most women are able to lose their extra weight gradually over a period of five to six months after the baby is born—that is, if they maintain sensible eating habits. Breastfeeding promotes the loss of these extra pounds because adequate milk production requires 900 to 1,000 calories per quart. The stored fat provides some of these calories; the rest comes from an additional 500 calories a day that should be taken in by the breastfeeding mother.

The point is that pregnancy is not the time to lose weight; it is a time to concentrate on a high-quality diet.

Other Nutrition Issues

Salt For years pregnant women were told to eliminate or restrict the use of salt. They were told not to use salt at the table or in cooking, and every pregnant woman was given a list of processed foods that were high in salt or sodium. The rationale for this treatment was based on the tendency of the pregnant woman to retain fluid—which was assumed to cause preeclampsia. (See chapter 3 for a discussion of preeclampsia.) It is now known that gradual, moderate fluid retention in pregnancy is not only normal, it is necessary to ensure an adequate volume of blood and amniotic fluid. The abnormal, sudden increase in fluid retention seen in preeclampsia is not due to excessive salt intake, but rather to the impaired functioning of the liver and kidneys, which normally regulate electrolyte and fluid balance. Adequate salt intake during pregnancy is now known to be important in maintaining fluid balance.* The wise pregnant woman will salt her food to taste.

By the same token, the use of diuretics, once prescribed almost routinely during pregnancy to "wash away" fluid and electrolytes, is now known to stress the system that controls blood pressure and fluid balance. Diuretics cause problems with fluid balance during pregnancy; they do not solve them.*

Fluid Retention

As stated above, you normally retain fluid as part of the process that ensures the increase in blood and amniotic fluid volume that is necessary to a healthy pregnancy. You need to retain more fluid because:

- Your blood volume increases by 50 percent or more (from approximately two and one-half to three and three-fourths liters).
- By the end of pregnancy, your baby is immersed in about one liter of amniotic fluid, which is replaced every three hours.

It also is estimated that tissue fluid increases by two to three liters during pregnancy. While the role of this extra fluid is not fully understood, it is thought to be necessary to ensure an adequate volume of blood and amniotic fluid. This requirement is met by hormonal changes that alter the way the kidneys handle fluid.

During pregnancy, try to drink at least two quarts of liquid a day (milk, fruit juices, and water). This is difficult if you are not in the habit of drinking very much. If so, it may be helpful to fill a one-quart pitcher with water, put it in the refrigerator, and drink from it throughout the day, making sure it is empty by bedtime. In addition, plan to have a glass of milk or other liquid with each meal and a glass of fruit juice at snack times. You can easily develop this habit with a little conscientious effort.

In summary, by gaining an appropriate amount of weight, eating a well-balanced diet, using salt as desired, drinking a generous amount of liquids, supplementing your diet with iron and folic acid, and avoiding diuretics, you are following the nutritional guidelines most likely to produce a healthy baby and mother.

Common Concerns

Several common nutrition-related problems arise during pregnancy due to normal changes in hormone production and the increased size and weight of the uterus. The following pages discuss some causes of and treatments for these ailments.

Nausea and Vomiting

Nausea and vomiting are sometimes referred to as "morning sickness" (although for many women it is not restricted to the morning). Pregnant women frequently feel nauseated and need to vomit when they have not eaten for several hours or when they smell certain odors, such as cigar smoke or certain foods being cooked. Although the "trigger" may vary from woman to woman, the problem is common.

With today's emphasis on good nutrition, you may worry about your baby's health if you vomit frequently. You will be reassured to know, however, that recent studies indicate that women who are healthy at conception have sufficient reserves to supply the growing embryo and fetus, even if they eat poorly for the first two or three months.* Another study indicates that the *presence* of nausea and vomiting (rather than their absence) is more likely to be associated with a favorable pregnancy outcome.*

Be assured that nausea is neither abnormal nor a sign of unconscious rejection of the baby, as is sometimes suggested. The cause is probably related to the body's increased production of twenty-six hormones, plus the manufacture of at least four other hormones produced only during pregnancy. Some of these hormones act to delay the emptying of the stomach. Other hormones, when present in large quantities, may be upsetting until the body adjusts.

Treatment

• Try modifying your eating habits. Some women find it helpful to eat several (five or six) small meals a day to avoid an empty stomach. Some protein should be included in each of these meals. Other women find that eating something like crackers or toast before getting up in the morning is helpful. Food can be left by the bed at night or brought to you in the morning. Drinking liquids between instead of during meals is also often beneficial.

• Try increasing your intake of vitamin B_6 (Pyridoxine), which helps some women. One way to do that, of course, is to eat more foods high in this vitamin (whole grains and cereals, wheat germ, nuts, seeds, legumes, corn). Another suggestion is to discuss with your caregiver whether you should take vitamin B_6 supplements. Self-prescribing extra vitamins in pregnancy is not advisable.

• Know that the condition will usually pass within three to four months.

• Have a sense of humor. For some women, throwing up is as much part of their morning routine as brushing their teeth and combing their hair. Their attitude has much to do with how well they cope with this and other annoyances.

• On very rare occasions, nausea and vomiting are so severe that a woman actually becomes dehydrated, loses a great deal of weight, and is unable to hold any food down. This condition is called hyperemesis gravidarum, and it may require medication or even hospitalization if the nausea and vomiting endanger either the mother or the baby's health.

• Medications are available to help control nausea and vomiting. They are prescribed either when the nausea and vomiting are severe and thought to be causing dehydration, or, more commonly, when the woman is upset or inconvenienced and requests medication. You should realize that these medications cross the placenta to the fetus and that neither their safety to the unborn baby nor their effectiveness has been established. Because they are used during the time of pregnancy when the fetus is most vulnerable, it would be wise to try the nonmedical forms of treatment first and to think twice before requesting medication. Until recently, Bendectin was available and widely used. Questions of a possible association between Bendectin and birth defects (cleft palate and heart deformities) led to expensive lawsuits persuading the manufacturer to withdraw it from the market.

Heartburn

Heartburn, a feeling of fullness, with some regurgitation of acid from the stomach, is a common complaint in late pregnancy. It is caused by a combination of hormonal effects that relax the muscular opening at the top of the stomach and cause the stomach to empty more slowly and the increased pressure from the growing uterus. Fatty foods, foods that produce gas, and large meals may also contribute to the condition.

Treatment

- Avoid fatty food and foods that produce gas.

- Eat several small meals (rather than a few large meals). Some women find that eating slowly and not eating just before bedtime also help reduce heartburn.

- Antacids or other drugs are sometimes used to control heartburn, but they should be used only if necessary. Consult your caregiver for recommendations and to learn about possible undesirable side effects.

Constipation

During pregnancy, the movement of food through the intestines is slowed. This allows more time for greater absorption of nutrients and water, but also tends to cause constipation. Pressure from the growing uterus on the large intestine magnifies the problem.

Treatment

- Drink plenty of fluids and eat foods with high-fiber content, such as raw or dried fruits and vegetables, whole grains, and prune juice, which encourage elimination.

- Exercise regularly. Exercise is an often neglected but effective aid to regularity. (See chapter 5.)

If proper diet and exercise are provided, laxatives can and should be avoided. Preventing constipation also alleviates the discomfort of hemorrhoids, another common problem during pregnancy.

Special Concerns

Good nutrition in pregnancy is always an important concern, but in some circumstances, you need to be even more conscientious about your diet. If your pregnancy is a "special pregnancy" or if you are on a special diet, your nutritional demands will be greater than normal.

In all these special circumstances, seek nutritional counseling and be particularly conscientious about eating nutritious foods. Nutritional counseling is available from your midwife, your physician, or a nutritionist. These professionals can help you plan your diet in a practical way.

Special Pregnancies

Multiple pregnancies. Two or more babies require the pregnant woman to consume more calories and more nutrients. For further information on nutrition in multiple pregnancies, see *Having Twins* by Elizabeth Noble.

Adolescent pregnancy. Because a teenager is still growing and has greater-than-adult requirements for most nutrients, she needs to eat particularly well when she is pregnant to maintain her own growth, while nourishing her fetus.

Pregnancies in rapid succession. Sometimes a pregnancy depletes your reserves of certain nutrients, such as calcium and iron. If you have sufficient time between pregnancies to replenish those reserves, no nutritional deficiency occurs. If you soon become pregnant again, however, your reserves may be depleted and you may need extra calories and nutrients. The length of time needed between pregnancies to correct deficiencies depends, of course, on your overall nutritional status and the quality of your diet.

Special Diets

A vegetarian diet. If you are a vegetarian, you can, with knowledge and careful planning, adequately nourish yourself and your unborn baby, especially if you include milk and eggs in your diet. Your major concerns are these: the need to take in sufficient calories; the (possible) need to supplement B_{12}, found mostly in animal meats; and the need to combine protein-rich foods to obtain all the essential proteins. (See the Recommended Reading for references on vegetarian diets.) The information in this chapter applies to both the vegetarian and the meat-eater.

Milk intolerance. If you cannot tolerate milk, you may have a problem getting enough calcium. Try cultured forms of milk, such as acidophilus milk and yogurt, which are often well tolerated by people who are upset by certain dairy products. Otherwise, you should learn about and eat other foods high in calcium (see chart 4b earlier). If you simply do not like the taste of milk, try cooking with dry powdered milk or eating cream soups and cheeses. These alternatives will give you the benefits of milk without its taste. If you are not meeting your needs through your diet, however, you may need calcium supplements. Consult your physician or midwife if this is a problem for you.

Allergies. If you have significant food allergies, you may need a nutritionist to plan a healthful diet for your pregnancy. Sometimes, eliminating problem foods leads to an inadequate diet, so you will need careful guidance.

Medical problems. If you are pregnant and have a medical problem, such as diabetes, anemia, heart or lung disease, you will need special nutritional guidance in conjunction with close prenatal observation and management. It is beyond the scope of this book to deal with such problems, except to emphasize the necessity of thorough prenatal care. Be sure you understand and follow the instructions you are given for any medical problems.

Drugs and Medications in Pregnancy

Until the early 1960s, it was assumed that the placenta protected the fetus from harmful substances. The Thalidomide tragedy of the sixties, however, dramatically altered that assumption. Effective in controlling nausea in early pregnancy, Thalidomide was thought to be harmless to the unborn child. Shortly after it was introduced, an epidemic of babies born without arms or legs led to an exhaustive investigation that linked these birth defects to the drug. Scientists and the public then began questioning whether other birth defects might be linked to other drugs and medications used during pregnancy.

For several reasons, it is difficult to trace the connection between drugs and birth defects. Because the risks are great, animals—not humans—are used as experimental subjects. While the information gained from animal studies is valuable, it cannot necessarily be applied to humans. In addition, it is difficult to isolate a single agent used in a pregnancy since most women consume numerous drugs and medications during their pregnancies.* Finally, it is possible that a drug may be harmful only when used at a particular time or only in conjunction with other agents.

Despite the complexities of tracing the specific effects of particular drugs, we do know that virtually all drugs and medications taken by a pregnant woman cross the placenta and reach the fetus. Their effect on the fetus is at least similar to and possibly greater than their effect on the mother because of the fetus' rapid growth and development.

Where does all this leave the pregnant woman? When should she take a drug? Are all drugs bad? What about social drugs? What about the medicines she has been using? This section reviews what is known about some of the most common social drugs and medicines, provides some guidelines on when and when not to use them, and suggests some substitutes. If you have already used some of these drugs during your pregnancy, you will find a practical discussion of your options.

Generally speaking, if you are pregnant, be very cautious about using any drug. No drug has been proven safe for the fetus, though many drugs are thought to be safe or at least have not been proven to be harmful. The best course to follow when considering the use of a drug is to weigh the possible risks against the possible benefits. If the benefits clearly outweigh the risks, then use the drug or medication; if not, look for alternative treatments or pleasures.

Alcohol   Until the mid-1970s, alcohol was thought to be harmless to the infant. It was even assumed that the large quantities of alcohol drunk by alcoholic women were not, in themselves, harmful to the fetus. Alcoholism was felt to be a problem because an alcoholic pregnant woman might tend not to eat nutritious food, resulting in malnutrition in the fetus. We now know, however, that alcohol has a direct toxic effect on the developing fetus. Alcohol quickly crosses the placenta and enters the fetus' blood in the same concentration as in the mother's blood. Babies born of alcoholic mothers are at substantial risk for suffering from Fetal Alcohol Syndrome, a cluster of disabilities that includes mental and physical retardation, tremors, and peculiar facial characteristics.

Lesser amounts of alcohol are also associated with some features of Fetal Alcohol Syndrome. An occasional drunken episode, depending on its timing during pregnancy, may have lasting harmful effects. Even moderate social drinking (about two drinks per day) has been associated with birth weights that are significantly lower (an average of five ounces) than the birth weights of babies born of nondrinking mothers.

If you are pregnant, you would be wise to give up drinking—the earlier the better. While drinking in early pregnancy is more likely to be associated with birth defects, drinking later in pregnancy is more likely to be associated with smaller fetal size. Stopping at any time, therefore, will allow your baby the opportunity to catch up in growth before birth.

Questions

• *What if you drink only occasionally, and then only lightly or moderately?* At this time it has not been shown that this type of drinking has lasting or measurable effects. We do know, however, that the baby receives alcohol when you drink, and no one has yet been able to determine a "safe" dose. Beer and wine are not less harmful than hard liquor. A four-ounce glass of wine or a can of beer contains as much alcohol as a mixed drink.

• *What if you not knowing the dangers of alcohol, have drunk too much during your pregnancy?* It would be difficult for you not to be concerned about the health of your baby. A few points may be helpful here. As stated above, whenever you stop drinking, it will probably be beneficial. Also, remember that the fetus is remarkably strong and resilient. Babies handle difficulties very well. Consider the very high percentage of healthy babies born to mothers who took drugs or medicines, or had illnesses or other problems during their pregnancies. Of course, you should not depend on the strength of the fetus and deliberately abuse drugs. But if you have used drugs, it should be reassuring to know that the fetus has resources to help her combat their effects.

It has also been shown that pregnant women commonly develop an aversion to alcohol (as well as smoking and caffeine). Many women cut down on their use of alcohol simply because it loses its appeal. Perhaps our bodies are trying to tell us something! In any situation when you might drink alcohol, it is wise to substitute fruit juice, tomato juice, or bottled water with a twist of lemon.

Tobacco   Tobacco smoking has been widely studied for its effects on the unborn baby. The evidence strongly suggests that if you are pregnant and you smoke, you should stop or cut down as much as possible as soon as possible—before pregnancy begins, if you can.

Cigarette smoke contains many substances—tars, nicotine, carbon monoxide, lead, and others—that are harmful to both you and your unborn child if you smoke. Compared to nonsmokers, pregnant women who smoke, on the average, give birth to smaller babies and have a greater chance of premature rupture of the membranes, premature birth, perinatal death, placental abnormalities, and bleeding during pregnancy. These conditions are directly proportional to the amount of smoking: the more you smoke, the greater the chance you will have these complications.*

Smoking may also produce harmful, long-term effects on the child. The incidence of respiratory illness is higher in children from households where adults smoke. Children of smoking parents are also more likely to smoke than are the children of nonsmoking parents. In one very large study that compared the children of smokers and nonsmokers, the children of smokers were an average of one centimeter shorter and three to five months behind the children of nonsmokers in intellectual ability. (The study allowed for associated social and biological factors.)*

What if you do not smoke, but your friends, family, or coworkers smoke in your presence? Passive smoking (breathing in other people's smoke) can be uncomfortable to you and possibly harmful to your fetus, depending on how poorly ventilated the area is and how much time you spend in it. Depending on how strongly you feel, and on how assertive you are, you may want to avoid smoky areas and smoking friends, colleagues, and family members, either by asking people not to smoke near you or by choosing to stay in nonsmoking areas as much as possible.

Marijuana

At this time, there has been little research on the effects of marijuana smoking on the fetus and infant. It is clear, however, that marijuana smoking affects the fetus at least as much as it does the mother. The amounts of tar and nicotine in marijuana are considerably greater than in cigarettes because no effort is being made to reduce these substances in marijuana.

Carbon monoxide, which is present in all smoke, including marijuana smoke, significantly reduces the blood's capacity to carry oxygen. It is not known how the active ingredients in marijuana and the substances added to marijuana affect the fetus. Nor are the possible long-term effects known.

Caffeine

Coffee, tea, colas and other soft drinks (read the labels), chocolate, and some over-the-counter drugs contain caffeine. Some animal studies have shown a connection between caffeine consumption and certain birth defects.* Another study on humans associated coffee consumption with abortion, stillbirth, premature delivery, and low birth weight. This study, however, did not consider the added effect of smoking.* Because many people who drink excessive amounts of coffee also smoke, it is difficult to distinguish the real cause of the problem. A recent Boston study of over 12,000 women who had babies in a three-year period found that birth problems were more common among heavy coffee drinkers (those who consume more than four cups per day). But when they eliminated those people who also smoked heavily, the association between caffeine consumption and these effects disappeared.* While this report is reassuring to coffee drinkers, it has not persuaded the United States Food and Drug Administration to change its position advising "prudent and protective" expectant mothers to limit caffeine use.*

Other effects, besides birth defects and prematurity, should concern you as an expectant parent. According to a National

Academy of Sciences report, pregnant women take in an average of 144 milligrams of caffeine per day, the equivalent of about one to two cups of coffee or two to three cups of tea. Caffeine causes an increased production of "stress" hormones—epinephrine (adrenalin) and norepinephrine (noradrenalin). These hormones constrict peripheral blood vessels, including those in the uterus, which results in a temporary decrease in the amount of oxygen available to the fetus. The more caffeine you take in, the more the fetus is affected in this way.* Caffeine readily enters the fetal blood stream. If the baby has caffeine in her circulation at birth, it takes a much longer time to clear her system than it would take an adult.*

Considering what we now know about caffeine, it seems wise to eliminate or reduce caffeine intake during pregnancy.

Herbal Teas

Hundreds of herbs are available commercially as herbal teas.* They are said to have various curative or restorative properties, helpful for most discomforts. It is not possible to comment on the safety or value of herbal teas for the fetus since there has been little scientific scrutiny and little is known about the active ingredients that produce the benefits. It is known, however, that some herbs produce undesirable side effects in some adults. For instance, teas made from juniper berries, buckthorn bark, senna leaves, duck roots, and aloe can irritate the stomach and intestinal tract, sometimes severely. People allergic to ragweed and related plants may develop unusual allergic symptoms after drinking camomile tea. A popular ingredient of tea—licorice root—if used in large quantities, is related to water retention and loss of potassium.

Sassafras root contains safrole, known to cause liver cancer in rats. The Food and Drug Administration recently stated that safrole cannot be considered safe for human use. Ginseng contains small amounts of estrogen, and there have been reports of swollen and painful breasts after its use. These ingredients almost certainly reach the fetus and affect the baby at least as much as they do the mother. Because little is known about the risks and benefits of most herbs, you should use them with caution.

Medicines

Drugs such as aspirin, acetaminophen, sedatives and tranquilizers, antihistamines, antacids, and antiemetics (to control nausea and vomiting) are widely used during pregnancy. These drugs do not treat or cure an illness; they relieve symptoms such as pain, headache, nervousness, sleeplessness, runny nose, heartburn, and nausea. Other medications, such as antibiotics, insulin, and steroids, either cure or control an illness, and their benefits are surely greater than those drugs that merely relieve symptoms. Even so, medication should be used only when the benefits greatly outweigh the potential hazards. Caution on the part of parents, physician, or midwife will lead to a far more sensible attitude on drug use in pregnancy. (See chapter 9 for more information about medications.)

Some conditions are in themselves risky enough to mother and child to require treatment. Conditions such as epilepsy, pneumonia, asthma, strep throat, high fever, arthritis, diabetes, and heart disease may require treatment with strong medications even during pregnancy. Under these circumstances, nontreatment would be far more harmful to mother and fetus than treatment. Therefore, in deciding whether or not to use medication, consider the seriousness of the condition, the benefit to be gained from the medication, other possible treatments and their benefits, and the risk of both condition and treatment.

Particular mention should be made of two widely used drugs that are generally considered to be harmless—aspirin (Anacin, Bayer, Bufferin, Empirin, etc.) and acetaminophen (Datril, Tempra, Tylenol, etc.). These drugs reduce pain and fever, but both readily cross the placenta and enter fetal circulation. Are they safe during pregnancy?

Aspirin. Even one tablet of aspirin affects the body's ability to clot blood and prolongs bleeding time. Two tablets, the usual adult dose, will double bleeding time, an effect that lasts from four to seven days after a single dose.* Although there is greater concern over aspirin taken toward the end of pregnancy, because normal bleeding after birth may be increased and prolonged, it is wise to avoid aspirin even earlier in pregnancy; using it could worsen any bleeding you have during your pregnancy.

Aspirin present in the baby's circulation at birth also prolongs bleeding time for the newborn, and it increases the likelihood of jaundice.* Therefore, you are better off avoiding aspirin during pregnancy, except when it is necessary for controlling certain diseases like arthritis, where its benefits outweigh these risks.

Acetaminophen. Acetaminophen is less potentially harmful than aspirin. No adverse fetal effects have been reported with the moderate use of acetaminophen. However, if you consistently use more than the recommended amounts, there may be kidney damage in the fetus. If you normally tolerate acetaminophen well, it would be preferable to use it in moderation rather than aspirin if you *really need* a pain or fever medication during pregnancy.* Generally speaking, it is wise to use nonmedical forms of treatment before resorting to medications.

*Home
Remedies*

Here are some suggested alternatives to the medical treatment of common ailments. If any of these discomforts persist or seem harmful to your well-being, however, consult your doctor or midwife for further treatment.

Headache. Instead of using aspirin or acetaminophen, or combination drugs, try a warm relaxing bath, a massage, tension-reducing exercises (such as shoulder circling) and relaxation routines. Hot packs on the back of the neck or shoulders and cold packs on the forehead also help relieve headache for many people.

Cold, hay fever, runny nose, and cough. A cool mist vaporizer, handkerchief, rest, liquids, and honey and lemon are safe and as effective in curing a cold as decongestants, aspirin, and cough syrups. All the drugs available treat only the symptoms and do nothing to cure the cold.

Nausea, vomiting, and heartburn. See the discussion on pages 62 to 64.

Backache. Backache is a common problem for pregnant women. You can best alleviate backache with massage, hot or cold packs, and exercises to strengthen the abdominal muscles and to decrease the curve in the low back. (See chapter 5 on comfort measures and posture.) Avoid aspirin and muscle relaxants unless the condition is severe; check with your caregiver before taking these drugs.

Sleeplessness. This is especially common in late pregnancy. Instead of drinking alcohol or taking a sleeping pill, try these helpful sleep aids. Take a brisk walk each day; this will help release tension that might keep you from sleeping. Try a warm bath, a glass of warm milk, a massage, or listening to soothing music before going to bed. If you find yourself wide awake in the middle of the night, try reading (a dull book is more likely to help you get back to sleep) or using the relaxation techniques described in chapter 5.

Harmful Environmental Agents

Pregnant women (and young children) should avoid the following environmental agents.

*Herbicides
and
Insecticides*

Weed- and insect-killing sprays are widely used along roadsides, in farming areas, and in residential communities. Their presence in the atmosphere and on food has been associated with both miscarriage and birth defects. While numerous chemicals are used against weeds and insects, their safety for the unborn and young child has not been established. Some, such as 2,4,5,-T, have already been banned because they are known to be harmful.

Radiation

During your pregnancy, you should avoid X-rays for medical and dental diagnosis and you should not work in areas where radiation levels may be high. This is especially important during your first trimester since radiation interferes with cell division and organ development. Fortunately, most X-rays in early pregnancy can be avoided or postponed until after the birth.

Although ultrasound is more often used today, X-rays are sometimes used in late pregnancy to assess the relationship between the size of the baby's head and the size of the mother's pelvis (X-ray pelvimetry), to find out if there are twins, and to determine fetal presentation. (See chapter 7, pages 126 to 127.) In such cases, the benefits of the information gained are thought to outweigh the risks of exposure. You may question your physician or midwife and ask what information he or she expects to gain from these X-rays and whether the clinical management would be altered by the results. Generally speaking, such exposure should not be done routinely or if there is reasonable doubt about the benefits.

Saunas and Hot Tubs

There is evidence that prolonged exposure to the extreme heat found in saunas or hot tubs may raise the mother's body temperature, creating a fever that endangers the fetus. The high temperature of a fever may interfere with cell division and may cause birth defects or even fetal death if fever occurs repeatedly, for extended periods, or at a crucial time in fetal development.* If you find saunas or hot tubs really relaxing and beneficial, it would be wise to take your oral temperature while you are exposed to the heat. When your body temperature rises one degree or more, it is time to get out and cool down. Ten minutes in a sauna or hot tub seems to be a reasonable limit since it does not seem to cause the body temperature to rise. If you become uncomfortably hot in a sauna or hot tub, get out, even if you have been there for a short time. You may also reduce the temperature in the sauna or bath water to allow you to use it safely.

Toxoplasmosis

Toxoplasmosis is a mild infection that causes coldlike symptoms or no apparent illness at all in adults. It can be very serious, however, to the unborn baby, causing possible eye and brain defects and prematurity. Cats are the common carriers of toxoplasmosis—especially outdoor cats who eat raw meat, such as rats and mice. The toxoplasmosis organism passes from the cat in its feces and lives for up to a year. You may pick up these organisms by handling cats or cat litter boxes, or by working in soil where a cat has buried its feces. Eating raw or undercooked meat is another way of acquiring this disease. To avoid getting toxoplasmosis and passing it on to your unborn baby, be sure to wash your hands after handling cats and cat litter boxes, and cook your meat.*

Drugs, Environmental Hazards, and the Father

At this time there is little scientific information available on how drugs, environmental hazards, or other influences affect the reproductive capability of the male. Evidence is growing, however, that the man's health and well-being are more important than previously suspected in producing a healthy baby. For example:

• A recent report on smoking and male fertility indicates that heavy smokers have much higher numbers of abnormal sperm than do nonsmokers.*

• The age of the father seems to be important for normal fetal development. Just as the mother's age at conception has been found to be very significant as a risk factor for Down's syndrome, the father's age is equally significant as a risk factor for other congenital disorders, such as dwarfism (achondroplasia). These disorders, termed "autosomal dominant mutations," are more likely in children born to fathers over forty. (They occur at a frequency of 0.3 to 0.5 percent.) It should be noted that few such disorders can be diagnosed before birth; amniocentesis is not a useful test.*

• Some herbicides, particularly Agent Orange, a defoliant used widely during the Vietnam war, are suspected of causing genetic mutations and birth defects in the offspring of Vietnam veterans.*

Other than a few reports on how certain drugs may alter the reproductive potential of men, the direct contribution by the father to his infant's health is poorly understood. His indirect contribution, however, is of great significance. A woman is much more likely to control her use of tobacco and alcohol, for example, if her partner also controls his use of these agents. If he supports her in her concern for a positive outcome of the pregnancy by joining her in any change she has to make, she is much more likely to be successful.

Conclusion

After reading this section, you may wonder if there are any pleasures left for the pregnant woman or expectant couple! Concentrate on the pleasures that have not been taken away: exercise, sports, dancing, good food, massage, love and sex, music, art, movies, reading, television, and, perhaps the best of all, the experience of "growing" a baby.

Chapter Five

Exercise and Comfort in Pregnancy

Exercise is particularly important for you during pregnancy. As your body grows and you gain weight, regular exercise helps you stay healthy and comfortable. Exercise helps tone and strengthen the muscles most affected by pregnancy, including the pelvic floor, the abdominal, and the low back muscles; it also helps maintain good respiration, circulation, and posture. Although prenatal exercise and physical fitness do not guarantee an easy labor, they may give you more stamina to cope with a long, hard labor and more body awareness to help you work with your body during labor. One of the major benefits of prenatal exercise comes after birth. Recovering your energy level, your strength, and your prepregnant size are unquestionably easier when you are in good physical condition during pregnancy.

This chapter suggests ways to improve your posture and to perform everyday tasks comfortably, and it provides specific exercises for the parts of the body most affected by pregnancy and birth. You will also find techniques to help you with pregnancy's common discomforts.

Posture and Movement

Good posture and body mechanics—the safe and efficient performance of everyday tasks—are the cornerstones of a comfortable pregnancy. As you gain weight and your body changes shape, you must adjust your posture to maintain alignment and balance. By observing the following principles, you can perform everyday activities with the least strain and effort, and can reduce fatigue and common aches and pains. In fact, these principles apply whether you are pregnant or not, and they are especially important in the first few months after your baby is born.

Posture

You can improve your posture by standing as tall as possible and by keeping your chin level. Imagine a string attached to the crown of your head, pulling it toward the ceiling. If you hold your head high, the rest of your body usually aligns itself properly.

Check the following list for signs of good and poor posture. Try both postures. Which one looks and feels better? Watch yourself in windows and mirrors to increase your awareness of your posture, and ask your partner to observe you.

Poor posture often causes backache. When your posture is poor, your abdominal muscles are relaxed, the curve of your back is exaggerated, and the small muscles of your low back must maintain your balance and alignment. This continual shortening and tightening of these back muscles creates low back pain.

During pregnancy, your center of gravity shifts as your baby and uterus grow, and it takes special effort to maintain good posture. Flat or low-heel shoes help. Exercises to maintain abdominal muscle tone and strength are also beneficial. (See the conditioning exercises, pages 84 to 90.)

GOOD POSTURE	POOR POSTURE
Head—high	**Head**—tilted forward
Chin—level	**Chin**—poking out
Shoulders—relaxed, down, and back	**Shoulders**—rounded or thrust back
Abdominal muscles—firm, working to straighten spine	**Abdominal muscles**—relaxed, causing a larger bulge
Back—subtle "S" curve; slightly curved lower back	**Back**—hollowed or swayed; exaggerated "S" curve
Buttocks—tucked in	**Buttocks**—sticking out
Knees—relaxed	**Knees**—locked or hyperextended
Feet—supporting body weight equally; weight supported equally on heel and ball of each foot	**Feet**—one foot supporting more weight or standing with weight mostly on heels or toes

Standing

When possible, avoid standing for a long time during late pregnancy. Standing inhibits the blood flow from your legs, which can make you light-headed. If you must stand, stimulate the blood flow from your legs to your heart by using your leg muscles. Shift your weight from leg to leg, rotate your ankles in small circles, and rock back and forth from your toes to your heels. Be fidgety; do not stand still in one spot.

To help prevent backache while standing, put one foot on a low stool or opened drawer. This helps flatten your back and reduces the strain on your low back muscles.

Sitting

During late pregnancy, try to avoid prolonged sitting since this impairs the return of blood from your legs. To improve circulation in your legs while sitting, do not cross your legs at the knees, but frequently move and rotate your feet at the ankles. Sitting with your feet up and calves supported is also a restful and beneficial position.

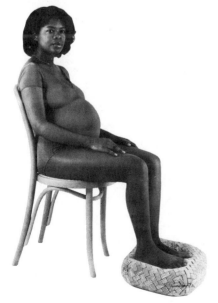

On a long car trip, stop hourly to get out and move around. In the car, shift your position occasionally and move your legs about. Remember to wear your seat belt when you are in the car. Place the lap belt over your lower abdomen, below the bulge of your uterus. Always wear the shoulder belt.

As your uterus enlarges, you will find a straight-back chair more comfortable than a low, deep one. A small, firm pillow in the small of your back and a low stool under your feet will provide additional comfort for your back. To avoid back strain when you get up, first move to the edge of the chair and use your leg muscles to raise your body.

Lifting

Joints and ligaments are softened and relaxed during pregnancy, so you are more likely to injure yourself if you lift heavy objects. You can safely lift light objects if you do so properly.

To lift or pick up an object, use your strong thigh muscles instead of the short, weaker muscles of your low back. Remember to bend at the knees when lifting, not at the waist. Follow these rules even if you are picking up a piece of paper:

1. *Get as close to the object as possible. Keep your feet wide apart, toes pointing out. (Feet can be parallel or one foot can be ahead of the other.)*
2. *Bend both knees (squat), keeping your back straight.*
3. *Grasp the object firmly, and hold it close to your body. Avoid twisting at your waist.*
4. *To avoid strain on your perineum, contract your pelvic floor muscles and do not hold your breath as you rise.*
5. *Stand up by straightening your legs. Remember to keep your back straight.*

Lying Down

As your pregnancy progresses, it becomes increasingly difficult to be comfortable while lying down. Pillows help. When you are lying on your side, put a pillow between your knees and puff a pillow under your head so it is well supported. It is often more relaxing to rest your arms and legs on the bed (or floor) than on other parts of your body.

If your blood pressure rises, your caregiver may encourage you to rest on your side during the day. If this is the case, it is preferable to lie on your left side because the placental circulation and heart function are most efficient in this position.

You may find side-lying comfortable if you lie more toward your front. If you are lying on your left side, put your left arm behind you. Straighten your left leg. Bend your right leg and rest it on a firm, fat pillow. Bend your right arm, bringing your hand toward your face. You will need only a flat pillow for your head.

Toward the end of pregnancy you may experience heartburn or shortness of breath when you are lying down. Propping your-self up with pillows to a semisitting position (about 45 degrees) or raising the head of the bed a few inches may help alleviate these problems.

In late pregnancy, lying flat on your back (the supine position) may cause your heavy uterus to press on the large abdominal vein (the vena cava), reducing the blood flow from the lower body to the heart, thus lowering your blood pressure. This condition, called *supine hypotension,* can inhibit the flow of blood to the placenta, decrease the oxygen available to the baby, and slow the fetal heart rate. If you feel dizzy or light-headed when lying on your back, it is almost certain that the fetal oxygen supply has also been reduced. You can correct this condition by rolling over to your side or sitting up. Even if you do not feel dizzy, it is a good idea to stay off your back while lying still. Some of the exercises in this chapter are done while lying on your back. Supine hypotension tends not to be a problem under these circumstances, since the exercises themselves shift the weight of the uterus. Do not remain on your back after exercising—roll to one side or sit up.

Lying on your side

Rolling toward your abdomen

Getting Up

Getting up from the floor or out of bed becomes more difficult as pregnancy advances. The usual "jackknife" style of getting up (a sudden jerking sit-up) may strain your abdominal and low back muscles. To get up properly from lying down on the floor:

1. Roll onto your side and bend your hips and knees. Using your arms, push up to a sitting position.

2. Get onto your hands and knees. Place one foot on the floor in front of you, while keeping the other knee on the floor.

3. Stand up, using your leg muscles. Use your knee or another object for balance.

Note: To get out of bed, put your legs over the side of the bed, then push yourself to a sitting position and stand up.

Comfort Measures

Even if you stand and move properly, aches and pains are still common during pregnancy. The positions and exercises described below can help relieve some of these discomforts.

For Low Backache

1. Tailor-Sitting
Tailor-sitting (or sitting cross-legged) is a comfortable way to keep the low back rounded and relaxed.

2. Squatting
Many women find that squatting (described on page 85) helps relieve low backache.

3. Pelvic Rock Exercise

Starting position: Get down on your hands and knees, with your hands directly under your shoulders and your knees directly under your hips. To prevent strain on the low back muscles, do not sway your back. Keep the small of your back flat or in a neutral position.

Exercise: Rock your pelvis, contracting your abdominal muscles and tucking your buttocks as you arch your low back. (Imagine a frightened dog, tucking his tail between his legs.) Hold for a slow count of five, then slowly release the contraction, returning your back to the flat position. Avoid sagging.

Repetition: Repeat five to ten times.

Relaxed

Contracted

4. Knee to Shoulder Exercise

Starting position: Lie on your back with your knees bent and your feet flat on the floor.

Exercise: Draw one knee up to your chest and hold it with one hand. Bring the other knee up and hold it, letting your knees spread apart around your abdomen. Keep your head on the floor while gently pulling your knees toward your shoulders until you feel a slight stretch in the lower part of your back. Hold for a slow count of five. Release the pull without letting go of your knees.

Repetition: Repeat five to ten times. Let one foot down to the floor, then the other.

Note: In late pregnancy, you may wish to raise and pull only one leg at a time. Roll onto your side as soon as you finish the exercise. If this exercise causes lightheadedness, do not do it.

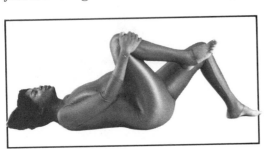

One knee up

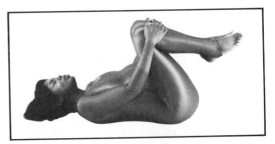

Both knees up

For Upper Backache

1. Shoulder Circling

Starting Position: Stand or sit with your back straight, your arms relaxed, and your chin level.

Exercise: Raise your shoulders toward your ears, then slowly roll them forward, down, back, and up again. Think of making large circles with your shoulders. Imagine that someone is rubbing your back as you slowly make circles with your shoulders. Feel the relaxation. Finish with your shoulders back and down in a relaxed position.

Repetition: Do five to ten rotations, then reverse the direction and repeat.

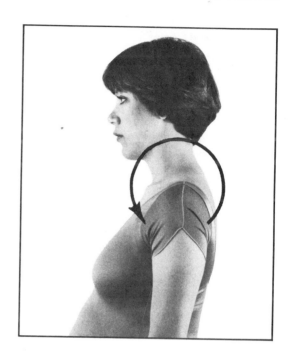

2. Upper Body Stretch

Starting Position: Sit tailor fashion (page 79) or stand with your arms straight and extended in front of you.

Exercise: Cross your arms at the elbows; feel your upper back stretch. While slowly breathing in, raise your hands toward the ceiling and gradually uncross your arms. Reach upward so you feel the stretch in your entire body.

Exhale as you lower your arms down to your sides and behind you with palms up. Feel the stretch across your chest and upper arms. When your arms are down behind you, stretch further with five gentle pulsing motions. Exhale with each stretch, making a "who" sound. Drop your arms to your sides and relax without slumping.

Repetition: Repeat five times.

For Aching Legs or Swollen Ankles

1. *If you are bothered by aching legs, swollen feet and ankles, or varicose veins, do the following to promote better circulation:*

• Walk, do not stand still.

• When you are sitting, rotate your feet at the ankles, and do not cross your legs at the knees.

• When you are resting during the day, lie on your side or elevate your feet (sit with your feet up, for example).

2. *To help prevent or reduce swelling in the legs, try the following:*

• Wear support stockings. Put them on before you get out of bed, since this is when there is the least amount of swelling.

• Raise the foot of your bed on two- to three-inch blocks. When you are lying down, your feet need be only a little higher than your heart to reduce the swelling in your legs, feet, and ankles. If this position causes more heartburn or shortness of breath, rely on the other measures described above.

For Leg Cramps

Cramps in the calves or feet commonly occur in late pregnancy when you are resting or asleep. Cramps are caused by fatigue in calf muscles, pressure on the nerves to the legs, impaired circulation, or a calcium-phosphorus imbalance in the blood. This imbalance can result from inadequate calcium intake or from eating large amounts of phosphorus—in foods such as processed meats, snack foods, and soft drinks. Even with a good diet and careful attention to circulation in the legs, you may still get cramps, especially when you point your toes or when you stand or walk on your tiptoes.

Relieving Cramps

A muscle cramp disappears when the muscle is slowly and gently stretched.

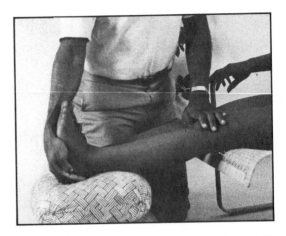

• To relieve a cramp in the calf, straighten your knee and bend your foot back with your toes pointing toward your nose. Bearing weight on the cramped leg is helpful. Keep your knee straight, your ankle bent, and your heel on the floor, then lean forward to stretch the calf muscle. When a leg cramp is severe, you may need help. While you sit in a chair or on a bed, your partner holds your knee straight with one hand and, while gripping your heel with the other, he uses his forearm to gently press your foot and toes back toward your face.

• A cramp in the foot tightens the muscles of the arch and curls the toes. To relieve the cramp, stretch out your toes and foot with your hand. To prevent cramping, do not curl your toes.

For Sudden Groin Pain

A common discomfort of pregnancy is a sudden pain in the lower abdomen or groin, on one or both sides. This may occur when you stand up quickly, or sneeze, cough, or laugh with your hips extended (lying down or standing). The sudden stretching of one or both of the round ligaments that support the uterus causes the pain. These ligaments, which connect the front sides of the uterus to either side of the groin, contract and relax like muscles, yet much more slowly.

Any movement that causes a sudden stretching of these ligaments causes pain. You can avoid this pain by moving slowly, allowing the ligaments to stretch gradually. If you anticipate a sneeze or expect to cough, bend or flex your hips to reduce the pull on these ligaments.

In labor, the contractions of the round ligaments during uterine contractions are beneficial, since they pull the uterus forward and align it and the baby with the birth canal for the most efficient and effective action.

Exercise

How much and what kind of exercise is best during pregnancy depend to some extent on the course of your pregnancy, your fitness, and your usual activity level. Physical changes during pregnancy directly affect your tolerance for exercise. Your ligaments relax and your joints become more mobile, due to hormonal changes; your center of gravity shifts, due to the enlargement of your abdomen.

Sports. Pregnancy is not a time to take up vigorous sports that require good balance or sudden jerky movements, such as softball, skating, or tennis. If you are already skilled in those or other demanding sports, however, continue playing them until you feel uncomfortable. In other words, as long as your pregnancy remains normal, you may continue any recreational sport or activity in which you feel competent, including tennis, swimming, cross-country skiing, jogging, or bicycling. Limit or avoid potentially dangerous activities, such as skydiving, scuba diving, springboard diving, or rock climbing. Talk with your caregiver if you have questions about a particular sport during pregnancy.

Aerobics. The goal of an aerobic exercise program is to improve heart and lung performance. Aerobic exercise programs usually include a warm-up, a period of sus-

tained, vigorous exercise during which the heart is expected to reach a specified rate, and a cool-down. Exercises for strength and flexibility are sometimes added. You will take your pulse (heart rate) frequently to make sure that it does not exceed the specified rate. Two studies of pregnant women—one describing a swim-conditioning program, and the other an aerobic exercise program—suggest that it is safe and beneficial for pregnant women to participate regularly in an aerobic program. Guidelines for aerobic exercise during pregnancy are based on your age and your fitness level.* If you choose an aerobic program, start slowly and gently. Avoid exhausting exercise, which may adversely affect you or your baby. Stop exercising if you feel pain, headache, nausea, severe breathlessness, dizziness, or loss of muscle control. You can let your body be your guide if you listen to it carefully.

GENERAL PRINCIPLES OF SAFE, EFFECTIVE EXERCISE

During exercise sessions, follow the principles outlined below to avoid injury and to provide the most benefit to you.

- *Exercise regularly—daily, if possible.*

- *Exercise on a firm surface.*

- *Exercise with smooth movements; avoid bouncing or jerking.*

- *While performing an exercise, do not hold your breath; it can increase pressure on the pelvic floor and abdominal muscles or make you feel dizzy.*

- *Stop the exercise if you feel pain. Your body might be telling you that muscles, joints, or ligaments are being strained. Check with your doctor or midwife if you have questions about exercising.*

- *To avoid strain and fatigue, start with the easiest position, then try others as your muscles strengthen. Start with a few repetitions, gradually increasing the number.*

Conditioning Exercises

Whether or not you participate in an organized exercise program, you can practice the following conditioning exercises along with an invigorating activity such as walking or swimming. The conditioning exercises are designed to keep your muscles (especially the pelvic floor and abdominal muscles) in good condition during pregnancy, to enable you to use your muscles effectively during birth, and to speed your postpartum recovery.

Conditioning the Pelvic Floor Muscles

The pelvic floor (or perineal) muscles act as a hammocklike support for your abdominal and pelvic organs. During pregnancy, these muscles may sag in response to the increased weight of your uterus and the relaxing effect of the hormones your body produces. Regular exercise of the pelvic floor muscles maintains tone and improves circulation, which can reduce the heavy, throbbing feeling that you might experience during pregnancy or post partum. Since the pelvic floor muscles are most affected by the baby's birth, and their condition is of lifelong importance, regular exercise of the pelvic floor is essential during pregnancy and throughout your lifetime.

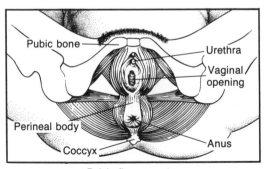

Pelvic floor muscles

The pelvic floor muscles, forming a figure 8, circle around the urethra, vagina, and anus. During childbirth, the circle of muscles around the vagina stretches to allow the birth of the baby. Birth is quicker, more comfortable, and easier if you relax these muscles rather than tighten them. Pelvic floor exercises during pregnancy will help you prepare for this process. Regular exercise of these muscles can also enhance sexual enjoyment for you and your partner. Problems such as leaking urine and the relaxation of the rectal wall can also be prevented or reduced if the muscle tone of the pelvic floor is maintained.

To check the strength of your pelvic floor muscles, try to stop the flow of urine in midstream. If you cannot, do not despair. These muscles respond quickly to exercise. You may also check by inserting two fingers in the vagina and tightening your pelvic floor muscles around them. During intercourse, check by tightening your pelvic floor muscles around your partner's penis; he can help evaluate your progress.

1. Pelvic Floor Contraction (also called perineal squeeze or Kegel exercise)

Aim: To maintain the tone of the pelvic floor muscles, improve circulation to the perineum, and provide better support for the uterus and other pelvic organs.

Starting position: Assume any position— sitting, standing, or lying down.

Exercise: Contract or tighten the pelvic floor muscles as you would to stop the flow of urine. You will feel a slight lifting of the pelvic floor. Hold tightly for a slow count of two or three. Release the tension, relax and lower the pelvic floor.

Repetition: Repeat three to five times, then rest for a few minutes. Repeat the sequence as often as possible during the day (100 per day are not too many).

Note: Always end this exercise with the pelvic floor muscles slightly contracted so they maintain their supportive function.

Variation A (*"elevator"*)

Aim: To become aware of pelvic floor muscle tension and relaxation, and to learn to tighten or relax these muscles when desired.

Starting position: Get into any position.

Exercise: Slowly tighten the pelvic floor muscles. Think of them as an elevator rising slowly and stopping at each floor. Second floor—tighten a little and hold. Fifth floor—tighten a little more and hold. Eighth floor—tighten even more. Feel the muscles in the vagina contract. Slowly release the tension; do not let the "elevator" drop too quickly. Sixth floor—release a little and hold. Fourth floor—release more and hold. First floor—relax muscles, but keep some tension to maintain their supportive function.

Repetition: Repeat once or twice a day.

Variation B (*pelvic floor bulging*)

Aim: To practice and prepare for the second stage of labor—pushing the baby out.

Starting position: Get into the tailor-sitting position, squat, or any of the birthing positions (see chapter 7, pages 142 to 143). Make sure your bladder is empty when practicing this one!

Exercise: Consciously relax the pelvic floor muscles. Gently bear down, as you do when you are having a bowel movement, letting the perineal muscles relax further and bulge downward. Putting your hand on your perineum will help you to feel this bulge. Do not bear down hard or strain; hold for three to six seconds.

Stop bearing down. Breathe in and tighten the pelvic floor up to a supportive resting position.

Repetition: Repeat once or twice a day.

Squatting
2. Squatting

Aim: To increase the mobility of the pelvic joints, stretch the muscles and ligaments of the inner thighs and calves, practice a position for assisting the descent of the baby during childbirth.

Starting position: Stand with your feet comfortably apart (one to two feet) and your heels on the floor. Squatting with your heels on the floor allows for greater stability, greater curve of the low back, and better alignment of the birth canal. To maintain your balance, you can hold onto your partner or a chair while squatting, or you can lean your back against a wall and slide down. If you cannot squat with your heels flat, try spreading your feet farther apart. You can also wear shoes with moderate heels or elevate each heel with a one- to two-inch book.

Note: If you have had a hip or knee injury, consult your caregiver before trying this exercise.

Exercise: Slowly squat with your weight on your whole foot, not just your toes. Do not bounce or let your feet roll inward. If your feet do roll inward, put a book under each heel, wear shoes with moderate heels, or squat with support so you can squat correctly. Stay down for thirty seconds to two minutes, then rise slowly.

Repetition: Repeat five to ten times daily. Progress to squatting for two minutes at a time.

Conditioning the Abdominal Muscles

The abdominal muscles are the ones most obviously stretched during pregnancy. However, keeping them in good condition helps you maintain good posture, avoid backache, push the baby out more easily, and hasten the full recovery of your figure after the birth.

There are four layers of abdominal muscles that, like a corset, support the contents of the abdomen. These layers work together to bend the body forward or sideways, rotate the trunk, tilt the pelvis, and help with voluntary breathing. Exercises that condition these muscles without causing excessive strain are described below. To avoid back and abdominal muscle strain in late pregnancy, do not do double-leg lifts or straight sit-ups.

3. Abdominal Tightening

Aim: To strengthen and tone the abdominal muscles.

Starting position: Sit up with your hands on your abdomen.

Exercise: Breathe in, allowing your abdomen to bulge. As you breathe out, gradually tighten your abdominal muscles by pulling in your abdomen toward your backbone until your lungs are empty. Imagine your abdominal muscles hugging your baby and pressing your air out. Breathe in, relaxing the muscles. Rest.

Repetition: Repeat two or three times. Stop if you feel dizzy or light-headed.

4. Pelvic Tilt

Aim: To strengthen the abdominal muscles, improve posture, and relieve backache.

Starting position: Lie on your back with your knees bent and your feet flat on the floor.

Exercise: Flatten the small of your back onto the floor by contracting your abdominal muscles. Hold the abdominal muscle contraction for a count of five as you exhale. Relax.

Note: To check that you are doing the exercise correctly, place your hand under the small of your back as you tilt your pelvis. You will press your back onto your hand.

Repetition: Repeat this exercise and each variation five times daily.

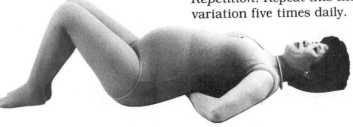

Variation A

Starting position: Get on your hands and knees (as you would for pelvic rocking, page 80). Keep your back straight—not hollowed, swayed, or arched—and your knees comfortably apart.

Exercise: Tighten your abdominal muscles to arch your low back. (Imagine a frightened dog who tucks her tail between her legs.) Hold for a count of five. Relax and return your back to the starting position—do not sag.

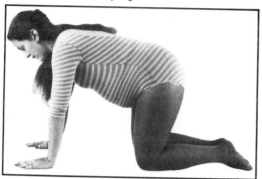

Relaxed

Contracted

Variation B

Starting position: Stand with your buttocks and shoulders against a wall, your feet apart and twelve to fifteen inches away from the wall, and your knees slightly bent.

Exercise: Press your low back against the wall as you contract the muscles of your abdomen. Hold for a count of five. Relax.

Note: To check yourself, put your hand between the wall and the small of your back. As you tilt your pelvis, you should feel your back press against your hand. To increase the efficiency of this exercise, move your feet closer to the wall.

Variation C

Starting position: After you have mastered the pelvic tilt leaning against a wall, try it while standing upright.

Exercise: By raising your pubic bone in front, as if you were tilting a basin, you can maintain good posture and help relieve or even prevent backache. To check, put your hands on your hips. You will feel your hip bones move as your pubic bone tips up toward your chest.

Relaxed

Contracted

5. Leg Sliding

Aim: To strengthen the lower abdominal muscles.

Starting position: Lie on your back with your knees bent and your feet flat on the floor. Your feet will slide better if you wear socks or stockings. Put your hand beneath the small of your back.

Exercise: Maintain a pelvic tilt with your low back flat against your hand while slowly sliding your feet, straightening both legs until you feel your low back come up off your hand. Stop sliding your legs and bring both knees up again, one at a time. Repeat the exercise, but straighten your legs only to the point where your back comes off your hand. Work in this range until your abdominal muscles are strong enough to keep your back flat until your legs are outstretched. Return your legs to the starting position, one at a time.

Repetition: Repeat five to ten times daily.

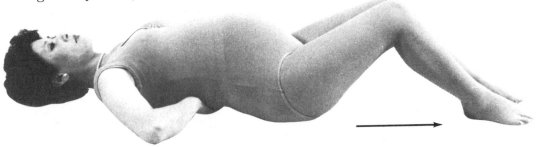

6. Diagonal Lift

Aim: To strengthen the diagonal abdominal muscles.

Starting position: Lie on your back with your knees bent, your feet flat on the floor, and your palms together.

Exercise: Breathe in, tilt your pelvis and keep your back flat on the floor. Tuck your chin and slowly lift your head and shoulders as you breathe out. Stretch your arms toward the outside of your left knee. Lift until your right shoulder is raised more than the left, but your waist is still on the floor. Do not jerk or strain. Hold for a count of five. Relax and lean back gently. Repeat, reaching toward the right side.

Repetition: Repeat five to ten times daily on each side.

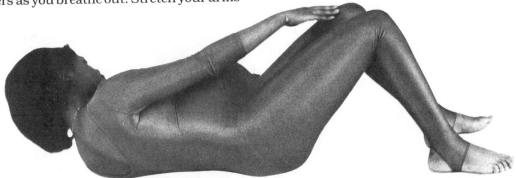

Stretching

Stretching helps increase flexibility and promotes comfort during pregnancy and birth. When you are stretching, remember to relax into the stretch, stretch slowly, and hold the stretch for thirty to sixty seconds.

1. Modified Tailor-Sitting

Aim: To stretch the muscles of the inner thighs and to practice relaxing the leg and pelvic floor muscles in preparation for birth. Caution: Do not try this exercise if you feel pain in the area of the pubic bone.

Starting position: Take off your shoes, and sit on the floor with your knees bent and the soles of your feet together, as close to your body as is comfortable. Hold your feet.

Exercise: Leaning forward from your hips and relaxing your legs, allow the weight of your legs to stretch the inner thighs. Then, using the muscles of your outer thighs and buttocks, gently press your knees toward the floor. Consciously re-

lease the muscles of the inner thighs and pelvic floor. When you feel the muscles stretching, hold that position for thirty to sixty seconds. Do not bounce your knees or press down on them with your hands.

Repetition: Repeat two to three times.

2. Hamstring Stretch

Aim: To stretch the hamstring muscles (at the back of the thighs). This exercise can help relieve backache.

Starting position: Sit tailor fashion. Extend your left leg straight out, with your kneecap toward the ceiling and your ankle relaxed.

Exercise: Reach slowly and gently toward your left foot with both hands. When you feel the back of your thigh stretching, hold that position for thirty to sixty seconds. Relax and sit up.

Repetition: Repeat two to three times. Then straighten the right leg and bend the left. Repeat two to three times stretching toward the right.

3. Calf Stretch

Aim: To stretch the tendons and muscles of the calf and ankle.

Starting position: Stand two or three feet from a wall with your shoes off. Resting your hands on the wall, place one foot about twelve inches in front of the other.

Exercise: Slowly and gently bend your front knee, putting your weight onto the front leg. Keep your back straight, your buttocks tucked in, and your heels on the floor. When you feel the calf muscle stretching in the rear leg, hold that position for thirty to sixty seconds. Then straighten and relax.

Repeat with the other leg forward. To increase the stretch, lengthen the distance between your feet or place the ball of your back foot on a book, keeping your heel down.

Repetition: Repeat, stretching each calf two to three times daily.

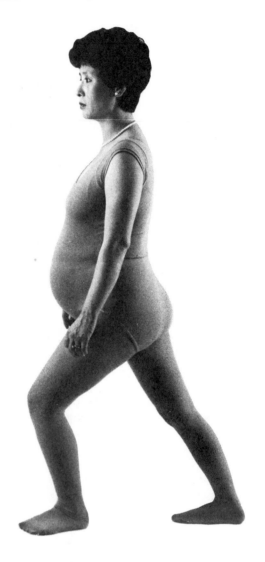

Chapter Six
Preparation for Childbirth:
Relaxation, Comfort, and Breathing Techniques

During pregnancy, you and your partner will want to prepare yourselves physically, emotionally, and intellectually for the extraordinary experience of having a baby. During labor you may use relaxation techniques, a variety of comfort measures, and patterned breathing to help you remain relaxed, maintain a sense of well-being, and cope with the stress and pain of labor and birth. This chapter includes complete descriptions of these techniques and how to master them, along with a daily practice guide—a step-by-step, week-by-week approach to childbirth preparation (pages 120 to 122).

While the use of these techniques cannot guarantee a pain-free childbirth, they can reduce pain and stress and give you some control over the experience. Along with the support you will have from your partner and others, these techniques and your adaptations of them are your own physiologic resources for coping with labor. You may use them instead of or in conjunction with medical interventions. When you use these techniques and participate fully, your birth is rewarding, exciting, and fulfilling—one to look back on with satisfaction and joy.

Historical Overview

Over the last half-century a number of outstanding individuals have contributed significantly to the methods now used in labor to enhance relaxation and to relieve pain.

Dick-Read   Grantly *Dick-Read*, a British physician, pioneered natural childbirth in the 1920s. He taught his obstetric patients about the natural physiologic process of birth to decrease their fear of the unknown. His approach was based on the need to prevent the cycle of fear, tension, and pain. He observed that when a woman is afraid, she becomes tense and the tension gives rise to pain. The more pain she feels, the more frightened she becomes, perpetuating and intensifying the cycle. To interrupt this "vicious cycle," he advocated education, relaxation, and controlled abdominal breathing.

Grantly Dick-Read taught that the mind and the body are so closely connected that the act of consciously relaxing the voluntary muscles of the body can lead to a more relaxed state of mind. "Where there is a state of relaxation of the body, there cannot be a state of tension or acute anxiety of the mind."* Dick-Read's beliefs about pain in childbirth have stood the test of time and are still significant today.

Lamaze

While Grantly Dick-Read was teaching about childbirth without fear, Dr. Fernand *Lamaze* of France was training women with the "Accouchement Sans Douleur" or "Childbirth Without Pain" method. In the 1950s, Lamaze developed his childbirth preparation methods after observing the techniques used by Russian women in labor. Based on the theories of conditioned response developed by Pavlov, Lamaze introduced the psychoprophylactic method in France. *Psychoprophylaxis*, which literally means "mind prevention," involves the use of distraction techniques during contractions to decrease the perception of pain or discomfort. These techniques include controlled deep chest breathing; a light massage of the abdomen, called "effleurage"; and concentrating on an object called a "focal point." Women trained in the Lamaze method are encouraged to respond to the stimulus of the contraction by relaxing and concentrating on these techniques. When a mother uses the Lamaze method, or psychoprophylaxis, her preparation can help reduce the pain of labor and birth. Elisabeth Bing and Marjorie Karmel introduced and popularized the Lamaze method in the United States.

Bradley

In the 1950s and 1960s, Robert *Bradley*, an American physician, influenced childbirth education by emphasizing relaxation and abdominal breathing for labor. Bradley's major contribution, however, was to encourage husbands to participate as labor coaches.

Kitzinger

Since the 1960s, Sheila *Kitzinger*, British anthropologist and childbirth educator, has influenced childbirth preparation with her psychosexual approach; she sees childbirth as a personal, sexual, and social event. Kitzinger encourages women to examine their feelings about their bodies, pregnancy, and childbirth. Because labor and birth involve others at a time of emotional and physical stress, the expectant mother and her partner should learn how to communicate with their caregivers. The Kitzinger method emphasizes body awareness, innovative relaxation techniques, and special breathing patterns. Her philosophy is that "the aim is not to retreat from contractions, but to adjust to them and respond actively, with control and concentration."*

Besides these four leaders, other individuals and organizations have contributed significantly to childbirth education as it is taught today. *La Leche League International*, founded in 1956, has been largely responsible for a renewed interest in breastfeeding. In the 1960s the voice of the consumer in maternity care was given a great boost by the formation of two prominent organizations—the *International Childbirth Education Association* (ICEA) and the *American Society for Psychoprophylaxis in Obstetrics* (ASPO). Their efforts helped launch the childbirth education movement and have greatly enhanced the quality of childbirth education.

In the 1970s the scope of childbirth preparation expanded beyond methods of pain relief to include a more holistic approach: emphasis on movement by the mother during labor and the use of the upright position to enhance the progress of labor (Roberto Caldeyro-Barcia and others); gentler pushing techniques for birth (Kitzinger, Caldeyro-Barcia, and Elizabeth Noble); bonding between parents and newborn (Marshall Klaus and John Kennell); and gentle birth procedures for the benefit of the newborn (Frederic Leboyer). The exercises and techniques offered in the following pages are drawn from the approaches described above and are relevant to childbirth today. In addition, you will learn ways to adapt these skills to suit your own individual needs and expectations.

Relaxation

Relaxation—the art of releasing muscle tension—is the cornerstone of comfort during labor. The ability to relax at will comes more easily to some than to others. With concentration and practice, however, everyone can master the skill of relaxing. Many approaches to relaxation are presented in this chapter. Try them all, but concentrate on those that appeal to and work best for you.

Relaxation skills, which are helpful in daily life, are essential during labor and birth. During labor they will help you:

• **Conserve energy and reduce fatigue.** If you are not consciously relaxing your muscles, you will most likely tense them during labor. By tensing the muscles not needed during labor, you waste energy, decrease the oxygen available for the uterus and baby, and become unduly tired.

• **Calm your mind and reduce stress.** A relaxed body leads to a relaxed state of mind, which in turn helps you reduce stress. There is evidence that distress in the laboring woman—in the form of anxiety, anger, fear, or illness—produces an excessive amount of catecholamines, the stress hormones—epinephrine (also called adrenalin) and norepinephrine (also called noradrenalin). A high level of catecholamines can prolong labor by decreasing the efficiency of uterine contractions and can affect the fetus by decreasing the blood flow to the internal organs, including the uterus and placenta.*

• **Reduce pain.** Relaxation decreases the tension and fatigue that intensify the pain felt during labor and birth. It also allows maximum availability of oxygen for the uterus, which may decrease pain, since a muscle deprived of oxygen is painful. The concentration involved in consciously relaxing all the muscles you do not need to maintain your position also reduces your awareness of pain by helping you focus your attention away from the pain of contractions.

Learning to Relax

The first step in learning to relax is to become aware of how your mind and body feel when you are resting or falling asleep. Since your mind and body influence each other, you probably will notice a simultaneous release of muscle and mental tension when you relax. Your breathing pattern will probably be slow and even, with a slight pause between each inhalation and exhalation. This type of breathing will aid you in the relaxation exercises and during labor.

When you practice relaxing, lie down, using pillows to make yourself comfortable, or sit in a comfortable chair with cushions for support. Do not lie on your back, a position that impairs circulation. After you have learned to relax in these positions, practice relaxing while sitting up, standing, and walking, since you will need to relax in a variety of positions during labor.

When you are learning relaxation skills, begin in a quiet, calm atmosphere and progress to noisier, more active surroundings. Remember, hospitals are busy places, so you will need to be able to relax in the midst of activity. After a practice session, lazily stretch all your muscles and get up slowly to avoid becoming light-headed or dizzy.

Becoming conscious of muscle tension (body awareness) is the next important step in learning to relax. The following techniques will help you recognize and reduce the unnecessary tension that may develop during labor.

Body Awareness Techniques

1. Tensing and Releasing Muscles

Starting position: Sit in a chair or on the floor. Try to relax all the muscles you do not need to keep yourself upright.

Exercise: Raise your right hand by bending your wrist. Pay attention to how the muscles in your forearm feel. They are hard when they are tense. Touch those muscles with the fingers of your left hand. Now lower your right hand and relax the forearm muscles. Notice how soft the muscles feel when you release the tension.

Next, raise your shoulders toward your ears. Notice how you feel when your shoulders tense. Relax and lower your shoulders. Now, release even more. Really relax. Did you notice a change? Often you can release residual muscle tension when you become aware of it.

2. Tensing and Releasing the Whole Body

Starting position: Lie down in a comfortable position.

Exercise: Tighten the muscles of your entire body: your abdomen, hips, and legs, then your back, neck, and arms. Keep the muscles contracted for a slow count of ten. Pay attention to how you feel—tense, tight, cramped, or uncomfortable.

Then let your body go limp, releasing the tension all over. You may start by relaxing your abdomen and releasing outward toward your arms, legs, and head. Think of the tension flowing out your extremities. Breathe slowly. Sigh, relaxing even more. Notice yourself relaxing.

3. Discovering the Effect of Mind on Body

Starting position: Get into a comfortable position.

Exercise: Imagine the following scenes. Notice how they can increase or decrease the tension in your body.

• **Scene A.** Imagine you are on vacation, spending the day at the beach. It is a beautiful, warm summer day. After spreading your blanket on the sand, you lie down. You can feel the warmth of the sand through your blanket and it feels good. You sigh and relax. You can hear a few birds in the background and the soft sound of the waves on the shore. A warm breeze blows over you. You relax even more. You are completely relaxed, calm, and at ease.

• **Scene B.** Imagine you are on a skiing vacation. You have just returned from a long day of skiing, and you are outside your rented ski cabin. The door is locked. You are tired. You realize that you left the key to the cabin inside. It is snowing, and the snow is dripping down the neck of your parka. You are cold. You decide to break a window with a snowball. You pick up some snow to make a hard snowball, and since you left your gloves somewhere, the snow is very cold in your bare hands. You need to press hard to make the snowball firm and solid. You wonder what the owner will think about a broken window. Notice the tension in your hands, arms, neck, and back.

Practicing with Your Partner

While you are developing an awareness of tension and relaxation, your labor partner should also learn to recognize when you are tense or relaxed. He can detect signs of tension in several ways:

• By looking at you when you are tense and when you are relaxed. How do you look when you are anxious, uncomfortable, calm, content, or asleep?

• By touching or feeling various parts of your body—arms, legs, neck, face. How do your muscles feel—hard or soft?

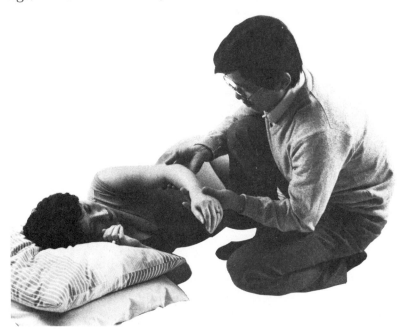

• By lifting one of your limbs, supporting it well, and moving the joints of the limb, feeling for the floppy heaviness that accompanies relaxation. How does it feel to your partner as he moves it? A relaxed arm or leg should neither help nor resist movement.

The way your partner checks you has a lot to do with your ability to relax. If he touches or moves you in a gentle manner—not dropping, shaking, or pinching your limbs—you will develop a sense of confidence and security. This trusting relationship carries over beautifully into labor. As you practice together, you will learn which parts of your body you have most difficulty relaxing. For instance, you may have a particular "tension spot." Many people, under stress, tighten their shoulders. Some reflect tension with a frown or anxious brow; others clench their jaws or fists. Your tension spots should receive special attention, both as you learn relaxation and during labor. Find out what eases tension in these areas: touch, massage, verbal reminders, warmth? After exploring the possibilities and discussing your responses, you will know what works best to help you relax and stay that way.

Once you both are skilled in relaxation and spotting tension, you can practice by deliberately tightening a muscle group and having your partner try to detect the part you have tensed. You could tense a whole arm or a finger. Try contracting the muscles most likely to be tense during labor—the buttocks, thighs, back, neck, face, or fists. Once your partner has found the tension, have him help you relax.

Relaxation Techniques

Passive Relaxation

Once you can recognize tension in your muscles, you can start to master the art of releasing tension. By focusing on different parts of your body and by releasing tension in each part, you can achieve a state of deep relaxation of both body and mind. This takes some concentration and conscious effort. When you start passive relaxation, have your partner read the following exercise in a calm, relaxed voice. He should read slowly, allowing you time to focus on and release each part of your body. Pleasant, relaxing music may also help. Once you have made a selection, use the same music each time you practice and then use it during labor to create a familiar and relaxing environment.

Starting position: Find a comfortable position lying on your side or semisitting, with all your limbs supported by the floor, bed, or pillows. Take plenty of time getting as comfortable as you can so you do not need to use any muscle effort to hold yourself in that position. Depending on the position you choose, you may want to put pillows under your knees, behind your head, or under your abdomen to help you get a comfortable, relaxed feeling. Soothing, restful music may help.

Exercise:

1. Take a long sigh, or yawn.

2. And now focus way down to your toes and feet. Just let go. Think how warm and relaxed they feel.

3. Think about your ankles—floppy and loose. Your ankles are very relaxed and comfortable.

4. And now your calves. Let the muscles go loose and soft. Good.

5. Now focus on your knees. They are supported and relaxed—not holding your legs in any position. They are very comfortable, flexed and loose.

6. Think of your thighs. The large, strong muscles of your thighs have let go. They are soft and heavy, and your thighs are totally supported. Good.

7. And now your buttocks and perineum. This area especially needs to be relaxed during labor and birth. Just let go. Think "soft" and yielding. When your baby is being born, the tissues of your perineum will ease open and let the baby slide out. You will release, allowing the perineum to give and open for the baby. Good.

8. And now the low back. Imagine that someone with strong hands has just given you a lovely rub. It feels so good. Your muscles are soft and warm, and your low back is comfortable and relaxed.

9. And now let your thoughts flow to your abdomen. Just let those muscles go. Let your abdomen swell as you breathe in, and collapse as you breathe out. Your abdomen is free. Focus on how it moves as you breathe. Good. Focus on your baby within your abdomen. Your baby is floating inside, free, warm and secure within you. Your baby is relaxing, too.

10. And now your chest. Your chest is also free. As you breathe in, bringing air into your lungs, your chest swells easily, making room for the air. As you breathe out, your chest relaxes to help the air flow out. Breathe easily and slowly, letting the air flow in and flow out, almost like sleep breathing. Ease the air into your chest, and ease it out. This easy breathing helps you relax more. The relaxation helps you breathe even more easily and slowly. Good. Now try breathing in through your nose and out through your mouth—slowly and easily, letting the air flow in and flow out. Listen as you breathe out. It sounds relaxed and calm, almost as if you were asleep. This is very much like the slow breathing you will be using during labor. Good.

11. And now your shoulders. Imagine you have just had a lovely massage over your shoulders and upper back. Let go. Release. Feel the warmth. Feel the tension slip away.

12. And now your neck. All the muscles in your neck are soft because they do not have to hold your head in any position. Your head is heavy and completely supported, so your neck can just let go and relax. Good.

13. Focus on your mouth and jaw. They are slack and relaxed. You do not have to hold your mouth closed or open. It is comfortable. No tension there.

14. And now your eyes and eyelids. You are not holding your eyes open or closed. They are the way they want to be. You are not focusing your eyes and your eyes are not moving beneath your eyelids. Your eyelids are relaxed and heavy.

15. Focus on your brow and scalp. Think how warm and relaxed they are. Just let go. You have a calm, peaceful expression on your face, reflecting a calm, peaceful feeling inside.

16. Take a few moments to note and enjoy this feeling of calm and well-being. You can relax in this way anytime—before sleep, during an afternoon rest or during a quiet break. This is the feeling to have in labor. During labor you will be walking, sitting up, showering, and changing positions; but whenever a contraction comes, you will allow yourself to release all over and let your mind relax, giving you a feeling of peace and confidence. It is this feeling that helps you focus on the positive accomplishment of each contraction, yielding to these contractions and letting them guide you in breathing and comfort.

17. Now it is time to end this relaxation session. Gradually open your eyes, stretch, tune in to your surroundings, and get up slowly.

Touch Relaxation

With touch relaxation, you respond to your partner's touch by relaxing or releasing tense muscles. During pregnancy, touch relaxation is a pleasurable way to practice relaxation. During labor, you use your companion's touching, pressure, stroking, or massaging as a nonverbal cue to relax.

The idea that touch and massage can decrease pain during labor is based on the "gate theory," which maintains that the pathway of pain sensations can be interrupted or blocked (as if by a gate) by messages from the touch receptors in the skin. Your perception of pain can be decreased when your skin is stimulated by touch.

Starting position: Lie down in a comfortable position.

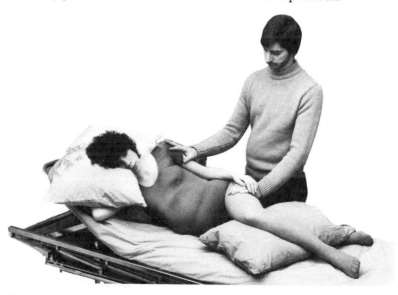

Exercise: Contract a set of muscles, then have your partner touch those muscles with a firm, relaxed hand, molding his hand to the shape of the part of your body being tensed. Release the muscle tension and relax toward your partner's hand. Imagine the tension flowing out of your body.

Note: Your partner can use several types of touch (listed below). Find out which you prefer, but practice all methods, since your preference could change during labor.

• **Still touch**—your partner holds his hand(s) in place until he feels the release of tension.

• **Firm pressure** applied by your partner on the tense area. Your partner gradually releases his pressure; you respond by releasing tension with him.

• **Massage**—your partner lightly or firmly strokes the tense area in one direction (away from the center of your body) or kneads the tense muscles.

PRACTICING TOUCH RELAXATION

Practice tensing, then relaxing, the following muscle groups:

Scalp. *Raise your eyebrows. Your partner strokes from the center of your forehead toward your temples.*

Face. *Frown. Your partner places his fingers or palms flat against your temples, pressing firmly then gradually releasing the pressure outward.*

Neck. *Tense your neck. Your partner massages it.*

Shoulders. *Raise your shoulders toward your ears. Your partner massages your shoulders.*

Upper back. *Press your shoulder blades toward each other. Your partner firmly strokes them from the center of your back outward..*

Arms. *Make a fist, tightening one arm at a time. Your partner strokes down the arm, from shoulder to hand.*

Abdomen. *Tighten your abdominal muscles. Your partner strokes the lower curve of your abdomen with his fingertips.*

Low back. *Tighten your low back, making a swayback. Your partner massages the small of your back from the center outward.*

Buttocks. *Squeeze your buttocks. Your partner firmly strokes them from your tailbone toward your hips.*

Legs. *Tighten your leg muscles one leg at a time. Avoid pointing your toes. Your partner strokes firmly down your leg, from hip to foot.*

Selective Relaxation

Selective relaxation, also called neuromuscular control or active relaxation, is the ability to relax the rest of your body while one set of muscles is contracted. During labor and birth, as your uterus contracts, the rest of your body should relax. Practicing the following exercise will help you relax the muscles that are not needed during labor.

Starting position: Lie down in a comfortable position.

Exercise: Breathe slowly in through your nose and out through your mouth. Relax more with each breath out. Contract one muscle group (for instance, the right arm), while relaxing all other areas. Have your partner check the rest of your body, telling you where there is tension (see pages 96 to 97).

After thirty to sixty seconds, release the tension and relax. Breathe deeply and slowly. Relax completely before selecting another area to contract. You can use the following progression as a guide:

Right arm	*Shoulders*	*Right arm and leg*
Left arm	*Abdomen*	*Left arm and leg*
Right leg	*Pelvic floor*	*Right arm and left leg*
Left leg	*Both arms*	*Left arm and right leg*
	Both legs	

A combination of other muscle contractions (for example, face, perineum, back, and so on)

Relaxation during Activity

If you practice relaxing during physical activity, you can prepare more realistically for labor, which will probably involve the same sort of activity. Your goal is to achieve the same relaxed feeling and mental state while active that you had with passive relaxation.

• Walk around your home or yard, paying attention to which muscles are needed to maintain your posture and to walk. Release the tension from all other muscles. Relax your shoulders, arms, and hands. Relax the muscles of your face.

• Practice relaxing in many positions—standing, sitting, semisitting, on your hands and knees, squatting, and lying on your side. Different positions require tension or activity in different muscle groups and allow for release of tension in others. Only by practicing in various positions will you be able to relax most effectively during labor.

• Practice relaxing while performing such activities as washing the dishes, typing, or driving a car. Active relaxation requires you to be awake and alert as you continue an activity; at the same time you have to release the tension from muscles that are not needed for the particular task.

• Practice relaxing while performing the stretching exercises in chapter 5. Relaxing while stretching enables greater stretch with less pain.

• Imagine that you are having labor contractions while you practice relaxation and breathing patterns. By visualizing the intense sensations of labor contractions while relaxing, you can make each practice session a labor rehearsal.

101

Relaxation Countdown

After you have become aware of body tension and have mastered relaxation, learn the following technique* to quickly release extra muscle tension. This is particularly helpful when you are trying to relax during labor. At the beginning of each labor contraction, your "organizing breath" (see page 109) can be a signal to relax completely, in just a few seconds. At first use three to four slow breaths to help you relax. With practice, you should be able to relax on the slow exhalation of one breath.

Starting position: Start by sitting in a comfortable position and progress to any position you might use in labor—standing, on hands and knees, or lying down (see pages 137 to 138 for more on labor positions).

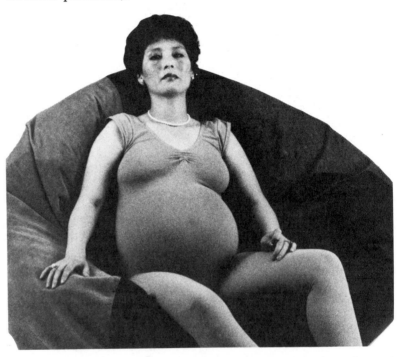

Exercise: Breathe in through your nose. As you breathe out through your mouth, release the muscle tension in your body. At first use more breaths to accomplish this. Count down from ten to total body relaxation. Think of this countdown as a wave of relaxation that passes down through your body. Use the following guide, releasing tension from head to foot.

10. *Head and face*

9. *Neck and shoulders*

8. *Arms and hands*

7. *Chest*

6. *Abdomen*

5. *Back*

4. *Hips and buttocks*

3. *Perineum*

2. *Legs and knees*

1. *Ankles and feet*

Comfort Measures for Labor

Women respond differently to labor, depending on the nature of their labor, their sense of readiness, their coping styles, and their goals and expectations. As you prepare and practice for labor, learn the various comfort measures and then adapt them to suit you. Analyze yourself and use this knowledge to develop your own style for labor. For instance, what helps you relax? Music, massage, soothing voices, meditation, a bath or shower, thinking about pleasant places and pleasing activities?

How do you cope with pain? Can you "tune into it"—focusing on it, thinking about it, and tailoring your responses to it? Some people find that if they acknowledge it, recognizing the pain as productive and positive—a part of the process that brings the baby—they can reduce pain to a manageable level. Others prefer distraction techniques, concentrating on outside stimuli to keep themselves from thinking about pain.

Many women successfully use both tuning-in and distraction. For instance, in early labor they relax, breathe slowly and easily throughout their contractions, close their eyes, and visualize the uterine contractions opening the cervix and pressing the baby downward. As labor intensifies, some continue in this way; others lighten and speed up their breathing. Then, during late labor (transition), many women find it necessary to open their eyes, focus outside (perhaps on their partner's face), and follow outside directions (their partners guiding their breathing, giving verbal directions, pacing their breathing with hand signals, or breathing with them). Sometimes more complex breathing patterns are more helpful.

All the following comfort measures are based on relaxation, the key to pain control in labor. Learn and adapt them to suit yourself.

Focal Point　During labor contractions, your attention should not drift; it should be focused on something. It can be an external focal point, such as your partner's face, a picture on the wall, a reminder of the baby (perhaps a toy), an object in the room, a flower, or even a crack in the plaster. Some people focus on the same thing for many contractions; others change focal points often. Others focus on a line like the edge of a window and follow that line visually during the contraction.

Some women prefer an internal focal point. They close their eyes and visualize something calming and pleasant—the beach, a mountain top, a happy memory. Others visualize exactly what is happening—contractions of the uterine muscle pulling the cervix open, the baby pressing down and pushing the cervix open. Music, soothing voices, or other pleasing sounds can all help you maintain your focus.

As you practice breathing and relaxing together through mock contractions, try all the focal points described above. You will probably develop a preference, but be ready to shift your focal point if it does not seem to be helping in labor.

Massage *Effleurage* is a light, rhythmic, stroking massage of the abdomen, back, or thighs. It can help with relaxation and pain relief when done on bare skin by you or your partner.

Some women prefer an extremely light, even "tickly" stroking, while others find a firmer touch more soothing. As you and your partner prepare for labor, try varying the pressure and rhythm of effleurage until you find the most appealing stroke. Then practice it as part of your labor preparation. Effleurage over the lower abdomen, following the lower curve of the uterus, is most popular. Some people think of it as stroking the baby's head. Others like to stroke the abdomen in circles with both hands.

Many women use effleurage during contractions in labor. Using cornstarch or powder will help your hands slide easily. Keep the massage rhythmic, even timing it with the slow breathing. If you find that your skin is becoming extra sensitive as the contractions intensify, you might try effleurage in a different area or discontinue it.

Other types of massage, such as *firm stroking* or *kneading* (squeezing and releasing a part), are soothing and relaxing both during pregnancy and during labor. Such massage of the face, neck, shoulders, back, thighs, feet, and hands can be very comforting. Work together massaging these different areas. Find out how and where massage is most helpful and plan to use it in labor.

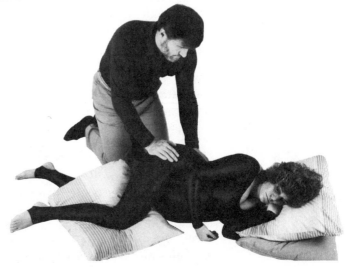

Another helpful form of massage for labor is known as *counter-pressure*, used particularly over the low back during contractions. This type of massage is especially helpful for backache during contractions. Your partner simply presses with his fist or the heel of his hand on a spot in your low back or sacrum. He usually presses with considerable force, holding your hipbone with his other hand to avoid pushing you over. The exact spot for applying pressure varies from woman to woman and changes during labor, so your partner should try various places until you tell him he has found the most helpful spot. You may need a surprising amount of pressure, so your partner may find himself physically exhausted after a few hours. It is worth the effort, however, because of the relief and comfort it brings. Your partner can take turns with another support person or the nurse to allow him to rest.

Perineal Massage

Perineal massage has a somewhat different purpose than most massage. It is used to soften the tissue around the vagina and increase the elasticity of the perineum by taking advantage of the hormonal changes that loosen connective tissue in late pregnancy. It also encourages you to relax the pelvic floor muscles when there is pressure as there will be during birth. The likelihood of avoiding an episiotomy or serious tear seems to be improved by perineal massage.* (Episiotomy is discussed further in chapter 8.)

If you are interested in avoiding an episiotomy, you may find it very helpful to massage the perineum daily for about six weeks before your due date. Be sure your caregiver knows what you are doing and why. Because perineal massage is unusual and personal, some caregivers are not familiar with it. Some women or couples find it distasteful and will not try it. Others feel it is worthwhile if it can reduce the chances of having an episiotomy. Some find it enjoyable, especially after doing it for a while and learning to relax.

If you have vaginitis, herpes, or other vaginal problems, be sure to check with your caregiver before beginning perineal massage as it could worsen the condition.

What to Do

Either you or your partner can do the massage. The first few times, take a mirror and look at your perineum so you know what you are doing. Be sure your fingernails are short. If you or your partner has rough skin, it might be more comfortable to wear disposable rubber gloves. Wash your hands before beginning.

Starting position: Make yourself comfortable, in a semisitting position, squatting against a wall, sitting on the toilet, or standing with one foot up on the edge of the tub or a chair.

Massage:

1. Lubricate your fingers well with oil or water-soluble jelly. Some people recommend wheat germ oil, available at health food stores, because of its high vitamin E content, but other vegetable oils or water-based lubricants such as K-Y Jelly can also be used. Do not use mineral oil or petroleum jelly. Wash your hands before dipping into the lubricant again.

2. Rub enough oil or jelly into the perineum to allow your fingers to move smoothly over the tissue and lower vaginal wall.

3. If you are doing the massage yourself, it is probably easiest to use your thumb. Your partner can use his index fingers. Put the fingers or thumb well inside the vagina (up to the second knuckle); move them upward along the sides of the vagina in a rhythmic U or sling-type movement. This movement will stretch the vaginal tissue (mucosa), the muscles surrounding the vagina, and the skin of the perineum. You can also massage by rubbing the skin of the perineum between the thumb and forefinger (thumb on the inside, finger on the outside or vice versa). In the beginning, you will feel tight, but with time and practice, the tissue will relax and stretch.

4. Concentrate on relaxing your muscles as you apply pressure. As you become comfortable massaging, increase the pressure just enough to make the perineum begin to sting from the stretching. (This same stinging sensation occurs as the baby's head is being born.)

5. Massage for about five minutes. If you have any questions after trying the massage, ask your caregiver.

Unfortunately, there have been no controlled studies of the benefits and risks of perineal massage, which makes it difficult to substantiate or refute the benefits claimed for it. Therefore, you need to decide if perineal massage seems to be a good idea and whether or not to do it.

Water Warm water—in the form of a lingering bath, shower, or hot wet compresses to the low abdomen, low back, or perineum and groin—is a comfort measure that most laboring women find very helpful. Contractions may seem less painful if you are in water. You are able to relax better because of the buoyancy of the bath water or gentle massage provided by the shower. Find out if you will have access to a bath or shower during labor. In the shower, lean against the wall or sit on a towel-covered stool so you can rest. Direct the spray where it helps the most. In the tub, lean back against a bath pillow or folded towels and relax. If your membranes have ruptured, you should not take a bath. In some birth settings the partner can accompany the laboring woman into the shower (he can wear his swimsuit). Hot compresses are simply washcloths or small towels soaked in hot water, wrung out, and quickly applied where you need them. As they cool they are replaced. Putting them into a plastic bag or using a hot water bottle retains heat longer. They can provide marvelous relief in a painful labor.

Cold   A cold pack—such as an ice bag or even a rubber glove filled with crushed ice, a hollow plastic rolling pin filled with ice, chilled silica gel packs (camper's "ice") or "instant" packs used for athletic injuries—can provide a great deal of relief. Placed on the low back for back pain during labor or on the perineum immediately after birth to reduce pain and swelling, a cold pack feels wonderful.

Movement   Moving around during labor is another extremely useful comfort measure. Changing your position every twenty to thirty minutes, or more often, from sitting to standing to lying down to all-fours to walking will help relieve pain and provide the benefits of gravity and changes in the alignment of the pelvic joints that can improve the pattern of labor. If labor is progressing slowly, walking may speed it up again. The upright position may give you a greater sense of control and active involvement than lying down. See chapter 7, pages 137 to 138, for further description of positions for labor.

Liquids   Most laboring women lose their appetites when they begin active labor, but their need and desire for liquids continues throughout labor. You should therefore take in liquids, either by drinking or by an intravenous drip. In a normal labor, you can drink water, tea, or juice, or suck on popsicles between contractions. By quenching your thirst you are also meeting your body's requirements for fluids. If your doctor does not allow fluids by mouth, if your labor is prolonged, or if you are nauseated, you probably should receive fluids intravenously. You can still move around and walk if you receive intravenous (IV) fluids, if the IV unit is placed on a rolling stand. Hourly trips to the bathroom to urinate will increase your comfort during contractions. If oral fluids are restricted, you may have a very dry mouth, so suck on ice chips, a wet washcloth, or a sour lollipop. You may also rinse your mouth and teeth with cold water and a toothbrush.

Breathing Techniques

In this section, you will learn a variety of breathing techniques to use during the *first stage of labor*, while the cervix dilates completely, and pushing techniques for the *second stage*, when the baby is born. (See pages 129 to 146 for more discussion.)

All skills involving physical coordination and control, such as swimming, running, singing, playing an instrument, public speaking, and meditation, require you to regulate your breathing for effective and efficient performance. Labor is no different. Along with relaxation and other comfort measures, patterned breathing is used during labor and birth to relieve pain. *Patterned breathing* simply means breathing at any of a number of possible rates and depths. The pattern you choose depends on the nature and intensity of your contractions, your preferences, and your need for oxygen. By learning and adapting breathing patterns before labor, you can use the breathing patterns to help calm and relax you during labor. Each method of childbirth preparation—Lamaze, Bradley, Kitzinger, Dick-Read, and others—relies on some form of patterned breathing.

No single method is promoted here; instead, a broad framework is offered, within which you can develop the breathing techniques that fit your preferences and needs. Some women, for example, find abdominal breathing more comfortable than chest breathing; others find just the opposite. The important thing is not where you breathe, but that the breathing calms and relaxes you. Through practice, experimentation, and adaptation, you and your partner will find your own best way to use the breathing patterns in labor.

Hyper-ventilation

Practicing and adapting your breathing patterns helps you avoid hyperventilation, a condition in which the balance of oxygen and carbon dioxide in your blood is altered, causing a tingling sensation in your fingers, feet, or around your mouth and a light-headed or dizzy feeling. Hyperventilation is caused by improper breathing (either breathing too deeply, too fast, or both), tension, or a combination of the two. While rarely serious, it is uncomfortable and can be prevented or corrected. If you have practiced and mastered the relaxation and breathing techniques before labor begins, you will be less likely to hyperventilate during labor.

If hyperventilation does occur, it can be corrected by:

• Rebreathing your own air (to increase carbon dioxide intake), by breathing into cupped hands, a paper bag, or a surgical mask.

• Holding your breath after a contraction until you feel the need to take a breath. This also allows carbon dioxide levels in the blood to increase. Do not hold your breath during a contraction.

• Relaxing and reducing tension. A shower, bath, massage, touch relaxation, or music may help here.

• Setting a slower breathing rate or making breathing more shallow. Your partner can help by "conducting"—setting a rhythm with hand movements—or breathing with you. *Note:* if your partner is breathing along with you, he can also hyperventilate. He should use the above measures, too, if necessary.

Three Levels of Patterned Breathing (First Stage)

Basically, there are three levels of breathing for labor: *slow, accelerated (or light)*, and *transition* breathing. You will use these breathing levels during your contractions to assist relaxation, ensure adequate oxygenation, and enable you to respond appropriately to the intensity of the contractions.

At the beginning of each contraction you will take an *organizing breath*—a deep, quick breath—to prepare you and your partner psychologically for the contraction, to establish the breathing pattern, and to encourage and assist relaxation. When you expel this organizing breath, release or breathe away all tension, as in the relaxation countdown (see page 102), so that when you begin your patterned breathing, you are relaxed. At the end of each contraction, take a relaxing, cleansing, or "good-bye" breath—another deep, quick breath—to help you release any tension built up during the contraction, to help you rest and relax between contractions, and to psychologically establish that the contraction is gone forever.

BREATHING THROUGH A CONTRACTION

Once the contraction begins, you will:

1. *Greet it with an organizing breath, releasing all tension as you breathe out.*

2. *Focus your attention, either internally or externally.*

3. *Begin patterned breathing—slow, accelerated, or transition—depending on the intensity of the contraction and your perception of the pain.*

4. *Use effleurage, counterpressure, or another form of massage, if desired.*

5. *Continue the breathing, relaxation, and comfort measures throughout the contraction.*

When the contraction ends, you will:

1. *Take a relaxing breath, blowing that contraction away forever.*

2. *Relax, move around, and sip liquids until the next contraction; then repeat the above.*

Practice the following breathing techniques in all the positions shown on the following page. Turn to the chart on pages 137 to 138 for a discussion of each position's advantages and disadvantages.

FIRST STAGE POSITIONS

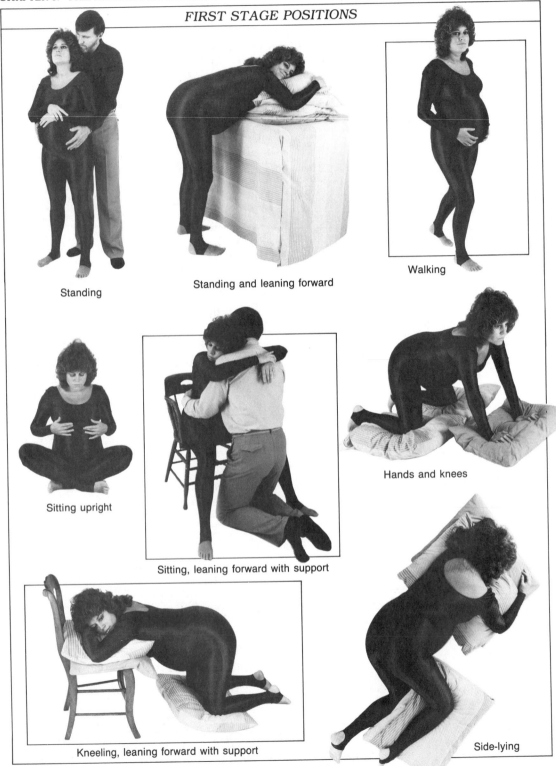

Standing

Standing and leaning forward

Walking

Sitting upright

Sitting, leaning forward with support

Hands and knees

Kneeling, leaning forward with support

Side-lying

Slow Breathing

Use slow breathing, the first level of patterned breathing, when you get to the point in your labor that it feels better to use it than not to use it. A good rule is to begin slow breathing when you can no longer continue walking or talking through the contractions without having to pause over the peak. Use slow breathing for as long as you find it helps you in labor—at least until you are well along in the first stage of labor. Some women use only slow breathing throughout the entire first stage.

Slow breathing may be done either by expanding your chest or your abdomen. More important than whether you breathe with your chest or abdomen is that the breathing helps you relax.

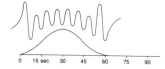

Slow breathing

How to Use Slow Breathing in Labor

1. *Take an organizing breath as soon as the contraction begins. Release all tension (go limp all over—head to foot) as you breathe out.*

2. *Focus your attention on your focal point.*

3. *Slowly inhale through your nose and exhale through your mouth, allowing all the air to flow out. Pause until the air "wants" to come in through your nose by itself. Breathe six to ten times per minute (about half the rate of normal respiration). If nasal congestion is a problem, use the same pattern and breathe in and out through your mouth.*

4. *Inhale quietly but make your exhalation audible to those close by, keeping your mouth slightly open and relaxed.*

5. *Keep your shoulders down and relaxed. Relax your chest and abdomen, so they can swell (rise) as you inhale and collapse (fall) as you exhale.*

6. *When the contraction ends, take a deep relaxing breath. Exhale as if sighing. Sometimes a yawn is a good relaxing breath.*

7. *Relax all over, change positions, take sips of liquids, and so on.*

Practice Sessions

Regular practice of five to ten contractions each session will ensure that you become comfortable, consistent, and confident with slow breathing and enable you to use it to relax deeply. Be able to use this pattern for sixty to ninety seconds at a time. Practice in different positions—sitting up, lying on your side, standing, on hands and knees, and even in the car. With each breath out, focus on a different part of the body to relax just a bit more. Think of blowing away tension in that part; then focus on another part for the next breath. Your partner should observe you for signs of tension by watching you, listening to your breathing (it should sound easy and relaxed), and by touching areas where you might develop tension. He can help you release if necessary.

Accelerated (Light) Breathing

Accelerated (light) breathing is the second level of breathing. Begin using it only if you find that slow breathing no longer relaxes you during contractions. Your partner may notice you are breathing more rapidly than six to ten times per minute or that you moan or tense at the peak of the contraction. This may not occur in your labor at all, in which case use only slow breathing. Most women, however, feel the need to switch to accelerated breathing at some time during the late first stage. Let your labor guide you in deciding if and when to use accelerated breathing.

Accelerated breathing begins slowly—in through the nose and out through the mouth—like slow breathing. Then it gradually lightens and quickens, becoming all mouth breathing as the contraction increases in intensity, and remains light over the peak of the contraction. Gradually, it slows and deepens as the contraction subsides. As in all breathing patterns for labor, your inhalations should be very quiet and your exhalations clearly heard.

How to Use Accelerated Breathing in Labor

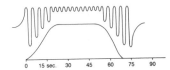

Accelerated (light) breathing

1. Take an organizing breath as soon as the contraction begins. Release all tension (go limp all over) as you breathe out.

2. Focus your attention on your focal point.

3. Inhale slowly through your nose and exhale through your mouth, gradually accelerating your breathing as the contraction increases in intensity. Keep your mouth and shoulders relaxed.

4. As your breathing rate increases toward the peak of your contraction, breathe in and out through your mouth, at the rate of about one per second.

5. As the contraction decreases in intensity, gradually slow your breathing rate, switching back to breathing in through your nose and out through your mouth.

6. When the contraction ends, take a deep relaxing breath—exhale as if sighing.

7. Completely relax, change position, take sips of liquids, and so on.

Practice Sessions

Add this breathing pattern to your daily session. Practice in a variety of positions. Be able to use this pattern for 60 to 120 seconds. Let the middle third of your contraction represent the peak, using light breathing with shallow movements in the upper chest or abdomen. The rate should be about one per second, ranging from two breaths per second to one breath every two seconds. Count your breaths for ten seconds. If you count five to twenty breaths, you are in this range. Find a rhythm that is effortless for you. This technique may be difficult and uncomfortable until mastered. At first you may feel tense or as if you cannot get enough air. Mastering this breathing technique is like learning to breathe when you do the crawl stroke in swimming. It is hard at first, but with practice becomes almost second nature and makes swimming much easier and more comfortable..

Breathing lightly through an open mouth may cause dryness, so use the following suggestions. With practice, you will be able to relax, tolerate your dry mouth, and get just the right amount of air.

• Touch your tongue to the roof of your mouth just behind your teeth as you breathe.

• With your fingers spread, loosely cover your nose and mouth so that your palm reflects the moisture from your breath.

• Sip water or other liquids between practice contractions.

Transition Breathing

Transition breathing, the third level, is really a variation of accelerated breathing. It is sometimes referred to as "pant-pant-blow" breathing, because it combines light shallow breathing with a periodic longer or more pronounced exhalation. Transition breathing is used late in the first stage if you feel the need to try something different from slow or accelerated breathing. If you feel overwhelmed, unable to relax, in despair, or exhausted, a switch to this variation may help.

Transition breathing begins with a quick cleansing breath, but rather than building slowly as accelerated breathing does, it starts with light, quick breathing at a speed ranging from two breaths per second to one breath every two seconds. After two to five of these quick, light breaths, blow out a longer, slower breath (about twice as long as the others). This "blow" helps steady your rhythm; it can also help if you need to keep from bearing down with a premature urge to push (discussed on page 114).

How to Use Transition Breathing in Labor

1. *Take a quick organizing breath as soon as the contraction begins. Release all tension (go limp all over) as you breathe out.*

2. *Focus your attention on your focal point. Your partner's face may be a reassuring focal point at this time in labor.*

3. *Breathe through your mouth, in light, shallow breaths, at a rate between two breaths per second and one breath every two seconds, throughout the contraction.*

4. *After every second, third, fourth, or fifth breath, blow out a longer breath with pursed lips. Some people emphasize this blowing breath by making a "puh" sound as they exhale. Find*

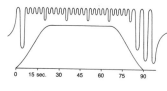

0   15 sec.   30   45   60   75   90

Transition breathing

the pattern you are comfortable with, then keep it constant throughout the contraction. Your partner might count for you ("one, two, three, four, blow") or you might count to yourself for added concentration.

5. *When the contraction ends, take one or two deep relaxing breaths.*

6. *Completely relax, sip liquids, move around, and so on.*

Variation: Scramble breathing is a further variation on transition breathing, where the number of pants per blow varies each time. Your partner tells you during the contraction how many pants, either verbally or by holding up a number of fingers. Thus you might breathe as follows: one, two, blow; one, two, three, four, blow; one, two, three, blow; one, blow; and so on. This variation adds a significant element of distraction, which may be a help during the most difficult part of the first stage.

Practice Sessions

Add this breathing pattern to your daily practice session. Late first stage contractions may last two minutes or come in pairs, so that you need to be able to use this pattern for up to three minutes. Practice in various positions. Relax for only thirty seconds or so between practice contractions to prepare yourself for the brief rest period between contractions in late first stage.

Controlling the Urge to Push

The urge to push is an instinctive reaction to the pressure of the baby on the pelvic floor. It is characterized by a feeling of pressure deep in the pelvis, a feeling similar to an urgent need to have a bowel movement. When the urge to push comes upon you, you will either hold your breath, make grunting sounds as you breathe, or have a catch in every breath. Ask your nurse or midwife to check for dilatation at this time. If your cervix is fully dilated, you generally can begin bearing down and pushing when you feel the urge. If your cervix is not fully dilated, you should either bear down only enough to satisfy the urge or avoid it altogether until the cervix dilates all the way. Your birth attendant will guide you at this time. Some birth attendants believe that a mother can damage or bruise her cervix if she bears down before full dilatation. Others believe it is better to bear down gently, following her urge. Although it is sometimes very difficult and uncomfortable to keep from pushing when you have a strong urge, it is not harmful to postpone bearing down until the cervix has dilated completely.

To control a strong, premature urge to push, lift your chin and use the "blow-blow-blow" breaths of the transition breathing pattern, until the urge subsides. It is helpful for some women to vocalize at this time, actually saying or singing, "puh, puh, puh." Then use transition breathing for the rest of the contraction.

Practice Sessions

Practice transition breathing two or three times each day, incorporating an imagined urge to push. When your partner says, "Urge to push," lift your chin and blow, blow, blow until he says, "Urge passes." As a variation, and to keep him alert, try occasionally holding your breath or grunting in the middle of a practice transition contraction. This should signal him to tell you to "blow, blow, blow." This blowing-breathing pattern, when used in labor, does not take away the urge to push; it only helps to keep you from holding your breath and joining in with the pushing effort.

Expulsion Breathing (Second Stage)

Once the cervix is fully dilated, the second stage of labor has begun. You may or may not feel an immediate urge to bear down (or push) with your contractions. Your baby's station and position in the pelvis, your body position, and other factors will determine whether the urge comes immediately or after a short rest. Usually, with time or with a change to an upright or squatting position, this resting (latent) phase of second stage subsides and the urge to push increases.

Your responses to second stage contractions are dictated by the sensations you feel—often a strong, even irresistible, urge to push lasting a few seconds several times in each contraction. Simply breathe in whatever pattern suits you best—slow, accelerated, or transition—until your body begins bearing down. Then join in with this unmistakeable and irresistible sensation by straining and holding your breath or gradually releasing air, while tightening your abdomen. Bear down for as long as it is comfortable, then breathe lightly until either another urge comes or the contraction is over. You will probably bear down three to five times per contraction, with each effort lasting about five to seven seconds. Between contractions take advantage of the opportunity to rest and relax.

This approach is called "spontaneous bearing down," and it is recommended when labor is progressing normally, without medication. Anesthesia diminishes the pushing sensations and your ability to bear down effectively. In such a case, your birth attendant and/or nurse will direct you with effective expulsive techniques.

When practicing bearing-down techniques for the second stage, try to imagine what will be happening when you use them in actual labor. By visualizing the baby descending and rotating, you will be reminded of the importance of relaxing and bulging the pelvic floor. (See exercise on page 85.)

Positions for the Second Stage

Just as movement in the first stage is helpful for both comfort and progress, movement or a change of position in second stage may be equally beneficial. Practice bearing down or expulsion breathing in the positions shown below. Turn to pages 142 to 143 for a discussion of each position's advantages and disadvantages.

SECOND STAGE POSITIONS

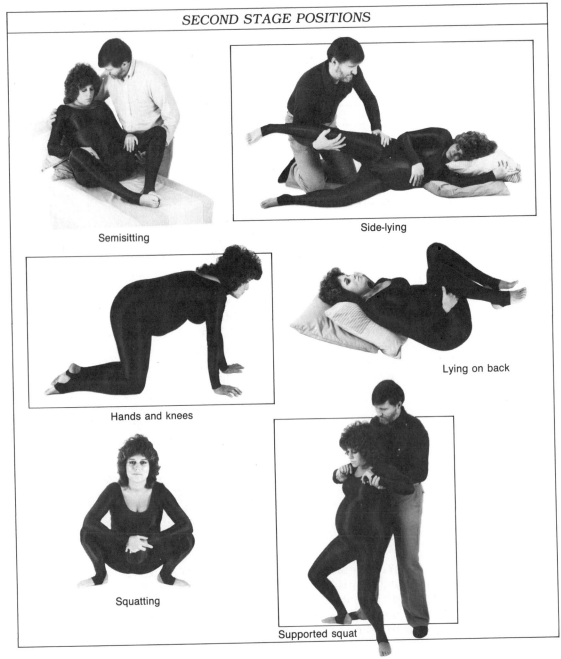

Semisitting

Side-lying

Hands and knees

Lying on back

Squatting

Supported squat

The positions you use will depend on a number of factors: the speed and ease of delivery (you may not have time to change positions if the baby is coming rapidly; if second stage is slow, however, you will have a chance to try them all); your willingness to move about; your mobility (electronic fetal monitors, catheters, anesthetics, intravenous equipment, and narrow beds discourage mobility); and your birth attendant's preferences. When you prepare your Birth Plan, discuss delivery positions. Although many doctors and midwives are most comfortable with the semisitting position (often with your feet in stirrups) on the edge of delivery table or bed, they may be willing to work with the other positions you choose at least until a few contractions before the actual birth. Then you can change to the position of your attendant's choice.

Spontaneous Bearing Down (or Expulsion Breathing)

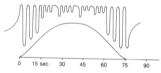

Spontaneous bearing down

What to Do

1. *Take an organizing breath as soon as the contraction begins. Release all unnecessary tension as you breathe out.*

2. *Focus on the baby moving down and out.*

3. *Breathe slowly, letting the contraction guide you in accelerating and lightening your breathing as necessary for comfort. When you cannot resist the urge to push (when it "demands" that you join in), lean forward, curling your body, and bear down, holding your breath or slowly releasing air by grunting or straining. Tighten your abdominal muscles. Most important of all, relax the pelvic floor. Let the baby out by releasing any tension in the perineum.*

4. *After five to six seconds, release your breath and breathe in and out lightly until, once again, the urge to push takes over and you join in by bearing down. You will continue in this way until the contraction subsides. The urge to push comes and goes in waves during the contraction, giving you time between to "breathe for your baby"—to oxygenate your blood to provide sufficient oxygen for the baby.*

5. *When the contraction ends, slowly lie or sit back and take one or two relaxing breaths.*

Note: This kind of breathing continues for each contraction until much of the baby's head can be seen, at which time you will feel the skin of the vagina stretch and burn. At this point you need to reduce your bearing-down efforts to allow the vagina to stretch gently to reduce the likelihood of tearing and to avoid a too-rapid delivery. While the stretching, burning sensation is a clear signal to let up on your bearing-down effort, your doctor or midwife will also give directions at this point, telling you when to push and when to blow to stop pushing. Continue blowing until the urge to push goes away or until you are able to bear down again.

Directed Pushing

The previous description of the second stage bearing-down technique is based on the assumption that you will feel a spontaneous urge to push, which will guide your response to your contractions. If, however, you do not feel your contractions because of anesthesia, or if you have no urge to push even after letting fifteen or twenty minutes pass and trying gravity-enhancing positions (squatting, sitting, or standing upright), then you may need to follow a routine of directed pushing.

What to Do

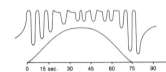

Directed pushing

In this technique your birth attendant, nurse, or partner tells you when, how long, and how hard to push.

1. *When the contraction begins, take two or three deep breaths, hold the last one in, tuck your chin on your chest and bear down, tightening your abdominal muscles.*

2. *Release your pelvic floor muscles. Bear down for five to seven seconds. Quickly release your air, take another breath, and repeat the routine until the contraction eases off.*

3. *When the contraction ends, slowly lie or sit back and take two relaxing breaths.*

Note: This routine continues for each contraction until the baby's head is almost out. At this point the doctor or midwife will tell you to stop pushing to allow the baby to pass slowly through the vaginal opening. At the attendant's direction, immediately relax and let all the air out of your lungs. Pant, if necessary, to keep from bearing down.

Practice Sessions

Use the practice sessions as rehearsals, going through the contractions as described for spontaneous bearing down. Remember the importance of relaxing the perineum while bearing down. In practice, bear down only enough to allow yourself to feel bulging of the pelvic floor. In actual labor, your body guides you in how hard to bear down.

In addition, occasionally rehearse directed pushing with your partner counting to five or seven while you hold your breath.

Prolonged Pushing

Prolonged breath-holding and pushing used to be taught for all births, whether the mother could feel her urge to push or not. It is still more familiar to many birth attendants than other methods, and it is more widely advocated by them.

Prolonged pushing differs from directed pushing in the length of time the woman is expected to hold her breath and bear down—ten seconds and more as compared to five to seven seconds. Although prolonged pushing may be beneficial under some circumstances (such as a very long second stage, inability to use a gravity-assisted position, a large baby, and so on), it is not a good idea to use prolonged pushing when progress is good. This kind of pushing, especially in the supine (back-lying) position, is associated with a decrease in the oxygen available to the fetus, a drop in the mother's blood pressure, and too rapid stretching of the vaginal tissues, increasing the possibility of a tear and the need for an episiotomy.

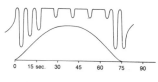

Prolonged pushing

Spontaneous bearing down and directed pushing efforts with breathing in between result in better oxygenation of the fetus* and more gradual distention of the vagina. Unless the woman uses positions that promote descent, the second stage may last longer than with prolonged pushing, but the fetus normally remains in good condition throughout.

The circumstances under which the advantages of prolonged pushing may outweigh the disadvantages are discussed in chapter 8; they involve situations when there is need to speed the second stage. Your caregiver is the best judge of this. Since you will be using this technique only under the guidance of your caregiver, there is no need to practice it before labor.

Partner's Support Role during Practice

Try to use practice time for more than simply practicing a number of techniques. Consider this time to be a rehearsal for labor. Think about and discuss when you might use the techniques and why. Review what you have learned about the emotional and physical events of labor. Use the Labor and Birth Guide, pages 152 to 154, to help you review. Most of all, use this time together to explore the basic techniques you have learned, to adapt them to fit your needs, and to learn how to work together.

Here are some suggestions for how your partner might work with you during practice. Many of these same suggestions will be useful in labor as well.

• To signal the beginning of a contraction, your partner says, "Contraction begins," or something similar. It might be in response to your organizing breath or whenever he wants to start a contraction. It is a good idea for you to take turns in "starting" the contraction. You both will get used to responding whether you are ready or not. (This is more like a true labor situation.) When the contraction ends, he acknowledges it by saying, "Contraction ends," or something similar.

• Timing contractions and calling off fifteen-second intervals may be helpful ("fifteen seconds, . . . thirty seconds, . . . forty-five seconds," and so on). This counting helps you know where you are in a contraction and about how much longer it will last. It is often helpful in labor, as well.

• To help simulate the pattern of intensity of labor contractions your partner might use physical pressure—squeezing your inner thigh or upper arm. He should gradually increase and decrease the intensity of pressure to follow a contraction pattern. Vary the length of practice contractions between 45 and 120 seconds. After you have mastered the techniques in a nonpainful situation, he might occasionally increase the pressure to painful levels so you can practice using the techniques as pain-relievers. It will be reassuring to both of you to discover how these techniques reduce your awareness of pain.

• While practicing the techniques, your partner should be aware of tension and help you regain a relaxed state. Touching, massaging, talking, breathing with you, steadying your rhythm by conducting —using his hand to set a pace for breathing— and reminding you to move around are all ways to help you during practice and during actual labor.

Suggested Guide for Daily Practice

Many techniques are offered in this chapter and in chapter 5. The following learning sequence, which is based on an eight-week preparation period, will help you master these techniques in a careful, organized way. Try to begin about ten weeks before your due date to assure finishing even if you have the baby early or to give ample time for review. You will have to condense the sequence, of course, if your preparations begin later in your pregnancy.

Week 1 **1.** Do all the conditioning exercises described on pages 84 to 90, except the variations.

2. Practice body awareness, pages 94 to 95.

3. Practice passive relaxation with slow breathing, ten to fifteen minutes daily. (See pages 97 to 99.)

Week 2 **1.** Continue the conditioning exercises, adding the variations.

2. Continue passive relaxation for shorter periods (about five minutes) with your partner checking and providing feedback. (See pages 96 to 97.)

3. Practice slow breathing in a contraction pattern (page 111), using many positions—side-lying, sitting, standing, leaning against a wall, on hands and knees, and squatting. (See page 110.) Once mastered, practice three one-minute contractions with time between for feedback, changing position, and so on. Have your partner observe and assist you in maximum relaxation in all positions; he should watch for consistency in your breathing pattern.

4. Learn accelerated (light) breathing, pages 112 to 113. This may take several days. Experiment with depth and rate to find the best way for you. Partner observes for relaxation. You may need to practice five to ten one-minute contractions per day for a few days. Once you have mastered the technique—when you can relax and do it consistently—reduce the number of practice contractions.

5. Incorporate an internal or external focal point (see pages 103 to 104) with all breathing patterns.

Week 3   **1.** Continue your conditioning exercises.

2. Learn touch relaxation, pages 99 to 100.

3. Continue practicing three slow-breathing contractions using different positions with your partner observing for relaxation and consistency and providing feedback, suggestions, and encouragement.

4. Continue accelerated (light) breathing for three ninety-second contractions in different positions.

Week 4   **1.** Continue your conditioning exercises.

2. Continue touch relaxation.

3. Learn selective relaxation, pages 100 to 101. Contract a single limb or muscle group.

4. Learn effleurage and other massage techniques, pages 104 to 106.

5. Continue practicing slow-breathing contractions.

6. Continue accelerated breathing as before, with your partner conducting.

Week 5   **1.** Continue your conditioning exercises.

2. Continue touch relaxation, effleurage, and other massage techniques with breathing patterns.

3. Continue selective relaxation, contracting two limbs or muscle groups.

4. Continue practicing slow breathing.

5. Continue practicing accelerated breathing.

6. Learn transition breathing, pages 113 to 114.

7. Learn counterpressure and other techniques for back pain, pages 105 and 165.

Week 6   **1.** Continue your conditioning exercises, particularly the pelvic floor contractions.

2. Continue with more complex selective relaxation exercises.

3. Practice relaxation during activity, page 101.

4. Continue practicing slow breathing.

5. Continue practicing accelerated breathing.

6. Continue practicing transition breathing.

7. Learn scramble breathing, page 114.

Week 7　**1.** Continue your conditioning exercises, particularly the pelvic floor contractions (and variations A and B).

2. Practice relaxation with patterned breathing.

3. Continue practicing slow breathing.

4. Continue practicing accelerated breathing.

5. Continue practicing transition breathing, along with "scramble" breathing.

6. Learn the relaxation countdown, page 102.

7. Learn spontaneous bearing down in many positions. Have your partner help you by describing how you should be pushing. (See pages 116 to 117.)

8. Learn directed pushing in many positions, with your partner telling you when and how long to bear down. (See page 118.)

Week 8　**1.** Continue your conditioning exercises.

2. Rehearse for labor. Discuss the physical and emotional characteristics of each phase of labor, as well as the support and comfort measures likely to be useful. Practice several contractions for each phase, incorporating relaxation techniques, breathing patterns, and comfort measures. Use the Labor and Birth Guide on pages 152 to 154 as a review sheet.

Chapter Seven Labor and Birth

D uring labor, the uterus contracts, the cervix thins (effaces) and opens (dilates), and the mother gives birth to the baby, placenta, umbilical cord, and amniotic sac. The entire process, which usually takes from a few hours to a day or more, is the transition to parenthood for the woman and man and the transition to an independent existence for the baby. Labor is the climax of pregnancy, when many seemingly separate systems work in harmony to bring about birth.

The onset of labor seems to be under the joint control of the endocrine (hormonal) systems of mother and baby. These systems function in synchrony so that most of the time the baby is ready to be born when the mother is ready to give birth. The fetus begins producing the labor-stimulating hormones, oxytocin and prostaglandins.* These pass from the fetus through the cord, across the placenta to the mother's circulation, thus apparently playing a part in the onset of labor contractions. The aging of the placenta also contributes to the onset of labor. As the placenta ages, its blood supply diminishes and the production of progesterone decreases. When the level of this hormone, which helps maintain a relaxed uterus, decreases, the uterus contracts more often. The mother also begins producing prostaglandins in greater amounts.

Although this physiological interaction between mother, placenta, and baby is complex and not yet fully understood, recent research indicates that the maturity of the fetus is of greater importance than previously suspected in triggering the mechanisms that begin labor. These findings have influenced a change in the use of induction of labor. In the 1960s and 1970s, doctors frequently induced labor for convenience—for instance, to take advantage of daytime work hours or to meet a deadline such as a vacation date, anniversary, or time when a relative was available to help. Under these circumstances, many babies were born before they were ready. When it was recognized that some prematurity could be prevented by not inducing labor for convenience, most modern hospitals stopped the practice. Today caregivers recognize the advantages of spontaneous labor to the baby, except where there is clear medical evidence that induction is necessary.

As you approach the end of your pregnancy, you may wish you could have the baby sooner. You may feel awkward, tired, fat, hot, and uncomfortable. Try to remember that the baby has probably not arrived because she is not yet ready to be born.

The Last Weeks of Pregnancy

The last weeks of pregnancy are a valuable preparation time for you and your baby. Your breasts, for example, produce more colostrum, the first food for the baby after birth. Your uterus becomes more irritable, contracting more frequently, both spontaneously and in response to minor disturbances such as sneezing and bumping the abdomen. These contractions, usually mild, contribute to cervical changes such as ripening (softening) and effacement (thinning). Before labor begins, your cervix may have dilated one or two centimeters. The ligaments and cartilage in your pelvis relax, allowing greater mobility in the joints, making it possible for the pelvic bones to spread during labor and birth, and giving your baby a bit more room in the birth canal.* At the same time, the tissues of the vaginal wall relax and become more elastic, which eases the baby's passage.

Fetal development late in pregnancy not only sets in motion some of the mechanisms that initiate labor, but also prepares her for life outside the uterus. The fetus stores iron at a rapid rate in the last weeks of pregnancy, taking in enough to meet her needs for the next four to six months. This iron buildup supplements the small amounts of iron present in breast milk. The fetus adds fat and develops the mechanisms to maintain her own body temperature. She gains weight and strength. As the fetal adrenal glands mature, they begin secreting steroid hormones that play a crucial role in lung maturation. As the aging placental membranes, which separate the fetal and maternal circulations, become more permeable, they permit antibodies to cross from you to your baby, providing months of protection for the baby against diseases to which you are immune.

Thus, your baby's readiness to survive outside your body coincides with her production of hormones, which feed back to your circulation and seem to play a key role in triggering at least some of the changes that start labor. Your own readiness for labor is the other key. Usually, when the time is right for both you and the baby, labor begins.

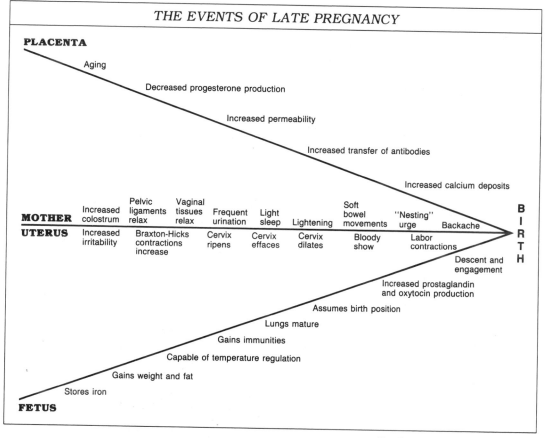

THE EVENTS OF LATE PREGNANCY

(developed by Penny Simkin, 1980)

Key Concepts for Understanding Labor

Descent   At some time during late pregnancy or labor the baby begins moving down through the pelvis. This process is called *descent*. If the baby is said to be "floating," his lowest part is still above the level of the pubic bone. For *primigravidas* (women pregnant for the first time), some descent—either gradual or sudden—usually takes place several weeks before the onset of labor. For *multigravidas* (women who have been pregnant more than once), it is not unusual for labor to begin with the baby still floating.

As the baby descends, his progress is measured in terms of *station*, which refers to the placement of the presenting part (the body part that comes first—usually the baby's head) in relation to the ischial spines (the bones marking the middle of the true pelvis). For example, if the top of the head is at O station, it means that it has descended to the middle of the pelvis. When the head is floating, it is at a minus (–) 4 station (four centimeters above the midpelvis). If it is at a – 1 or – 2 station, the top of the head is one or two centimeters above the midpelvis. If the head is at a plus (+) 1 or a + 2 station, it is one or two centimeters below the midpelvis. When the head is at the vagina and on its way out, it is at a + 4 station. In other words, descent means that the baby moves from the highest station (– 4) down to the lowest (+ 4) station and is then born. Many women begin labor at a – 1, 0, or + 1 station, meaning that some descent has already taken place.

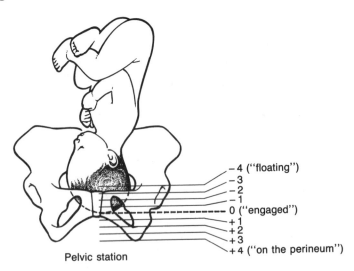

– 4 ("floating")
– 3
– 2
– 1
0 ("engaged")
+ 1
+ 2
+ 3
+ 4 ("on the perineum")

Pelvic station

Other terms used to describe descent include "lightening," which refers to the relief of pressure in the women's chest and stomach when her baby moves down. "Dropping" refers to descent that is physically noticeable. "Engagement" means that the presenting part is "engaged," or at about O station, and fixed in the pelvis.

Presentation and Position

The doctor or midwife uses these terms to describe how your baby is lying within your uterus. *Presentation* describes the part of the baby that is lying over the cervix. For example, the most favorable and most common presentation (occurring 95 percent of the time) is the vertex presentation, with the crown or top of the baby's head down over the cervix. Other presentations are the frank breech (buttocks), footling breech (feet), complete breech (buttocks and feet), shoulder, face, and brow presentations. (These rarer presentations, which may cause difficulties in labor, are discussed in chapter 8.) *Position* refers to the direction in which the baby lies within your body. The positions are anterior, referring to your front; posterior, your back; and transverse, your side.

If your doctor or midwife tells you the baby is occiput anterior (OA), it means that the back of the baby's head (the occiput) is pointing toward your anterior (front). Here are some other common descriptions of the baby's presentation and position:

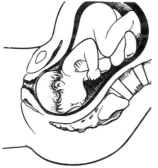

Occiput anterior (OA)

Left Occiput Anterior (LOA)—the back of the baby's head toward your left anterior (front).

Right Occiput Anterior (ROA)—the back of the baby's head toward your right anterior (front).

Occiput Posterior (OP)—the back of the baby's head directly toward your posterior (back).

Left Occiput Posterior (LOP)—the back of the baby's head toward your left posterior (back).

Right Occiput Transverse (ROT)—the back of the baby's head toward your right side.

Left Occiput Transverse (LOT)—the back of the baby's head toward your left side.

Right Sacrum Anterior (RSA)—the baby's tailbone or buttocks (sacrum) toward your right front. This is how a breech presentation is described.

Occiput posterior (OP)

Ripening, Effacement, and Dilatation

These terms refer to changes in the cervix that begin gradually before labor starts and end just when the baby is about to be born.

• *Ripening* is the softening of the cervix that begins in late pregnancy. Before ripening takes place, the cervix is firm.

• *Effacement* is the thinning of the cervix. For a primigravida, a substantial degree of effacement has usually taken place before dilatation (opening) begins. Multigravidas usually have simultaneous effacement and dilatation. Effacement is determined during a vaginal exam and is measured in percentages. "Zero percent effacement" means the cervix has not begun to thin; "50 percent effacement" means the cervix has thinned about halfway; "100 percent effacement" means the cervix has thinned completely.

• *Dilatation* refers to the opening of the cervix. Although it is usual for the cervix to dilate slightly before the onset of labor, most dilatation takes place during labor. Dilatation is estimated during a vaginal exam and is measured in centimeters. When the cervix is opened only a fingertip, it is one centimeter dilated; at the halfway point, it is five centimenters; and when fully dilated, it is ten centimeters dilated.

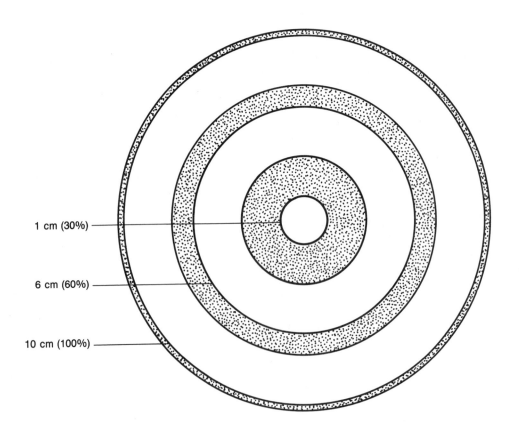

1 cm (30%)

6 cm (60%)

10 cm (100%)

Labor—The Physiologic Process

The rest of this chapter contains a description of the physiologic (normal and healthy) process of labor, along with what you can expect physically and emotionally, and what you can do to help the process and make it more comfortable. The next chapter deals with labor situations that are more difficult or complicated, along with the solutions you and your doctor or midwife might use.

THE FOUR STAGES OF LABOR

Labor is divided into four distinct stages, according to the physiologic changes that take place.

1. First Stage—the Dilating Stage, during which the cervix opens completely.

2. Second Stage—the Expulsion Stage, or the actual birth, which begins when the cervix is fully dilated and ends when the baby is born.

3. Third Stage—the Placental Stage, which begins with the birth of the baby and ends with the delivery of the placenta.

4. Fourth Stage—the Recovery Stage, which begins after the placenta is born and ends one to several hours later when the mother's condition stabilizes.

The First Stage of Labor —the Dilating Stage

At some point in your pregnancy (usually within two weeks before or after your due date), you will recognize that you are in labor. You will probably miss the exact moment labor begins; the process starts gradually and most of the early signs are subtle. Usually it takes a period of time (a few hours to a full day) for you to perceive the progression and recognize labor.

Signs of Labor By familiarizing yourself with the following signs, you will probably recognize labor and not be caught by surprise. The signs are not listed in order of occurrence because there is no consistent pattern. You may not experience all these signs of labor.

• **Backache that comes and goes**, accompanied by a feeling of uneasiness or restlessness—an inability to feel comfortable in any position for very long. This backache differs from the backache most women have in late pregnancy. This subtle sign of labor may occur for days before or along with other signs of labor.

• **Frequent soft bowel movements**, often mistaken for an intestinal upset. This is probably another hormonally induced change, which clears the lower digestive tract, making more room for the baby to move down. Diarrhea-like symptoms on or near your due date may be a subtle sign of early labor.

• **Passage of a thickened mucus plug or "bloody show."** Throughout pregnancy, the cervix has contained a thick mucus plug (the operculum), which is loosened and released when the cervix begins thinning and opening. The mucus may be tinged with blood from the ruptured blood vessels in the cervix. This bloody show can appear days before any other signs of labor are noticed so, by itself, it does not mean you are in labor. But note when you pass it and watch for other signs.

In late pregnancy, women often pass some brownish, bloody discharge about a half-day after a vaginal exam because the exam often causes some cervical bleeding. It is easy to mistake that discharge for the show. If you are not sure whether it is show or a postexam discharge, note the appearance of the blood. With the show, it is bright red and mixed with mucus; after an exam, it is usually brownish.

• **Contractions of the uterus that progress and intensify over a period of time.** That is, they become longer, stronger, and closer together as time passes. In early labor, contractions are usually felt as a tightening with some backache. Contractions usually become painful as labor advances. Uterine contractions shorten the muscle fibers in the body of the uterus, pull open the cervix, and push the fetus down and out of the uterus.

PRELABOR AND TRUE LABOR		
Before the cervix begins to dilate, many women experience nondilating contractions that may continue for hours or even days. Sometimes called "false labor," this prelabor can be tiring and confusing. The following comparison chart will help you decide if you are in true labor. If you are still unsure, however, call your caregiver or the labor and delivery nursing staff at your hospital.		
	Labor or True Labor	*Prelabor or "False" Labor*
Uterine contractions	• Become longer, stronger, and closer together with time. • Accompanied by abdominal discomfort or pain. • Rarely exceed 1 minute in early labor. • Often accompanied by increasing backache and restlessness. • Are not reduced by mother's activity; may increase with activity, but will never subside because of a change in activity.	• Tend to stay at about the same length, strength, and frequency. • Are usually not painful. If painful, the pain stays at the same level. • May last 1/2 to 4 minutes. • Are affected by change in mother's activity; will subside as the mother becomes more or less active.
Show	• Bloody show is often present before or during early labor.	• None
Intestinal symptoms	• Frequent soft bowel movements, often mistaken for digestive upset.	• None
Changes in the cervix *(determined by your caregiver)*	• Progressive effacement or thinning. • Progressive dilatation.	• Effacement not progressive. • Dilatation not progressive.

To assess your contractions, time them and keep a written record (see the Early Labor Record, page 132). To time contractions you need a watch or clock with a second hand. When the contraction begins, write down the time (it is easy to forget after a few contractions). When the contraction ends, figure out how many seconds it lasted. *Duration* refers to the number of seconds the contraction lasted. *Interval* refers to the length of time between the beginning of one contraction and the beginning of the next. You use the interval to determine the *frequency*, which refers to how often the contractions are coming; for instance, every five minutes.

• **Rupture of the membranes (ROM) or breaking of the bag of waters** begins labor about 10 to 15 percent of the time. In such cases, contractions usually begin immediately or within twenty-four hours. In most pregnancies, the membranes rupture late in labor. When the membranes break, there may be a sudden "pop" followed by a gush of amniotic fluid, or there may be a slow, uncontrollable leak of fluid. ROM may feel like urination; sometimes women believe they have lost control of their bladders. When ROM occurs and labor does not begin, the risk of infection increases as time passes. If your membranes rupture early, follow these rules:

1. *Note the time, color, odor, and amount of fluid.*

2. *Notify your doctor or midwife. Know his or her plan for your care. Some birth attendants induce labor soon after ROM if it occurs at term. (If it occurs before term, they may try to prevent labor.) Some caregivers are comfortable waiting to see if you will go into labor spontaneously or if you can get labor started by yourself. See "Ways to Start or Stimulate Labor," pages 157 to 159, for suggestions.*

3. *Do not put anything into your vagina (no tampon to control the flow, no fingers, do not have intercourse or take a tub bath) that could increase the possibility of infection. Your caregiver also may limit the number of vaginal exams done to reduce the chance of infection.*

• **Effacement and dilatation as confirmed by vaginal examination.** Your caregiver performs this examination to determine whether or not your cervix is opening.

Early Labor Record

To help you decide if you are in true labor, keep track of what is happening by making an Early Labor Record form like the one on the following page. You may find this form helpful when trying to decide when to call your caregiver or go to the hospital. If there is no progression in your contractions (if they do not become longer, stronger, and closer together) for an hour or more, stop timing. Resume timing later if there seems to be a change.

When you call your caregiver be prepared to furnish the following information: how long your contractions are lasting (duration); how far apart they are (interval) or how frequent; how strong contractions seem (intensity); how long your contractions have been like this; status of your membranes; show; and any other pertinent information.

EARLY LABOR RECORD

Date __2-29-84__

Contractions Time	Duration	Interval or Frequency	Comments
(Starting time.)	(How many seconds long?)	(How many minutes since the beginning of the last one?)	(Intensity of contractions, food eaten, breathing level, bloody show, status of bag of waters, other events.)
2:03 a.m.	25 sec.		show at 6 p.m. (2-28)
2:15 a.m.	28 sec.	12 min.	
2:30 a.m.	35 sec.	15 min.	loose B.M.
2:41 a.m.	30 sec.	11 min.	
2:55 a.m.	38 sec.	14 min.	Can't sleep

In Labor   When labor is established and your cervix is dilating, you will be in the first stage, which normally lasts from two to twenty-four hours. The average length of the first stage for a primigravida is twelve and one-half hours; for a multigravida, seven and one-third hours. Prepare yourself for a short, average, and long first stage, since it is impossible to predict just how long it will take.

Contractions continue intermittently throughout labor, shortening the muscle fibers in the body of the uterus and pulling the cervix open. Each contraction follows a wavelike pattern: it builds to a peak where it stays for fifteen to forty seconds, then gradually goes away, allowing the uterus to rest for a time. Early in labor, contractions may feel like a dull, low backache or menstrual cramps. These early contractions are usually short and mild, lasting thirty to forty seconds, and the interval between them may be as long as fifteen to twenty minutes. As labor advances, you will feel the contractions more in your abdomen or in both your abdomen and low back, and the backache may persist even between contractions. By the end of the first stage, the contractions may last as long as 90 to 120 seconds, and the interval may be as short as two to three minutes.

By the end of pregnancy your uterus has become the largest and strongest muscle in your body. When your uterus contracts, it hardens and bulges like any other muscle. It is capable of powerful contractions, which become increasingly stronger and longer as labor progresses. Usually these stronger contractions are more powerful and more effective both in dilating the cervix and pressing the baby downward. Labor contractions, under the control of various hormonal and other physiological factors, are involuntary. Once the process begins, it does not usually stop until the baby and placenta are born. Then you can rest and rejoice in your baby.

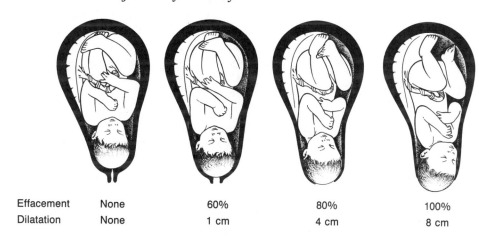

Effacement	None	60%	80%	100%
Dilatation	None	1 cm	4 cm	8 cm

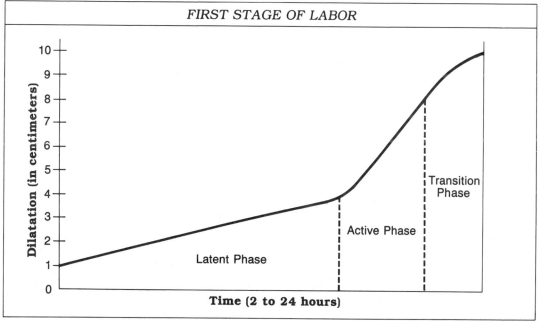

FIRST STAGE OF LABOR

The first stage of labor is subdivided into three phases: *latent*, *active*, and *transition*. The phases become shorter and more intense as labor progresses. Each phase is usually distinguished by its own physiological and emotional characteristics. If you and your partner understand each phase, you will be better prepared to recognize each phase and cope with your labor.

The Latent Phase

The latent phase is usually the longest phase of the first stage, and the contractions are farther apart, shorter, and less intense than during the later phases. During this phase, your cervix will efface and dilate to three, four, or possibly five centimeters. You will probably spend most of this phase at home, doing whatever activity is appropriate for the time of day—resting if it is nighttime, keeping busy if daytime. You and your partner will also probably spend a good portion of this phase uncertain whether you are in labor or not. The Early Labor Record will help you decide.

During this phase, it is a good idea to keep your mind active and not become preoccupied with the labor. You will probably feel excited and a bit nervous. Try to do things that are calming, not exhausting. Pack your bag (see suggestions on page 151) for the hospital or prepare your bedroom for a home birth. Focus on relaxing your muscles and your mind during your contractions. Have a massage. Take a bath if your membranes are intact or a shower if they have ruptured; do not underestimate the soothing, pain-relieving properties of water. Eat and drink easy-to-digest, appealing foods such as gelatin desserts, fruit, juice, and toast. Pass the time with pleasant activities; go for a walk, visit friends, listen to music, dance, watch television, or play games. When you reach a point where you cannot walk or talk through a contraction without pausing during the peak, it is time to begin the first level of patterned breathing, slow breathing, page 111.

When to Call Your Caregiver

When should you call your doctor, midwife, or hospital? During the last month of your pregnancy, ask your caregiver when and whom to call. Unless you live far away or have received other instructions, a primigravida should call when her membranes rupture or when the contractions are very strong, requiring total concentration and breathing. Contractions may be about five minutes apart. The multigravida should call when her membranes rupture or when she has experienced several of the signs of labor. Be ready to report the information on show, membranes, and contractions that you recorded in your Early Labor Record. Of course, if you are anxious or have questions even without evidence of true labor, call to allay your concerns.

The Active Phase

As the latent phase draws to a close, your labor pattern changes. Your contractions may be painful, though manageable, each lasting a minute or more and coming close together—some three to five minutes apart. This is the time when most people go to the hospital or birth center, or when the midwife or doctor arrives for a home birth. You may feel as if this now-intense labor has gone on for a long time without much progress. You may be tempted to calculate how long it took to get to four or five centimeters and multiply to predict how much longer it will take to get to ten centimeters. This will seem so long it may be discouraging and you may wish you could call it quits for the day. You may feel trapped in the labor, with no way out but to go on and complete the process.

These are typical reactions to the more demanding—and more productive—active phase of labor. In the latent phase, your spirits were high; in the active phase, you become serious and preoccupied with the contractions. Earlier your partner's jokes were fun and his conversation entertaining; now you cannot listen. You may even feel resentful of the "small talk" around you. As you become more centered on your labor, your partner should move in closer, focus more on your labor, and share your serious, quiet mood. He should help you relax, find comfortable positions, and maintain your focus and breathing. Most importantly, he can help you interpret what is going on. You may be discouraged because you seem to be progessing as slowly as before, yet the contractions are demanding so much more of you. The truth is, when you enter the active phase, labor is speeding up and you are accomplishing something with each of these intense, painful contractions. It is the knowledge that you are finally getting somewhere that renews your confidence and optimism.

Also, getting settled in at the hospital or with your birth attendant and support people helps you shift your frame of mind to accepting these intense, productive contractions. At this time, your nurse or birth attendant will assess your labor with a vaginal exam and evaluate the fetal heart rate. He or she will also check your blood pressure, temperature, and pulse, and may take urine and blood samples.

After these procedures, make yourselves comfortable. Try pressure and cold packs on your back, or hot compresses on your lower abdomen, groin, and back. Go to the bathroom at least once an hour because a full bladder is uncomfortable and can slow labor. Change position frequently; try to walk and sit rather than lie in bed. Some laboring women make the mistake of staying immobile in bed throughout labor. Lying down may increase the pain of contractions and slow the progress of labor.* Take advantage of gravity by standing and walking for at least part of the time. (See the photos on page 110 and the following chart for a discussion of positions.) Try to keep fairly active from the beginning, unless you are very tired and really need to lie down. You may want to alternate activity with rest. It is important to get fluids, so drink something after each contraction or suck on ice chips. To gauge your progress, at each vaginal exam find out the effacement and dilatation, as well as the station and position of the baby.

Continue your relaxation and breathing techniques. This is a good time for lots of encouragement from your partner, who can praise your efforts, rub your back and legs, count off every fifteen seconds in the contraction, and remind you to move around, drink fluids, and go to the bathroom. Relaxation is the key at this time. Make a special effort to keep from tensing during contractions.

You will want to continue slow breathing (page 111) for as long as it helps you relax. If your breathing begins to sound tense or labored if you are unable to keep the rate slow, or if you find you cannot maintain your focus and remain relaxed, even after renewed efforts and more active encouragement from your partner, switch to accelerated or light breathing (page 112). This may give you just the boost you need. Accelerated breathing follows the pattern of your contractions, lightening and quickening as the contraction intensifies, then slowing and deepening as the contraction subsides. Used in this way, the accelerated breathing pattern can help you tune in to your labor contractions and calm you with its rhythm.

POSITIONS FOR FIRST STAGE		
Position	Advantages	Disadvantages
Standing	• Takes advantage of gravity during and between contractions. • Contractions less painful and more productive. • Fetus well aligned with angle of pelvis. • May speed labor.	• Tiring for long periods. • May be impossible with anesthesia.
Standing and leaning forward	• Takes advantage of gravity during and between contractions. • Contractions often less painful and more productive. • Fetus well aligned with angle of pelvis. • May speed labor. • Relieves backache. • May be more restful than standing.	• Tiring for long periods. • May be impossible with anesthesia.
Walking	• Takes advantage of gravity during and between contractions. • Contractions often less painful and more productive. • Fetus well aligned with angle of pelvis. • May speed labor. • Relieves backache. • Encourages descent through pelvic mobility.	• Tiring for long periods. • Difficult or impossible with anesthesia, analgesia, or electronic fetal monitoring.
Sitting upright	• Good resting position. • Some gravity advantage. • Can be used with electronic fetal monitor.	• Prolonged sitting associated with slower progress.
Semisitting	• Good resting position. • Some gravity advantage. • Can be used with electronic fetal monitor. • Vaginal exams possible.	• Increases back pain. • May slow labor progress if used for long periods.

POSITIONS FOR FIRST STAGE

Position	Advantages	Disadvantages
Sitting, leaning forward with support	• Good resting position. • Some gravity advantage. • Can be used with electronic fetal monitor. • Relief of back pain. • Good position for back rub.	• May be associated with slower labor if used for prolonged periods.
Hands and knees	• Helps relieve backache. • Assists rotation of baby in OP position. • Allows for pelvic rocking. • Vaginal exams possible.	• Hands and knees go to sleep or hurt. • May interfere with external fetal monitor tracing. • May be tiring for long periods.
Kneeling, leaning forward with support	• Helps relieve backache. • Assists rotation of baby in OP position. • Allows for pelvic rocking. • Less strain on wrists and hands than on hands and knees.	• May interfere with external fetal monitor tracing. • May be tiring for long periods.
Side-lying	• Very good resting position. • Convenient for many interventions. • Helps lower elevated blood pressure. • Safe if pain medications have been used. • May promote progress of labor when alternated with walking.	• Contractions may be less effective and longer. • May be inconvenient for vaginal exams.
Squatting	• Takes advantage of gravity. • May be comfortable and relieve backache.	• May not enhance descent of baby if station is high. • Tiring for long periods.
Back-lying *(supine)*	• Convenient for caregiver for procedures and vaginal exam. • May be restful. • Convenient for electronic fetal monitoring.	• Supine hypotension. • Increased backache. • Psychologically vulnerable. • Labor contractions found to be longest, most painful, and least productive.

The Transition Phase

The transition phase represents the peak of intensity, pain, and difficulty in most labors. The cervix dilates the last one or two centimeters, the baby presses down lower in the pelvis, and your body prepares for the expulsion stage. Relatively short, the transition phase usually lasts from five to twenty contractions. These contractions, the longest of your labor, will give you the shortest rest between. You will probably be tired, restless, and irritable, totally consumed by your efforts to cope. The intensity of transition is almost overwhelming and you will need much reassurance and help to get through.

During this phase you are truly in a transition—from first to second stage. Your body shows some signs of the second stage, although it is still in the first stage. For example, your diaphragm may become irritable, beginning involuntary spasms that are the precursors of bearing down. As a result you may begin hiccuping, grunting, or belching. Nausea and vomiting are common. The baby's head pressing on your rectum feels like a bowel movement and may cause a backache or aching thighs. Trembling of the legs, which may spread throughout the body, and a heavy discharge of bloody mucus from the vagina reflect the increased downward pressure. Contractions may be irregular, with double peaks, and may last 90 to 120 seconds with only thirty-second rests between. Amidst the intensity and pain of transition, you may doze off during these short rests between contractions, as if your body is conserving every bit of energy for the work of contractions.

During transition, you become very focused on your labor; nothing else matters. You may worry that something is wrong. You may feel frightened by the intensity of labor and very dependent on those around you. You may feel transition will last forever, that you cannot take any more. But as one woman said, "When you can't take any more, there's no more to take." Transition pushes you to your limits, but with good support and knowing where you are and what you need to do, you will weather the storm because transition is short.

Getting through Transition

• Recognition is one of the keys to coping with transition. If you are experiencing the extreme sensations of transition and believe you are only five or six centimeters dilated, you will probably become discouraged. Remember that labor is a progressive process. "You are not where you were at the last vaginal exam. You are beyond that point," is a guideline to remember after you have passed the latent phase, especially if your sensations and emotional responses change during contractions. Know the signs of transition described above and be ready for them any time after you enter the active phase of labor. When women or couples know where they are, they are heartened by their progress and see the pain and difficulties of transition in a more positive light—transition is bringing the baby closer.

• Understanding the normal feelings, reactions, and events of transition is another key. Pain, nausea, trembling, despair, dependence, crying, inability to relax and breathe "perfectly" are *normal* responses during transition. They do not mean anything is wrong. It is when you think that your labor is worse than it is supposed to be that you begin to worry and seek a way out with pain medications or anesthesia. Pain medications, of course, are an option, but do not take them because you fear your transition is abnormal. The medication is to relieve pain, not to improve your or your baby's health (except in very rare instances where labor stops because the pain and stress are so great that a woman cannot respond to emotional support).

● Reassurance from your partner and caregiver is essential. You need to know that you and your baby are all right, that your sensations are normal, that you are coping well, and that this difficult time will be short.

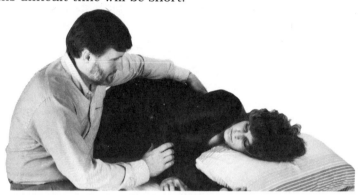

● Finally, more active support and coaching from your partner and caregiver helps you through transition. Your partner might "conduct" your breathing by pacing you with his hand or breathing with you. Switch to transition or "scramble" breathing (page 113) if accelerated or slow breathing seem ineffective. Many women like being held close at this time; others do not want to be touched, but find visual and verbal contact very helpful. Hot, moist towels on the low back, lower abdomen, and perineum can be a godsend. Changing positions between contractions sometimes brings relief.

Women often worry that transition will be too much for them, that they will lose control, panic, and behave in a way they will later regret. They have heard of women who struggled, screamed, or begged to be put to sleep. These impressions of childbirth are carryovers from the days when most women were given drugs such as scopolamine that took away their control. It was not labor, but these drugs, rarely used today, that altered women's behavior.

You can get through transition without drugs, especially if you prepare in advance, have good support, know what is happening, and use relaxation, breathing, and comfort techniques. Be assured that you will not lose your ability to respond to clear, simple directions. Your labor partner should not mistake moans, groans, or other sounds during transition with cries of agony. Many women find transition easier if they vocalize or make noise during the contractions. One nurse said, "When I walk down the hall, I can tell what stage of labor a woman is in by the sounds I hear."

The Second Stage of Labor —the Expulsion Stage

After dilatation is complete, transition ends and the second stage of labor begins. A new series of physiological events begins; your baby leaves the uterus, rotates within and descends through the vagina, and is born.

Signs of Second Stage

• The most significant sign of the second stage is *the urge to push*, which coincides roughly with full dilatation, although many women experience this urge before full dilatation and others experience it sometime later. (See page 114 on how to handle a premature urge to push.) The urge to push is a combination of powerful sensations and reflex actions caused by the pressure of the baby in the vagina during contractions. As difficult to describe as labor contractions, the urge to push is a strongly felt need to hold your breath and strain. It occurs several times within a contraction, and is responsible for your pressing the baby downward. It is as compelling and difficult to control as a sneeze, an orgasm, or vomiting. For many women, joining in with the urge to push is one of the most satisfying aspects of the entire birth experience. For others it is disturbing and painful.

• Another sign of the second stage is *relief from the sensations of transition*. The pain lessens, you calm down and cheer up, and become less focused on your labor and more aware of those around you. Now you can collect yourself for the effort of pushing your baby out of your body. During the first stage, you assisted your uterus to open up by staying relaxed and using positions to enhance the process. Now you will assist your uterus to empty itself, by voluntary bearing-down and using appropriate positions.

Key Concepts

Two key concepts should guide you during the second stage.

• The importance of *not rushing*. Although both you and the staff are anxious to get that baby out, do not rush. Follow your body's signals, bearing down or pushing spontaneously as the urge demands and giving your tissues time to spread open. By not rushing, your vagina can stretch open gently, decreasing the likelihood of damage.* You will also use your energy more efficiently. By joining in, holding your breath and bearing down only when you cannot resist the urge to push, you will be working in synchrony with your uterus and not wasting your effort.

By bearing down for five to six seconds at a time and breathing in and out several times between bearing-down efforts, you make more oxgyen available to the fetus. Although there is very little exchange of oxygen across the placenta during contractions, when the uterus relaxes, exchange resumes and the fetus benefits.*

• The importance of *different positions*. Progress and comfort should guide your choice of position. Feel free during the second stage to use positions that are comfortable; that alter progress, either by enhancing or slowing the baby's descent; or that provide other advantages.

Positions for Second Stage

The chart on the following page lists a variety of possible positions for second stage and their advantages and disadvantages. (Also, see the photos on page 116.) The most common position in North America is semisitting, with legs raised in stirrups or with feet in footrests or resting on the bed. Although this is convenient for the birth attendant, it is not always the best for comfort or progress. It is a good idea to know all of the following positions, their advantages and disadvantages, and be prepared and willing to try them all. Sometimes switching to a new position makes medical intervention (such as a vacuum extractor or forceps) unnecessary. If one position is very uncomfortable, or you make no progress in that position, try another. Positions that take advantage of gravity are an asset and may aid progress and descent.

When the second stage is progressing at a reasonable pace—not too fast or slow—use whatever position(s) seem most comfortable. If the second stage is going very fast, try a gravity-neutral position to slow it down. Sometimes, even if it hurts, you may have to get into another position, especially if descent has not been progressing. When birth is imminent, assume the position favored by your doctor or midwife.

POSITIONS FOR SECOND STAGE

Position	Advantages	Disadvantages
Semisitting	• Convenient for birth attendant. • Some gravity advantage. • Easy to get into on bed or delivery table.	• May aggravate hemorrhoids. • May restrict free movement of sacrum when more room is needed in the pelvis. • May slow passage of head under pubic bone.
Side-lying	• Gravity-neutral. • Useful to slow a very rapid second stage. • Takes pressure off hemorrhoids. • Easier to relax between pushing efforts.	• May not be familiar to birth attendant, who may need to adjust his or her technique for delivery. • Is unfavorable if you need to speed second stage.
Hands and knees	• Helps assist rotation of an OP baby. • Takes pressure off hemorrhoids. • Allows for free movement, rocking back and forth, tilting pelvis. • May reduce backache.	• Same as above. • Tiring for long periods.
Lying on back with legs pulled back, raising head to push	• Pulling legs back and apart helps widen pelvic outlet.	• Supine hypotension. • Maintaining the position exhausts the mother and may work against gravity.
Squatting	• Takes advantage of gravity. • Widens pelvic outlet to its maximum. • Requires less bearing-down effort. • May enhance rotation and descent in a difficult birth. • Helpful if mother does not feel an urge to push.	• Difficult to get into on a bed. • Difficult for birth attendant to see perineum. • May promote too rapid expulsion, leading to perineal tears. • May be uncomfortable.
Sitting on toilet or commode	• May help relax perineum for effective bearing-down. • Gravity advantage.	• Toilet may not be available nearby. • Mother must move for birth.
Supported squat *(mother leaning with back against support person who holds her under the arms, and takes all her weight)*	• Allows the baby to spread the bones of the pelvis as he descends by eliminating external pressures (bed, chair, etc.) and permitting relaxation while avoiding stretching of the muscles connected to the pelvis. • Gravity advantage.	• Hard work for the support person. • Requires birth attendant to bend down to assist birth.
Semilithotomy *(back-lying with head and shoulders elevated, legs in stirrups, and hips on edge of delivery table)*	• Some gravity advantage. • Mother able to view birth. • Convenient for attendant. • May be necessary for interventions (forceps, episiotomy, etc.).	• Leg cramps are common. • May be frightening to give birth over the edge of a table. • Restricts sacral movement. • Possible supine hypotension.
Lithotomy *(lying on back with legs raised in stirrups and hips on edge of delivery table)*	• Convenient for attendant. • May be necessary for interventions (forceps, episiotomy, etc.).	• Works against gravity. • May be frightening to give birth over the edge of a table. • Leg cramps are common. • Difficult to view birth. • Supine hypotension.

The second stage lasts from fifteen minutes to over three hours. The multigravida's second stage is usually faster than it was with her first birth. The second stage can be divided into three phases: latent, active, and transition.* These may be less distinct than the phases of the first stage.

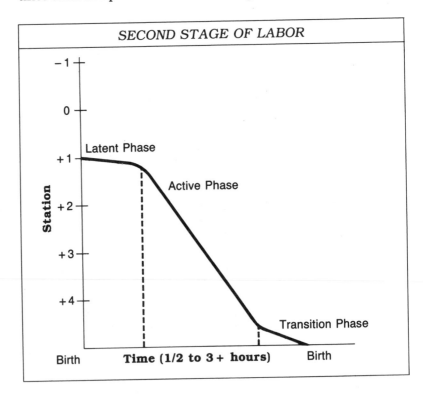

SECOND STAGE OF LABOR

Station: −1, 0, +1, +2, +3, +4

Latent Phase

Active Phase

Transition Phase

Birth   **Time (1/2 to 3 + hours)**   Birth

The Latent Phase

The latent or resting phase of the second stage is characterized by excitement over the imminence of the baby's arrival, relief that transition has passed, and a brief period of rest for the uterus. Contractions may be weak and further apart for ten or twenty minutes, descent may slow or stop temporarily, and the urge to push may be nonexistent or easily satisfied with slight bearing-down efforts. This resting phase may take place after the baby's head slips through the cervix, causing the uterus, which had been stretched tightly around the baby, to become a bit flabby. It needs time to tighten down around the rest of the baby's body. Then strong contractions resume and the urge to push becomes powerful. This temporary lull is normal and very welcome as a chance to rest and recuperate after transition; it is no cause for alarm.

If your baby is at a very low station when the second stage begins, you may not experience the latent phase, but move right into the active phase as soon as your cervix is fully dilated.

The Active Phase

During the active phase of the second stage, the baby descends and you will feel powerful contractions and an irresistible urge to push. You may find bearing down with all your strength extremely rewarding. You can feel progress. The baby's head distends the vagina and presses on the rectal wall. You may feel alarmed by the full, bulging feeling. You may be afraid to let the baby come down and may tense the pelvic floor against it, while raising your hips as if to escape from it. This will cause pain and slow progress. The most important thing for you to do during pushing efforts is relax your pelvic floor and bulge your perineum.

Your partner's reminders to "relax," "let the baby out," "open up," and "ease the baby out" are very important at this time, certainly more important than directions to "push, push, push." Pressing hot, moist towels against your perineum will help you relax and appropriately direct your bearing-down efforts. Clenching your jaw and clamping your mouth shut is a sign that you are probably tensing the muscles in your vagina. By relaxing your face, particularly your mouth, you may be more able to let go below.

As the active phase progresses, the perineum begins to bulge, the labia part, and the vagina opens as the baby's head descends with each bearing-down effort. Between efforts, the vagina partially closes and the head recedes. Soon, the baby moves farther down and her head becomes clearly visible. The joy and anticipation you now feel gives you renewed strength. If you are in a birthing room or at home, where sterile procedures are not required, you may reach down and touch your baby's head. You may be able to see the baby in a mirror. These concrete reminders will enhance the efficiency of your bearing-down efforts. During this phase, the baby descends and usually completes rotation to the occiput anterior position.

The Transition Phase

The third phase of the second stage is the transition phase, when the baby passes from inside the mother's body to outside. It begins when the baby's head no longer recedes between bearing-down efforts. This phase represents the maximum stretching of the vaginal opening and is characterized by a stinging, burning sensation sometimes called the "rim of fire." Strong bearing down at this time increases the pain and the likelihood of a serious tear of the vagina or perineum. Think of the "rim of fire" as your body's signal to reduce your bearing-down efforts. Breathe with a light panting or blowing pattern—do not hold your breath—and relax your vagina as the head crowns and emerges. Some birth attendants support the perineum with hot compresses or their gloved hands. Others massage with a lubricant to assist the slow stretching of the perineum. Still others maintain steady pressure on the baby's head to keep it from coming too rapidly.

Your baby emerges, first the top of the head to the ears, then her face—bluish-gray and soaking wet—is born. Then her head rotates to the side. This allows her shoulders to slip more easily through the pelvis. After the head is born, one shoulder (the one near your pubic bone) emerges and then the rest of the baby comes rather quickly. The entire baby appears bluish at first and may be streaked with blood. She also will be partially covered with the white, lotionlike vernix. With her first breath, which comes within seconds, her skin begins to turn more normal flesh-tones. All babies, whether dark- or light-skinned, go through these color changes in the first minute or two of life. Some are quite ruddy until their respiration and circulation adjust to normal. To assist respiration, the doctor or midwife may suction the baby's nose and mouth as soon as the head is out and again later. The baby may be placed on your abdomen or in your arms to await the delivery of the placenta. (See chapter 11 for more information about the appearance of a newborn.)

The Third Stage of Labor —the Delivery of the Placenta

The third stage, the shortest of all, begins with the birth of the baby and ends when the placenta is born. It lasts about ten to thirty minutes. After your baby is born, there is a brief lull, then the uterus resumes contractions and pulls itself away from the placenta. You might need to continue relaxation and patterned breathing because the uterus sometimes cramps vigorously. You might, on the other hand, be so engrossed in your baby that you hardly notice the third stage. Some parents enjoy seeing the placenta after it is delivered.

Immediately after the birth, your baby will receive close medical attention. As soon as his breathing is established and the baby is dried off, your caregiver performs a routine examination. The baby's overall condition is evaluated twice—at one minute and again at five minutes—using the Apgar score, a grading system devised by Dr. Virginia Apgar. Five areas are graded, each with a maximum of two points, making ten the highest possible score. The table on page 148 illustrates how newborns are evaluated.

The baby receives a total score each time the test is done. A first (one-minute) score of seven to ten indicates a normal baby (babies seldom receive a "ten"; most babies' hands and feet are bluish for a while, lowering their Apgar score); four to six indicates mild to moderate depression; zero to three indicates severe depression. The second (five-minute) score is usually higher than the first, indicating improvement with time and/or medical assistance. While Apgar scores are helpful, they do not indicate

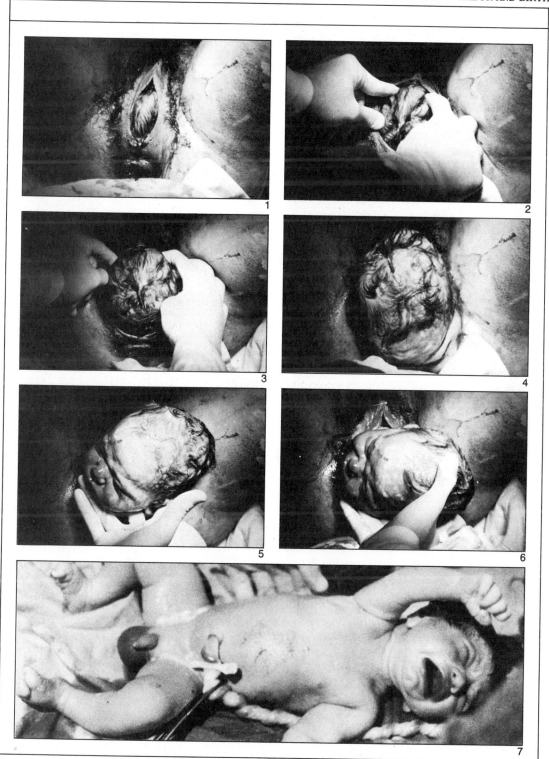

perfectly the baby's overall health. A physician or midwife will perform a thorough newborn exam within a few hours of birth to provide a more complete assessment of your baby's condition.

APGAR SCORING			
Sign	0 Points	1 Point	2 Points
Heart rate	Absent	Below 100/minute	Above 100/minute
Respiratory effort	Absent	Slow, irregular	Good, crying
Muscle tone	Limp	Arms and legs flexed	Active movement
Reflex irritability (often checked by being suctioned in nose)	No response	Grimace	Sneeze, cough
Color	Blue-gray, pale	Normal skin tones, except bluish hands and feet	Normal skin tones all over

Cutting the Umbilical Cord

The cord is cut within a minute or more after the birth. It is first clamped in two places and then cut with scissors between the two clamps. Sometimes the father makes the cut. The exact timing of cord clamping and cutting is a subject of some disagreement.

Advocates of early cord clamping (within one minute) believe that clamping the cord encourages and stimulates early breathing by depriving the baby of oxygen from the placenta. Early clamping prevents the baby from receiving excess blood from the placenta—a possible cause of newborn jaundice (see page 221 on newborn jaundice).

Those who advocate late clamping believe in waiting until the cord stops pulsating (usually a few minutes), which indicates that blood has stopped flowing between the baby and placenta. They believe that the baby benefits from the oxygen available in the cord blood while establishing respiration. This is thought to decrease the urgency of getting the baby to breathe. They also believe that by placing the baby on the mother's abdomen, which is at about the level of the placenta, excessive amounts of blood will not pass to or from the baby.

There are no clear answers to the question of the optimal time to clamp the cord. If you have strong feelings about it, discuss it with your doctor or midwife and be sure to include your preferences in your Birth Plan. There are some circumstances when immediate cord-cutting is necessary—a short cord and a cord wrapped tightly around the neck.

The Fourth Stage of Labor
—the Recovery Stage

The fourth stage begins when the placenta is born and lasts until your condition is stable, as indicated by your blood pressure, pulse, *lochia* (the normal vaginal discharge of blood from the uterus), and uterine tone. This usually takes about one or two hours. If anesthesia was used or if labor was difficult or prolonged, the fourth stage may last longer.

After birth the uterus immediately begins the process of *involution* (returning to its nonpregnant state). By continuing to contract, the uterus shuts off the open blood vessels at the site of the placenta and sloughs off the extra lining that built up during the pregnancy. You will begin passing lochia immediately and will need to wear a sanitary napkin.

Your nurse or midwife will check your uterus frequently to make sure that the fundus remains firm after the birth. If it is relaxed, she will massage it firmly to cause it to contract, which can be very painful. You might check your fundus yourself and, if it seems soft, ask how to massage it yourself. This way you can keep your uterus firm with less discomfort. This cannot be ignored, because the uterus can bleed excessively if it is not firm.

During the first minutes after birth, you may experience trembling of your legs, pain as your uterus contracts (*afterpains*, a common occurrence, especially in multigravidas), and swelling and discomfort in the perineum from the stretching and, perhaps, stitches. A warm blanket helps relieve trembling, and an ice pack on your perineum reduces the discomfort and may control swelling. Use slow breathing if necessary for the afterpains. You may feel hungry and thirsty—not at all surprising since you have been working hard and have probably missed some meals.

Your New Family While your body is settling down after the birth, your family is settling down also. You and any other family members or close friends will savor these first moments with the baby. The labor stimulates a state of wakefulness and alertness in the baby that may last for several hours. During this time, your baby is likely to become calm and begin observing and sensing the new sounds, smells, sights, touches, and tastes around him. He stares, particularly at faces. As your baby cuddles to you, stares into your face, or suckles at your breast, you will find him fascinating and irresistible. This is a time of falling-in-love and is a significant step in attachment, or bonding. Your partner also will want to hold him close, perhaps skin-to-skin, and enjoy these first moments with the baby. If you are breastfeeding, you will give your baby his first feeding as soon as he is ready after birth.

In some hospitals, routine care of the healthy newborn does not include time for the baby and his parents to be together. Check your hospital's policies; if you wish to be together in privacy for an hour or more after birth, discuss the possibility with your doctor or midwife and the nursing administration. If necessary, include this wish in your Birth Plan. Routine observations or procedures can be performed on the normal newborn in the presence and even in the arms of the parents.

After one to several hours, the baby usually falls deeply asleep. The initial exhilaration that you feel after the birth may give way to fatigue, the aftermath of labor. At this time, someone who is awake and alert should observe you and your baby's vital signs. In the hospital, a nurse will do the job. After a home birth, the observations are made by the midwife, a birth assistant, or an informed friend or relative.

In most parts of North America the government requires that all newborns receive *eye prophylaxis*—medication to prevent eye infection and possible blindness from gonococcus, the organism that causes gonorrhea. All babies are required to receive treatment because the tests for gonorrhea are not accurate enough to detect every mother who has the disease and could pass it to her baby. The rule is strict because gonococcal blindness is serious, but entirely preventable. Silver nitrate is commonly used for eye prophylaxis, but other medications, such as erythromycin and tetracycline, have recently been approved for use by the American Academy of Pediatrics and many state legislatures. Ask your caregiver which are available for your baby. (See page 197 for a discussion of these medications.)

The fourth stage is filled with adjustments to your nonpregnant state and the new state of parenthood. Your "real" baby replaces your "imagined" baby; your body begins the process of involution; and you begin the important work of reliving, understanding, and placing in perspective your labor and birth experiences.

Things to Do Before a Hospital Birth

The following lists will help you get ready for a hospital birth. If you are planning a home birth, much from these lists will be relevant. In addition, ask your midwife or doctor what preparations to make in your home and what supplies to have on hand.

Early Preparation

1. *Write a Birth Plan and go over it with doctor or midwife.*
2. *Tour the hospital.*
3. *Preregister at the hospital.*

Pack Your Bags for the Hospital

For Use during Labor

Pack these in a separate bag from your suitcase, which may not be handy during labor:

- Chapstick or lip gloss; toothbrush
- Small paper bag (for use if hyperventilation occurs)
- Warm socks in case your feet get cold
- Cornstarch or powder in shaker for effleurage and back rub
- This book
- A watch with second hand to time contractions
- Tennis balls, rolling pins, campers' ice for pressure on back
- Favorite juice, tea, honey, or popsicles if not provided
- Partner's snack (if hospital does not provide food in the labor room)
- Partner's swimsuit (so partner can accompany you in the shower)
- Phone numbers of people to call after the birth (money if needed)
- Camera, film, tape recorder
- Personalized focal point (a picture, design, or figure)
- Tapes of relaxing music

For Postpartum Stay

- Nightgowns or pajamas for nursing; may prefer hospital gowns
- Robe and slippers
- Usual cosmetic and grooming aids
- Shower cap
- Nursing bras (2)
- Reading and writing materials
- Money for newspaper, etc.
- Going-home clothes (a comfortable size, as you probably will not be back to your prepregnant size yet)
- Other personal items

For the Baby

- Diapers (2) and diaper pins (hospital may put a disposable diaper on baby)
- Undershirt
- Nightgown or stretch suit
- Waterproof pad or pants
- Receiving blanket
- Outside blanket, bunting, booties, and cap
- Dynamically tested car seat to be used for the ride home

LABOR AND BIRTH GUIDE

	Prelabor (Late Pregnancy)	Stage I — Effacement (percentage) and Dilatation (centimeter) of Cervix		
	Cervical Changes—some effacement, ripening, possible dilatation	*Latent Phase* 1 cm 2 cm 3 cm 4 cm	*Active Phase* 5 cm 6 cm 7 cm	*Transition* 8 cm 9 cm 10 cm
Breathing pattern	• No breathing pattern needed.	• Slow breathing. Use as long as possible.	• Accelerated breathing. (Begin when slow breathing no longer keeps you relaxed or it becomes difficult to keep the breathing slow.)	• Transition breathing, or "scramble" variation if necessary to change breathing pattern.
Contraction pattern	Irregular			
Possible physical signs	• Braxton-Hicks contractions. • Engagement of head. • Increased energy (nesting urge). • Light sleep.	• Bloody show. • Contractions becoming longer, stronger, and more frequent. • Small chance of rupture of membranes. • Possible backache. • Possible loose bowel movements.	• Contractions more intense, closer together, longer. • Possible rupture of membranes.	• Strong contractions, may have double peaks. • Pressure on vagina and rectum. • Nausea, vomiting. • Leg cramps. • Uncontrollable shaking. • Sensitivity to touch. • Drowsiness. • Hiccups. • Cold feet. • Flushed face. • Possible rupture of membranes.

		Latent Phase	*Active Phase*	*Transition*
Possible emotional signs	• Premonitions. • Exhilaration. • Anticipation.	• Excited. • Confident. • Talkative. • Apprehensive.	• Tired. • Feel trapped and discouraged. • Serious and uninterested in everything but labor.	• Restless. • Irritable. • Forgetful. • Fearful. • Have difficulty with relaxation and breathing pattern. • Overwhelmed, want to give up.
What to do: mother	• Prepare and pack bag. • Alternate mild activity with rest or nap. • Walk. • Sleep (at night). • Bathe or shower. • Eat and drink normally.	• Alternate rest and activity (appropriate to time of day). • Frequently empty bladder (every hour). • Time and record contractions. • Eat and drink sensibly, according to desire. • Bathe (unless ROM) or shower as desired. • Relax. • Begin slow breathing when you are unable to walk or talk through a contraction. • Call doctor or midwife (with membrane rupture, progressive contractions, or other concerns).	• Go to the hospital or birth center (or caregiver arrives at home). • Settle in, go over Birth Plan. • Use relaxation and breathing techniques (focal point, effleurage). • Alternate rest and activity (walking, sitting, and so on). • Use positions of comfort. • Drink liquids, chew on ice chips, or suck on damp cloth. • Empty bladder. • Relieve backache (pelvic tilt, change positions every 30 minutes: hands and knees, walking, side-lying, sitting forward).	• Take contractions one at a time. • Remember—transition is intense, but short. • Use relaxation and breathing pattern (transition, scramble, pant to control urge to push). • Use focal point and effleurage as desired. • Change position as needed for comfort.
What to do: partner	• Help pack. • Rest or sleep (at night). • Give moral support. • Encourage mild activity (during day). • Make sure you can be reached while away.	• Help pass the time with walking, talking, music, TV, games, and so on. • Time contractions. • Help her relax as necessary. • Suggest comfort measures as indicated (effleurage, back rub, food, fluids). • Follow her lead.	• Help her relax and use breathing pattern. • Use touch, stroking, or massage. • Apply cool cloth to her forehead, warm towel to abdomen, and so on. • Offer ice, liquids. • Help her move in bed or walk. • Match her mood.	• Be alert to signs of transition. • Encourage and reassure her; give clear, simple directions. • Stay with her. • Help with relaxation and breathing pattern; be her focal point if necessary. • Comfort her (back rubs, warm or cold packs, ice chips).

LABOR AND BIRTH GUIDE

	Stage II	Stage III	Stage IV
	Birth of the Baby	Delivery of the Placenta	Recovery—First Hours after Birth
Breathing pattern	• Bearing down or pushing (spontaneous, directed, or prolonged).	• Slow or accelerated breathing. • May push to expel placenta.	• Slow breathing if necessary for afterpains or perineal discomfort.
Possible physical signs	• Possible lull in contractions. • Urge to push becomes stronger with descent of baby. • Pressure of stretching vagina. • Crowning ("rim of fire"). • Birth of baby's head, then body.	• Mild to moderate contractions. • Uncontrolled shaking.	• Shaking. • Afterpains—painful uterine contractions, especially with multigravidas. • Perineal discomfort. • Difficulty with urination. • Hunger. • Nausea.
Possible emotional signs	• Cheerful. • Excitement and optimism. • Fatigue. • Amazement at effort. • Relief.	• Excitement. • Fatigue. • Relief. • Engrossment with baby.	• Excitement, elation. • Fatigue, exhaustion. • Relief. • "Empty" feeling. • Need to talk and recall labor and birth. • Surprise or fascination with appearance of baby. • Desire to see and hold baby.
What to do: mother	• Relax perineum, buttocks, and legs. • Bear down with the urge to push during contractions. • Change position for comfort and as necessary. • Pant as necessary, keeping chin up. • Keep eyes open, listen to doctor or midwife. • Touch baby's head if allowed.	• Use breathing patterns as necessary. • Push placenta out as directed. • Hold baby (skin to skin). • Relax and enjoy baby. • Watch initial care of baby.	• Rest, relax. • Interact with baby (cuddle, stroke, kiss, nurse, talk to). • Drink or eat. • Urinate (sitting up helps). • Massage fundus. • Ask for ice pack to perineum to decrease discomfort and swelling.
What to do: partner	• Help her change positions. • Support her in her chosen position. • Remind her to relax her perineum and keep her eyes open. • Help with panting or pushing as necessary. • Watch the birth.	• Help with breathing pattern if needed. • Hold baby. • Watch initial care of baby.	• Hold, touch, talk to baby; family time. • Comfort her as necessary (change positions, cool cloth to forehead, fluids, back rubs). • Talk through the birth experience. • Call family and friends.

Chapter Eight

Labor Variations, Complications, and Interventions

E ach birth experience is unique. Some labors and births are very short, some are taxingly long, and some require surgical intervention (episiotomy, forceps, cesarean birth). You can expect that your experience will be different from your mother's, your sister's, or even your prior experiences. Because no one can predict what kind of labor and birth you will have, you will want to prepare for all possibilities and include your ideas and wishes in your Birth Plan. This chapter discusses variations and complications in labor and birth and how they can be handled by you or with medical or surgical interventions.

Variations and Complications

A labor *variation* presents additional problems and challenges beyond the typical, normal labor, but it is still within the wide range of normal. A variation in itself does not pose dangers to either the mother or the baby, but it does pose problems that require the mother and her partner to make a greater effort to draw on their resources.

A labor *complication* presents problems to the mother or baby that cannot be solved by the extra efforts of the mother and her partner. Such labors require medical assistance and intervention to ensure an optimal outcome. Some variations become complications when, despite all the mother's efforts, the problem remains unsolved. Other complications are emergencies that pose immediate problems for the mother or baby and require prompt medical intervention.

Monitoring Techniques

By monitoring you and your baby during labor, your doctor or midwife becomes aware of labor variations and can detect most complications. The monitoring techniques described below serve several purposes: they gauge the progress of your labor; they help identify variations and complications; and they help your caregiver decide how to manage your labor, especially if it is a difficult one.

Monitoring the Mother

Periodic vaginal exams determine the dilatation of the cervix, and the station, presentation, and position of the fetus. They are often recorded on a time chart or labor graph, showing how your labor is progressing. The frequency and intensity of your contractions will be observed by the nurse, who will either put her hand on your abdomen or use an electronic monitor. Throughout labor, nurses or your midwife will assess your blood pressure, temperature, pulse, urine output, and fluid intake.

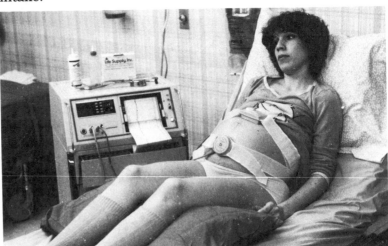

Monitoring the Fetus

Fetal heart rate. The fetal heart rate responds to changes in the availability of oxygen or to other stresses; it is an indicator of fetal well-being. Caregivers monitor the fetal heart rate by *auscultation* (listening) with a special fetal stethoscope or with a hand-held ultrasound stethoscope called "the Doppler." They also monitor the fetal heart rate with an electronic fetal monitor (EFM), a machine that records and prints out graphs of uterine contractions and fetal heart beats. Wires connect the machine to various sensing devices placed on your abdomen or within your uterus. (See pages 183 to 184 for more information.)

Amniotic fluid. The appearance of the amniotic fluid gives useful information about the baby's condition. An offensive odor may mean infection. A green or dark color may mean the baby may have expelled meconium from his bowels, which is a warning sign that the fetus has been under stress. If meconium is present, your caregiver will check the fetal heart tones often to determine if there is fetal distress or a serious slowing of the heartbeat.

Fetal scalp blood sample. If your caregiver suspects fetal complications, he or she may take a sample of scalp blood from a small cut in the fetus' head. The blood sample is analyzed for changes in the blood due to a lack of oxygen.

The Need to Start Labor

Sometimes problems arise for either the mother or the fetus in late pregnancy, and the doctor or midwife and the parents agree that the best way to handle the problem is to start labor. The decision is usually made after examining the mother and testing for fetal well-being and maturity. (See chapter 3.)

Some of the most common reasons for starting labor are a clearly prolonged pregnancy, prolonged rupture of the membranes, preeclampsia, a fetus who is small-for-gestational age, and certain illnesses in the mother (diabetes, heart disease, and so on). When any of these conditions is suspected or known, the mother and fetus are watched closely. If it appears that one or the other might be harmed if the pregnancy continues, labor is started.

In such a situation, there is often time for you to try some ways to start your labor. If you are successful, you may be able to avoid a medical induction of labor, which has some disadvantages. If time does not permit you to try these techniques or if you are unsuccessful, your caregiver has several methods available (Pitocin being the most common) for inducing labor. See pages 182 to 183 for information on medical methods of inducing labor.

Ways to Start or Stimulate Labor

At times, when it is important that labor start, or when labor is progressing too slowly, you might try these measures. Consult your caregiver before trying any of these techniques.

Nipple stimulation. Stimulating your nipples causes the release of your own oxytocin, which contracts the uterus and often succeeds in either ripening the cervix or starting labor. You may have to repeat these measures after a few hours or for half a day.

1. *Self-stimulation.* Lightly stroke or brush your nipples with your fingertips. Often within a few minutes you will feel contractions. You may have to do this off and on for several hours. Or massage your breasts gently with warm, moist towels an hour at a time, three times a day.*

2. *Electric or manual breast pump.* Use a pump for ten to twenty minutes per breast.* (Electric pumps are often available in the hospital.)

3. *Caressing and oral stimulation by your partner.* Try this for as long as you find it effective and pleasant, or until contractions become strong.

4. *Nursing a borrowed baby.* Suckling by a six- to twelve-week-old baby seems the most effective form of nipple stimulation. At this age, babies are usually efficient nursers, but are not too fussy to suckle from the breast of someone other than their mother. The baby needs to be awake and not very hungry; a sleepy baby will not suck, and a hungry baby gets frustrated. The baby's fussy period is a good time because the baby often wants simply to suck, not to eat. Suckling for at least ten minutes on each side seems to be effective. Your breasts and hands should be clean. Sit on a waterproof pad because your membranes might rupture.

Walking. Walking may help start labor, but it is more effective in keeping it going.*

Orgasm, clitoral stimulation, intercourse. Sexual excitement, particularly orgasm, causes contractions of the uterus. Prostaglandins are released into your bloodstream under these circumstances and act on the uterus and cervix. Prostaglandins are also present in semen and after intercourse, they act directly on the cervix. Manual or oral stimulation of the clitoris, even without orgasm, may also be effective. Intercourse, manual stimulation, and orogenital stimulation can be done as long as the membranes are intact, but not if they have ruptured. Blowing into the vagina is dangerous and should never be done. If you choose these techniques, make them as pleasant as possible. Try to forget your goal of starting labor and enjoy the sexual experience.

Bowel stimulation. You can sometimes start labor by stimulating and emptying your bowels. No one really understands how this works, but the contractions of the bowels may increase the production of prostaglandins, which cause the uterus to contract. It may also work simply by the mechanical irritation of the uterus by an active bowel.

1. *Enema.* Sometimes an enema will start labor by causing enough bowel action to initiate uterine activity. You can buy complete, compact disposable enema units at your drugstore, and give yourself the enema at home. You might also be able to get an enema in the hospital.

2. *Castor oil.* This causes powerful contractions of the bowel, making it a strong laxative. Castor oil induction has been used with limited success for years. Take two tablespoons at first. You can make it more palatable by mixing the castor oil with two or three tablespoons of orange juice and a teaspoon of baking soda.* Stir and quickly swallow. Thirty minutes later, you may take another tablespoon, and again thirty minutes after that. Since castor oil may cause painful cramping and diarrhea, it is not a pleasant way to begin labor, and it may not be preferable to Pitocin. It is sometimes used in combination with an enema.

Tea. Some caregivers recommend teas, such as blue cohosh, to induce labor. Teas should be used only with the knowledge and guidance of your caregiver since they contain active ingredients that enter the bloodstream and therefore represent a medical approach to inducing labor.

Short, Fast Labor (Precipitate Labor)

A *precipitate labor* lasts less than three hours. Though the shortness of the labor probably sounds appealing, a precipitate labor presents its own special problems and challenges. The latent phase of a precipitate labor passes unnoticed or so quietly and uneventfully that you miss the early signs of labor. Suddenly, you find yourself in active, hard labor without time to prepare psychologically. The first noticeable contractions can be long and overwhelmingly intense, and accompanied by feelings of panic and confusion.

If a hospital birth is planned, you will hurriedly leave home, trying to cope with strong, late labor contractions. If you are unaware that your labor is progressing rapidly and think you are in early labor with very painful contractions, you may feel unprepared, discouraged, and unsure of your ability to handle labor. At the hospital, you may be met with a flurry of activity and an unfamiliar doctor or midwife. You may feel anxious if your partner was unable to accompany you. As a result, you may experience feelings of loneliness, a lack of direction, and panic. In fact, you may feel like giving up and taking all the medication available to you to make the pain go away.

What You Can Do Take deep, relaxing breaths and trust your ability to get through this. Try each level of breathing, starting with slow breathing, to find the level that helps you cope. Have a vaginal exam before you make any decision about anesthesia. You may be dilated to eight or ten centimeters. If labor has progressed this rapidly, birth will soon follow and anesthesia may be unnecessary or may take effect too late to help you. What you need more than anything is reassurance that the labor is normal, if fast, and that you can handle it.

Because your contractions will be intense and very effective, you may have the urge to push before the hospital staff is ready. When the second stage begins, lie on your side and pant or gently bear down, rather than using a gravity-assisted position. This will give your birth canal and perineum more time to stretch, decrease the likelihood of tearing, and protect your baby's head from being pressed through the vagina too rapidly.

After the birth, you will probably experience feelings of relief that you made it to the hospital and that you and the baby are safe. You may need to review what happened. Talk with the staff and your partner to put the pieces together. You may also experience disappointment because your labor passed so quickly you were not able to savor it, use all the breathing and relaxation techniques, or share it with your partner as you had planned.

Emergency Delivery

If you have arranged to have your baby in a hospital, you may find it very disturbing to change your plans and have the baby at home. Initially, you may panic and temporarily forget all you know about labor, birth, and coping techniques.

However, when birth is truly imminent, it is far better to stay home, where it is warm and comfortable, than attempt to rush to the hospital. Usually, babies born without much warning are in excellent condition. The following suggestions will help you maintain control of an emergency situation and ensure the best possible outcome.

Signs of an Imminent Birth

• You feel a strong urge to bear down.

• You see the baby's head or presenting part visible at the vagina.

• You feel the baby coming.

What You Can Do

• Call the emergency care number and request an aid car. Paramedics are trained to handle emergency childbirth. If there is no aid service in your area, call the local fire department or police.

• Call your caregiver's office or the labor and delivery ward of your hospital. Ask for help or emergency instructions.

• Call for someone to help you at home—your partner, a relative, a neighbor, or a friend. Even children can help if they know specifically what to do.

Before the Birth

• Remove the clothing from the lower half of your body.

• Lie on your side or in a semisitting position in a warm, comfortable place (usually in bed) with clean towels or folded linen under your buttocks. A waterproof sheet will protect the mattress.

• Stay as relaxed as possible. Let the uterus do the work. Try not to push or bear down with the contractions, but pant or blow through them.

• Your partner or attendant should quickly, but calmly, gather a clean cloth handkerchief, tissues, clean towels, and receiving blankets. Keep these supplies nearby. If possible, put the receiving blankets in a clothes dryer or warm oven so they will be warm when the baby arrives.

• Your partner should thoroughly scrub his hands and arms up to the elbows.

During the Birth

When you first see the baby's scalp at the vagina, it will be wet and somewhat wrinkled, and it may be streaked with blood and vernix in places. The pressure of the baby's head bulges your perineum and anus. With the contractions, you will see more and more of the baby's head. With labor progressing so rapidly, there is no need to bear down. Instead, raise your chin and pant or "puh, puh" as lightly and rapidly as you can. Sometimes, as your baby's head descends, you will expel the contents of your lower bowel. If this happens, the attendant should remove the feces with tissues or paper towels to keep the area clean. He should remind you to keep your thighs and pelvic floor relaxed. Gradually, as the head emerges from the vagina and as "crowning" begins, make extra efforts to relax, pant, and not push. If the head is delivered slowly, it lessens the risk of tearing the perineum.

Once the head has fully emerged, your partner or attendant should use the clean handkerchief to wipe away excess mucus from around the baby's nose and mouth. If the membranes cover the baby's face, he should break them with his fingernail and peel them away. Wipe the baby's face.

A baby's head is usually born facing your back. After the head is born, the baby will turn 90 degrees to face your thigh so the shoulders can be born. At this time your attendant can gently support the baby's head, but should not pull on it. If the cord is around the baby's neck, your partner or attendant should lift it gently over the baby's head.

With the next contractions, you can bear down smoothly to deliver the shoulders and the rest of the baby's body. Your partner can support the body as it emerges; remember that it will be wet and slippery.

After the Birth

Care of the baby. Usually the baby begins breathing and crying immediately. Place the baby on her side on your bare abdomen, with her head slightly lower than her body to drain any mucus remaining in her nose and mouth. Wipe away any mucus, and dry the baby completely, especially her head. Keep the baby warm. She will stay warmest with her skin next to yours (no blanket in between) and a warm blanket over both of you. Keep her head covered to prevent heat loss.

Do not cut the cord. It will constrict when exposed to air, automatically stopping the blood flow. You will know the blood flow has stopped when the cord stops pulsating.

Care of the mother. Your contractions will resume after a slight lull and they will cause the placenta to separate from the uterine wall and slide down into the vagina. Bear down to deliver it. Wrap the placenta in a towel and place it on the bed. Place a sanitary napkin, folded diaper, or small towel on your perineum.

You can start breastfeeding right away. It will stimulate the uterus to contract and reduce bleeding. Even if the baby does not suck, her nuzzling your breast stimulates your uterus. Your uterus will be at the level of your navel, and should feel firm, like a large grapefruit. If your uterus is not firm, massage the fundus (top of the uterus) until it contracts. Do not continue the massage if the uterus is hard, but check it from time to time and massage again if necessary.

Possible Problems

Baby does not breathe spontaneously. Place her head lower than her body and rub her back or chest briskly but gently. If she does not respond within thirty seconds, hold her feet together and smack the soles sharply. If she still does not respond, repeat the procedure. If the baby still does not breathe, check her mouth with your finger for mucus, then do mouth to mouth resuscitation. Gently tilt the baby's head back to straighten the airway from face to chest. Place your mouth over her nose and mouth and your fingers on her chest. *Blow gently* with only the air in your cheeks until you feel or see the chest rise a little. *Do not blow hard.* Remove your mouth. Continue this sequence, one blow every five seconds, until the baby responds or medical help arrives.

Excessive bleeding from the birth canal. Some bleeding will occur after labor and delivery, in the third stage. However, if you lose more than two cups of blood, you may be hemorrhaging. Hemorrhage is characterized by a steady flow of blood and symptoms of shock (rapid pulse, paleness, trembling, cold, and sweating). If you suspect hemorrhage, firmly massage the uterus through the abdominal wall until it contracts, and encourage the baby to nurse (or massage the nipples). To avoid shock, elevate the lower half of your body.

If the bleeding appears to come from tears at the vaginal opening, pad the perineum with an ice pack and towels. Apply firm pressure. Go to a hospital where the staff will assess you, your baby, and the placenta and give you the attention you need.

In an emergency situation, your options are limited. Luckily in most areas aid cars and experienced paramedics are only minutes away. If an emergency home birth becomes necessary, remember what you have learned about relaxation, breathing techniques, and the birth process. An emergency birth can be hectic, but if you respond appropriately, calmly, and wisely, the experience will always be precious to you, despite its unconventionality.

Prolonged Labor (First Stage)

A labor that lasts longer than twenty-four hours is considered a prolonged labor. More important than the length of labor are the phase of labor in which progress is slowed and the rate of cervical dilatation. A labor with a long prelabor or long latent phase can discourage, exhaust, and emotionally drain you, but may not present an obstetrical problem. On the other hand, a labor that slows or stops in the active phase or later may turn into a complication.

Prolonged Latent Phase

If your labor is slow in starting or you are experiencing a long latent phase, do not assume that your entire labor will be prolonged. In most cases, labor will progress normally once you reach the active phase. It may simply mean that your cervix has not ripened or effaced before labor and that your early contractions are accomplishing these things before getting on with the job of opening the cervix.

What You Can Do

Try not to become discouraged or depressed. Nurture yourself with food or drink, baths and showers, walks and backrubs. Alternate between rest and activity. Try various methods to stimulate labor (see pages 157 to 159). Try distractions, such as a movie, a walk in the park or on the beach, a shopping trip, or a visit with friends or relatives. Think of something to do that helps keep your mind off the contractions.

Medical Care

Occasionally, when a latent phase becomes exhausting or lasts over twenty-four hours, you and your caregiver may turn to medical interventions. There are two possible approaches: attempting to stop contractions with medication (such as morphine) and let you rest, or stimulating effective contractions with procedures such as stripping the membranes, administering an enema, or giving drugs that ripen the cervix or induce labor (such as Pitocin).

Prolonged Active Phase

Labor that slows or stops once the active phase has begun is considered a more serious problem than a prolonged latent phase. A prolonged active phase can result from inefficient uterine contractions, an unfavorable presentation or position of the baby, a small pelvis, or a combination of these factors. Immobility, restriction to bed, a full bladder, drugs that slow or stop labor, fear, anxiety, and stress can all contribute to a prolonged active phase.

What You Can Do

The solution will depend on the problem. For instance, a full bladder can prevent the baby's descent, so empty your bladder every hour. If you have received drugs that slowed your labor, they will wear off with time. It may be possible to speed excretion of the drug by walking and drinking liquids. If you have been lying still in one position, try walking or standing (positions that make use of gravity), or try shifting positions in bed from side to side, then sitting, then resting on your hands and knees. You can use these positions even if you are attached to intravenous fluids and an electronic fetal monitor. To enhance the effectiveness of contractions, try nipple stimulation, walking, and standing.

If you are discouraged, tired, anxious, or fearful, you will need reassurance, encouragement, help with relaxation, and other comfort measures such as a massage or shower. Ask for help, not only from your partner, but also from the staff caring for you. Do not neglect these resources—they can sustain you.

The Occiput Posterior

Sometimes the position of the baby in the pelvis slows progress and descent. The most common such position is occiput posterior (OP), where the back of the baby's head is toward the mother's back. About one woman in four starts labor with the baby in the OP position, which is associated with longer labors because the baby must rotate further to get to the anterior position for birth. Dilatation and descent do not take place as efficiently when the baby is OP. By transition, however, most babies in the OP position turn to an occiput anterior position, though some turn even later. Other "persistent" occiput posterior babies are born in that position with their faces toward their mother's front (sometimes called a "sunny side up" delivery).

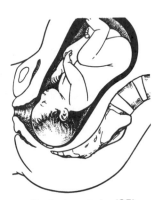
Occiput posterior (OP)

If your baby is OP, you may have considerable back pain during and sometimes between contractions because the hard round part of your baby's head (the occiput) presses on your sacrum (low back), straining the sacroiliac joints and causing pain in the entire low back area.

There are specific, effective ways to deal with the occiput posterior position and the resulting backache.

• Encourage the baby to turn by changing position every twenty to thirty minutes to take advantage of gravity and movement.

   1. *Stand or walk to try to align the baby's body with the entrance to the pelvis and enhance pelvic mobility.*

   2. *Get into the hands and knees position so gravity can assist rotation. (In the hands and knees position, gravity encourages the OP baby's trunk to drop toward your abdomen.)*

   3. *Do the pelvic rock while on your hands and knees to provide movement which may free the baby's head from the pelvis and allow it to turn to an anterior position.*

• Use these measures to help relieve the back pain.

   1. *Use positions that prevent the baby's head from pressing on your back. (See the chart in chapter 7, pages 137 to 138.)*

   2. *Ask your partner or birth attendant to use counterpressure on the painful area. To apply counterpressure yourself, press your fists into your low back or lean back on your fists or another hard object such as a tennis ball.*

   3. *Ask your partner for a back massage.*

   4. *Use cold or hot packs on your low back during or between contractions.*

   5. *Stand or sit in the shower and let the water spray on the painful area.*

   6. *Continue using relaxation and breathing techniques.*

   7. *If necessary, use pain medications.*

Medical Care

During a prolonged active phase, you can expect your caregivers to evaluate closely the progress of your labor and the well-being of your baby. Nurses will give you more vaginal exams, checking for progress in dilatation, descent, or rotation. They will monitor the fetal heart rate more, probably with the electronic fetal monitor. Intravenous fluids to prevent dehydration and medications for relaxation and pain relief become more likely and more welcome if your labor is unduly long. Eventually the doctor or midwife may rupture the membranes in an attempt to speed the labor or administer Pitocin to increase the frequency and intensity of your contractions.

If the baby is under stress, as indicated by the fetal heart rate in response to contractions, and labor continues to lag, your doctor may decide a cesarean birth is necessary. Remember that you can participate in these decisions.

Prolonged Labor (Second Stage)

Your labor may slow or stop after the cervix is fully dilated for many of the same reasons that cause a prolonged active phase. Most prolonged second stages can be handled as described previously. In addition, there are other possible problems that can arise only in second stage. A delay in progress can occur if the inlet (upper part) of the pelvis is large enough for the baby to enter, but the outlet (lower part) is too narrow to allow rotation or descent. If this is the case, problems do not arise until the baby is quite low in the pelvis. Another possible, but rare, problem is a short cord, which limits the descent of the baby or causes the fetal heart rate to slow during contractions.

A third, also rare, problem occurs if a baby has very broad shoulders—*shoulder dystocia.* This serious complication arises after the head is born and when the shoulders are so broad they are unable to pass through the pelvis. It is not possible in such cases to do a cesarean section. Instead, skilled maneuvers by the doctor or midwife, with the cooperation of the mother, are used to twist the baby and deliver the shoulders. Time is of the essence, since the baby's oxygen supply from the cord may be reduced.

What You Can Do

If you have a problem with descent during the second stage you should change to gravity-enhancing positions (pages 142 to 143). If there is no apparent progress after twenty to thirty minutes in one position, change again. Do not continue doing something if it is not effective. Squatting is perhaps the best aid to descent, since it not only uses gravity, but also causes maximum enlargement of the pelvic outlet.* This position may provide enough room for a baby in the occiput posterior position to rotate, or enlarge a relatively small pelvic outlet enough for the baby to pass through. You might also try the standing, semisitting, and hands and knees positions.

If tension in the perineum seems to interfere with effective bearing down, even with hot compresses and reminders to relax, sitting on the toilet may encourage release of the perineum. If changing positions does not enhance progress, you may need to use prolonged pushing with more forceful bearing down in order to get the baby moving. At this time the advantages of prolonged pushing may outweigh the disadvantages described in the earlier discussion of expulsion breathing in chapter 6. Your birth attendant directs your pushing at this time.

Medical Care

Close medical observation is necessary if second stage is prolonged. Your caregiver will carefully monitor the fetal heart rate.

If the fetus seems to be tolerating the contractions and positions (remember that lying on your back often causes fetal distress), they will encourage you to continue your efforts. If, however, your attempts are unsuccessful, if you are exhausted and unable to push effectively, or if you have received medications that inhibit your efforts and slow your labor, or if the fetus is responding poorly, procedures such as vacuum extraction, episiotomy, forceps delivery, and cesarean section may be used. (See page 169 for information on cesarean birth and the intervention chart that begins on page 182.)

Difficult Presentations

About 5 percent of the time, the baby is in a presentation other than vertex. Face and brow presentations occur less than 0.5 percent of the time. These usually cause prolonged labors and are managed as such. The shoulder presentation (transverse lie) occurs rarely, in about 1 in 500 births. Because a baby in this position only occasionally turns to a head-down presentation, a cesarean delivery is usually necessary. Finally, the breech presentation (with buttocks, legs, or feet over the cervix) occurs 3 to 4 percent of the time. (The incidence rises with prematurity or twins.) This is the most common of the difficult presentations.

Breech Presentation

There are four types of breech presentations: *frank*—buttocks down and legs straight up toward the face; *complete*—sitting cross-legged; *footling*—one or both feet down; and *kneeling*—one or both knees down. The frank breech is most common. Although breech deliveries usually turn out well, they are riskier to both baby and mother than the vertex presentation.

Risks to the baby. A breech presentation increases the chances of *cord prolapse*, the descent of the umbilical cord through the cervix into the vagina. This very rare, but extremely serious, complication is most likely to occur if the membranes rupture. Cord prolapse drastically reduces oxygen to the baby because the cord is pinched between the baby and the birth canal, especially during contractions. This is a life-threatening emergency. If you know that your baby is breech (or transverse) and your membranes rupture, try to lie down and stay flat or even get into a knee-chest position to prevent gravity from pressing the baby onto the cord. Someone needs to arrange for immediate transportation to the hospital, and you should lie down in the car.

Complete breech

Vaginal birth of a breech is more risky because the baby's feet and body are delivered before his head. After the feet and body are out, the baby's head can compress the cord within the pelvis, reducing the oxygen flow from the placenta to the baby. The feet and buttocks are small enough that they can be born before the cervix dilates enough for the birth of the head. This may result in the entrapment of the head in the bony pelvis and inhalation of amniotic fluid by the baby. Another risk is spinal cord injury, if the head of the fetus is hyperextended (bent back).

Risks to the mother. The mother's risks during vaginal breech delivery are considerably less than the baby's and consist of possible lacerations of the birth canal and possible hemorrhage.

What You Can Do

Try to keep informed about your baby's presentation and position, which are checked at each prenatal visit during late pregnancy. Most babies assume their birth position by thirty-four to thirty-six weeks. Others turn later, even during labor. If your baby is breech at thirty-six weeks, you may try the "breech-tilt" position to encourage your baby to turn. This position involves tilting your body so your hips are higher than your head. Lie on your back with your knees bent and your feet flat on the floor. Raise your pelvis, and slide enough firm cushions beneath your buttocks to raise them ten to fifteen inches above your head. You may also lie head down on an ironing board or a similar flat surface tilted from a chair to the floor. Lie in this position three times a day when the baby is active; make sure your stomach and bladder are empty. Relax your abdominal muscles and stay in the position for ten minutes. Your baby will probably squirm as his head presses into the fundus, and he may seek a more comfortable position. This technique does not always work, but since it is harmless, it is worth trying.

Medical Management of the Breech

There are several medical approaches to breech presentation: external version, vaginal birth, and cesarean birth.

1. *External version.* Though not widely practiced in North America, some physicians favor this procedure, which involves the manual rotation of the baby to a head-down position. The practitioner gently presses and pushes on the baby through your abdomen. Sometimes drugs are used to relax the uterus. Because the procedure carries some risk of separation of the placenta and cord problems, the baby is carefully monitored and ultrasound is often used. Sometimes the procedure does not work or works only for a short time and then the baby reverts to the breech presentation. Recent medical reports indicate a high success rate with external version when it is performed carefully by skilled practitioners.*

2. *Vaginal or cesarean birth of the breech.* Many physicians evaluate each breech presentation individually and weigh the risks carefully before deciding whether a vaginal or cesarean birth is best. The doctor considers the size and gestational age of the baby, the type of breech presentation, the size of the pelvis, and other factors. Before attempting a vaginal breech birth, many doctors require that a woman have had a previous vaginal birth. The best candidate for a vaginal breech birth is a term baby estimated to weigh less than eight pounds who is in a frank breech presentation with a well-flexed head (chin on chest) within a roomy pelvis. Careful monitoring and medical interventions are likely in this situation.

Some women are not candidates for a vaginal breech birth because of obstetrical factors or because their physicians prefer to deliver all breech babies by cesarean. In addition, some women attempting a vaginal breech birth develop problems requiring a cesarean birth. Therefore, the cesarean birth rate for breeches is very high.

Cesarean Birth

Today, cesarean birth is a relatively safe, surgical operation in which the baby is born through an incision in the uterine and abdominal walls instead of through the vagina. Hospital personnel refer to this abdominal birth as a cesarean section or a C-section. Although a cesarean is done for the safety of the mother or baby (or both), it is often a disappointment for a couple that had planned for a vaginal birth.

Approximately 10 to 20 percent of all births in the United States are cesarean births, with higher rates in large medical centers treating a large percentage of high-risk mothers and in rural areas where potentially difficult vaginal births are often avoided by doing cesareans.

Reasons for a Cesarean Birth

A cesarean birth may be indicated for the following reasons:

• **Cephalo-pelvic disproportion (CPD)**—a space problem resulting from a large baby, a small pelvic structure, or a combination of the two.

• **Malpresentation**—the baby is situated unfavorably for a vaginal birth. This includes the transverse lie (lying horizontally) and certain breech presentations (bottom or feet first).

• **Failure to progress** (or prolonged labor)—often means that contractions are of poor quality or that dilatation and descent are not progressing, or both, even after attempts have been made to rest and to stimulate the uterus.

• **Fetal distress**—is signaled by particular changes in the fetal heart rate, which are interpreted to mean the baby's oxygen supply has been reduced.

• **Prolapsed cord**—occurs when the umbilical cord descends through the vagina before the baby. The baby's oxygen supply is drastically reduced, necessitating immediate intervention.

• **Placenta previa**—a condition in which the placenta covers or partially covers the cervix. As the cervix dilates, the placenta separates from the uterus, depriving the fetus of oxygen and causing painless bleeding in the mother.

• **Abruptio placenta**—a condition in which the placenta prematurely separates from the uterine wall. This may cause vaginal bleeding or hidden bleeding with abdominal pain. The separation decreases the fetus' oxygen supply.

• **Maternal disease**—increases the chances of a cesarean birth. If a mother has toxemia, diabetes, high blood pressure, heart disease, or other conditions, she or her baby may not be able to withstand the stress of labor and vaginal birth. An active case of *herpes genitalis* is an indication for a cesarean birth since the baby may acquire the infection when passing through the birth canal.

• **Repeat cesarean**—may be performed because the original problem still exists or because the doctor is concerned about uterine rupture. Vaginal delivery may be possible for subsequent births, depending on the reason for the original cesarean, the mother's condition, and the doctor's philosophy. A discussion of vaginal birth after a cesarean (VBAC) appears later in this chapter. If you have had a cesarean birth and plan to have more children, discuss this option as well as your plans for a satisfying cesarean birth experience with your doctor.

In some cases a cesarean birth is planned in advance for medical reasons. Recognizing that labor rarely begins before the baby is mature, your doctor may wait until you go into labor and then perform the surgery. Or, after considering your due date, the fetal size and maturity, and the urgency of need, your doctor may schedule the surgery shortly before your due date. If there are any doubts about the maturity of your baby, fetal maturity tests are done. (See pages 49 to 50.)

If you are scheduled for a cesarean, you will check into the hospital for routine blood and urine tests. Then, the anesthesiologist will discuss the type of anesthesia and preoperative medications he or she will use, and ask about your allergies or sensitivities to drugs. The thought of surgery may make you feel nervous, jittery, and afraid. Calm yourself by using slow breathing and relaxation techniques. By asking questions and making requests, you can participate in the experience and make it more positive and less unsettling. Discuss your Birth Plan for cesarean birth and your partner's role with your physician, the nurses, and the anesthesiologist.

Before the Cesarean Birth

Whether the cesarean is planned or unplanned, a nurse usually prepares you by shaving your abdomen and the upper portion of your pubic hair. You may be given an enema and you will be catheterized. The nurse will insert a thin, flexible tube (a catheter) through your urethra into your bladder to keep it empty; the catheter will be removed twenty-four to forty-eight hours after surgery. The nurse will also start an intravenous drip in a hand or arm vein; this will remain in place for about twenty-four hours after the delivery.

Anesthesia

Anesthesia is necessary for the surgery. Most doctors use a regional anesthesia, which allows you to be awake without feeling pain. There are three basic types: spinal, epidural, and caudal. A *spinal* numbs you from your chest to your toes, and you cannot move your legs. An *epidural* or *caudal* numbs you in the same area as a spinal, but you may feel more pressure and pulling during surgery. Nausea, burning sensations, shoulder pain, trembling, and shortness of breath are all common during a regional anesthesia. To relieve these sensations the anesthesiologist can give you other medications, although they may make you drowsy during recovery and unable to enjoy your baby.

On occasion, particularly in those extremely rare cases of life-threatening emergencies where immediate intervention is required, a doctor may use a general anesthetic because it acts quickly. In such cases, you will receive an intravenous drug to relax your muscles and put you to sleep. An airway is put in your throat through which an anesthetic gas is administered. Physicians prefer to avoid this type of anesthesia, however, because of its undesirable side effects on the mother and baby. (See chapter 9 for further information on medications.)

The Surgery During surgery you will lie on your back, possibly with a wedge under one hip to reduce the likelihood of supine hypotension. The wedge helps displace the uterus from the large blood vessels. A member of the operating team will wash your abdomen with an antiseptic solution, drape it with sterile sheets, and place a screen between your head and abdomen to maintain a sterile field for the surgery. This prevents you and your partner from viewing the surgery. If you wish, ask the attendant to lower the screen for the moment of birth. Cesareans take about one hour, but the baby is usually born ten to fifteen minutes after surgery begins.

During a cesarean, the doctor makes two incisions: one through the abdominal wall—the skin, muscle, fat, and connective tissue; and the other through the uterus. Both incisions may be vertical or transverse (horizontal), or one may be vertical and one transverse. For example, you may have a transverse skin incision with a vertical uterine incision. It is important for the medical management of future births to know which type of incision you have had, so ask the doctor to write it down for you.

Skin Incisions

There are two types of skin incision for a cesarean. The *transverse skin incision* (or bikini cut) is the more common of the two; it is made horizontally just above the pubic bone. The *midline incision* is made vertically between your navel and pubic bone. It allows for a quick delivery in an emergency.

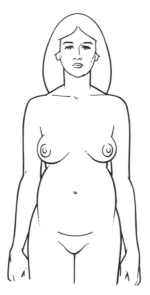 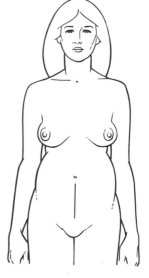

Transverse skin incision   Midline incision

Uterine Incisions

There are three types of uterine incision. The *classical incision* is made vertically in the fundus. It is rarely done today except for fetal emergencies, placenta previa, and transverse lie. Vaginal delivery is usually not feasible for future births after this type of incision.

The most common uterine incision is the *lower segment transverse*. Associated with less blood loss and reduced postpartum infection, this incision requires a little more time to perform than the classical. After a lower segment transverse incision, a future vaginal birth is possible.

The *lower segment vertical incision* is not commonly performed except when it is thought that a larger incision might be needed.

After the incisions are made, the amniotic fluid is suctioned out of the uterus, the baby is lifted out, and the placenta is manually separated and removed. The baby's nose and mouth are suctioned to remove the fluid and mucus. The baby is dried off, examined, and given an Apgar score (pages 146 to 148).

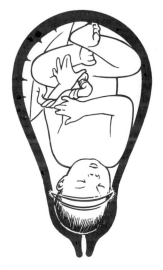
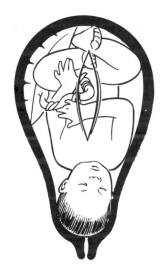

Lower segment transverse incision   Classical incision

After surgery, the uterus and abdominal muscles are closed with absorbable thread. The skin is closed with nonabsorbable thread, clamps, or staples that are removed before you go home.

After the Cesarean Birth

After your baby is born, you may see her before she goes to the nursery. If the father or partner is permitted in the delivery room and the baby's condition is good, the baby can be held by her father so that both parents can see and touch her. If the father is not permitted in the delivery area, the nurses usually show him the baby as soon as possible. During the next twelve to twenty-four hours, nurses will observe the baby for any respiratory problems. If the baby is breathing well and is generally healthy, she can be brought to the recovery room to be held, admired, and breastfed. (See page 245 for help with the initial breastfeeding.)

Soon after surgery, you will receive Pitocin intravenously to contract your uterus. Uncontrollable trembling and nausea are common reactions after a cesarean birth. Medications are available, but be aware that they may make you so sleepy that you will be unable to enjoy your baby for several hours. In recovery, the nurses will check your blood pressure, the abdominal incision, the firmness of your uterus, and the flow of lochia on your sanitary napkin.

If you have had a spinal anesthetic, you will probably be told to lie flat for eight to twelve hours to avoid headaches. If you had a general anesthetic, your throat and neck may be sore for a few days from the insertion of the airway used to administer the anesthesia.

Recovery from a Cesarean Birth

Your first venture out of bed usually occurs twelve to twenty-four hours after the birth. The nurse or aide will help you sit or stand. You may feel dizzy and light-headed at first. Take your time to stand. Do not slump. Stand tall and move around as much as possible, since movement helps alleviate gas pains and will speed your recovery. Use the cesarean postpartum exercises in the following section as soon as you feel able.

Your doctor and your condition will determine how long you stay in the hospital; the usual stay is from three to six days. The first day is usually the most uncomfortable, and your doctor will prescribe medication for pain. Be sure to use relaxation and slow breathing along with the medication. As the days progress, you will feel stronger and more able to move around. Your baby will be brought in for feedings and, depending on how you feel, rooming in may be available. Having a roommate who has also had a cesarean can be a great source of comfort and reassurance during your recuperation.

It is possible and desirable to breastfeed after a cesarean, but finding a comfortable position can be a problem. To protect your incision from the weight and wiggling of the baby, it is helpful to lay your baby on a pillow placed on your lap while sitting; or put your baby in a "football hold" at your side supported by pillows; or lie on your side.

Postpartum changes are similar in cesarean and vaginal births. Because of the incision and surgery, however, it will probably take you longer to feel strong enough to resume normal activities. Rest, a good diet, and plenty of fluids are top priorities. You may need help around the house; arrange for it in advance if possible. Lochia varies among individuals but is similar to lochia after a vaginal birth, and it gradually decreases after a few days. Avoid overexertion, which may cause excessive bleeding.

Even though you feel grateful for a healthy baby, you may feel disappointed, inadequate, or depressed about missing the planned vaginal birth, and these feelings may be more pronounced if you had an emergency cesarean that gave you little time to adjust. This lonely, let-down feeling may persist for both you and your partner, or you may adjust to it at different rates. If possible, talk honestly and openly about the birth and your feelings—it can help. Mixed feelings about the birth may make it difficult to relate to your baby. Caring for the baby soon after birth, talking about your feelings, and getting help with baby care will help you gain perspective and adjust to your new role as a mother. Your childbirth education group, physician, or midwife might know of a cesarean support group in your area that will help you adjust to your cesarean birth.

Activities and Exercises

After a cesarean, the soreness and stretching around the skin incision may make you reluctant to move and exercise. The following exercises, chosen with this in mind, are safe. Some encourage closure of the incision, some prevent possible complications, and some speed your general recovery.

When your condition permits (which is largely up to you and your doctor), probably within a week or two, you may then begin the other postpartum exercises described on pages 206 to 211.

1. Huffing

Aim: To prevent lung congestion after general anesthesia.

Exercise: As soon as you awaken from the anesthesia, combine deep breathing with coughing or "huffing" to clear any accumulated mucus. While in bed, bend your knees slightly. Put your hand, a small pillow, or folded towel flat over the incision, and press gently and firmly. Take in a deep breath, filling your lungs completely. Breathe out completely—forcefully and quickly, but evenly—pulling the abdomen in rather than pushing it out. Make a "huff" sound. Repeat. (You might try "huffing" a few times before your cesarean to get the idea and make it easier to do afterwards.)

Repetition: If there is mucus in your lungs, you will feel it or hear a bubbling or rattling sound in your chest. If so, repeat the deep breathing and "huffing" every fifteen minutes until you feel your chest is clear. If there is no excess mucus, repeat this deep breathing and "huffing" every half hour, while awake, for the first twenty-four hours after surgery.

2. Foot Circling

Aim: To maintain adequate circulation in the legs and prevent the formation of blood clots while confined to bed.

Exercise: Keep bedclothes loose to make movements easier. Rotate your feet in large circles, as if you were painting large circles with your toes, first in one direction, then the other.

Repetition: Repeat, doing ten circles each way every hour, while awake, when confined to bed.

3. Leg Bends

Aim: To maintain adequate circulation in the legs and encourage intestinal activity for the relief of gas.

Exercise: Begin with one knee bent, the other straight. Slide the heel of the bent leg down and back up. Repeat with the other leg. When you can, simultaneously bend one knee while straightening the other.

Repetition: Repeat ten times every hour, while awake, when confined to bed.

It is a good idea to do foot circling and leg bends before getting out of bed the first few times to help keep you from feeling faint when you stand. Add the following exercises when you feel ready.

4. Standing and Walking

Aim: To aid circulation and reduce intestinal gas. The first several times you get out of bed, you may feel faint, short of breath, and weak. Pain in your incision may make you slouch or bend over as you walk. The sooner you stand straight and walk, the better you will feel. Recovery is hastened with this mild activity.

Exercise: Before getting out of bed, do the leg-bending exercise. Be sure a nurse or two is ready to assist you. Rise slowly. Dangle your legs over the edge of the bed and do the foot-circling exercise. Stand as tall and straight as you can. It will not harm your incision. Try not to slouch. You can expect some pain, but it does not mean that you are stretching your incision too much or that something is wrong. Take your time when standing and walking. Try to increase the distance you walk each time.

5. Prolonged Expiration with Abdominal Tightening

Aim: To help alleviate gas pains and start gentle exercise of the abdominal muscles.

Exercise: Lie with knees bent and your hand or pillow supporting your incision. (You can do this exercise in a sitting or standing position.) Take a deep breath. Let the air out and at the same time pull your abdomen in toward your backbone. Continue until you have no air left in your lungs. Relax and breathe in.

Repetition: You can do this exercise often throughout the day—two or three times every hour. You will feel a pulling sensation in the incision caused by the contraction of the muscles, which actually brings the edges of the incision more tightly together.

6. Gentle Arm Stretch

Aim: To increase flexibility in the incision area.

Exercise: Stand upright against a wall. Raise both arms slowly and gently above your head as high as you can until you feel your abdomen stretch, then go a fraction higher. Hold for a slow count of five. Relax.

Repetition: Repeat five times daily.

7. Hip Lifting and Twisting

Aim: To increase flexibility in your trunk, to help alleviate intestinal gas, and to help you roll from back to side.

Exercise (for hip lifting): Lie flat on your back with your knees bent and feet flat on the bed. Tighten your buttocks, lift your hips off the bed, leaving your head, shoulders, and feet on the bed. Try to straighten your trunk from shoulders to knees. Hold for a slow count of five. Do not hold your breath. Lower your hips to starting position.

Repetition: Repeat five times.

Exercise (for twisting): Lie flat on your back with your knees bent and feet flat on the bed. Tighten your buttocks, lift your hips off the bed, leaving your head, shoulders, and feet on the bed. With your hips raised, twist them at the waist, first to the left, then to the right. Lower your hips to the starting position. This will build strength in the abdominal muscles without straining your incision. Many mothers find hip lifting and twisting helpful in rolling over from back to side. Rolling over is least painful if it is done this way.

Repetition: Repeat five times daily and use to reduce pain whenever rolling from back to side.

Vaginal Birth after Cesarean (VBAC)

Studies show that under proper conditions, many women who have had cesarean births may safely consider a vaginal delivery. The advantages of a vaginal birth over a cesarean include a lower risk of infection, less postpartum bleeding, fewer anesthesia complications, the financial savings of a shorter hospital stay, and a more rapid recovery. If a woman is considered a good candidate for VBAC, she is given a *trial of labor*, which is considered successful if it leads to a vaginal birth and unsuccessful if problems arise that require a cesarean.

Guidelines for selecting candidates for a trial of labor and a possible vaginal birth include:*

- Desire by the mother or parents for a vaginal birth.
- Adequate prenatal discussion and planning by the mother and her physician.
- Absence of the indications for the previous cesarean.
- A previous lower segment, transverse uterine incision.
- A normal, uncomplicated pregnancy.
- Expectation of an uncomplicated labor and birth.
- Pregnancy with one baby (not twins) in a vertex presentation who is expected to weigh less than eight and one-half pounds.
- Once labor has begun, normal and uneventful progress with no indication for a cesarean birth.

Labor that follows a previous cesarean is usually considered high risk. Therefore, the following facilities and services should be available in your hospital when you are having a trial of labor.

• A competent medical staff (doctors and nurses) present throughout labor and birth.

• The capability to monitor the fetal heart rate and uterine activity, and to administer intravenous fluids.

• Twenty-four-hour availability of an anesthesiologist and anesthesia.

• Twenty-four-hour access to blood-bank facilities.

• A pediatrician or neonatologist advised of trial of labor and available if needed.

If you and your caregiver follow the above guidelines, the safety of VBAC is comparable to the safety of any vaginal birth.* The main concern in the management of VBAC is the possibility of the uterus separating at the site of the old incision. In reality, such a separation is less likely with a VBAC than in women "who have weakened uteruses from many pregnancies and deliveries or who received too much oxytocin during labor, causing excessive strain on the uterus."*

Premature (Preterm) Birth

A *premature birth*, by definition, occurs before the thirty-seventh week of gestation. If you experience any of the signs of labor (see page 130) before thirty-seven week's gestation, call your caregiver. If you are in doubt about uterine contractions, lie down and time the contractions for one hour. If the contractions continue and occur every ten minutes or less or if you have any concerns, call your doctor or midwife.

Because the premature baby is small, immature, and not yet prepared for extrauterine life, caregivers may attempt to stop preterm labor. Bedrest is usually the first measure, followed by medications to inhibit contractions (see page 196). These methods, however, are frequently unsuccessful. When labor and birth appear inevitable, the focus of care shifts to managing the labor for the best possible outcome and preparing for a baby in need of special care.

Your caregiver will use an electronic fetal monitor to continuously assess the baby's condition. Pain medications that depress the fetal respirations and heart rate will probably not be used. Therefore, in early labor you should expect to use relaxation and breathing techniques as pain relievers. In active labor or during birth, you may receive regional anesthesia. Episiotomy and forceps are likely to be used to keep the vaginal wall from pressing too tightly on the baby's soft skull.

Since the health of the baby is paramount and he may be in need of medical attention, you may not be able to hold him immediately after birth. Most premature infants are put in a special nursery. Care of the preterm baby usually involves hospitalization and possibly long periods of separation from you. In many hospitals, parents can visit and care for their babies in the special-care nurseries. Participating in the care of your baby benefits both of you. (For more information on care of the premature, see page 220.)

Twins

The birth of twins is more complicated than the birth of a single baby. The excess stretching of the uterus and the combined weights of the babies and placentas often cause premature labor. Early rupture of the membranes is more common with twins and is another cause for prematurity. Generally, labor with twins progresses normally; but sometimes the over-stretched uterus cannot work as efficiently, slowing labor. Because of the high incidence of prematurity and increased chance of postpartum hemorrhage, you should expect more medical supervision and less medication.

The most common and favorable presentation for twin birth is with both babies head down. Ultrasound or x-ray during labor might be indicated to identify the positions of the babies. The results will determine the best type of birth—vaginal or cesarean. The second twin is usually born within thirty minutes of the first. The delivery of the placenta(s) will occur after both twins are born. The probability of cesarean birth is higher in twin or multiple pregnancies due to the increased likelihood of complications such as preeclampsia, prematurity, breech presentation, and prolapsed cord.

Third Stage Variations and Complications

Postpartum hemorrhage, which occurs in about 5 percent of women who deliver vaginally, is the most common problem of the third stage of labor.* It is defined as a loss of at least 500 milliliters (about two cups) of blood during the first twenty-four hours after birth.

The three major causes of postpartum hemorrhage are *uterine atony* (poor uterine muscle tone), *lacerations* or tears of the cervix or vagina, and *retention of the placenta* or placental fragments. Of these, uterine atony is the most common cause of hemorrhage.

Uterine Atony To encourage the uterus to contract effectively, nurse your baby to stimulate the release of your body's oxytocin. Uterine massage by your caregiver also stimulates it to contract. If these measures do not control bleeding by causing your uterus to contract, your caregiver may check for placental fragments; check your cervix, vagina, and vulva for lacerations; or give you drugs, such as Pitocin or Ergotrate. If hemorrhaging is serious, you may need a blood transfusion.

Lacerations Lacerations or tears of the cervix, vagina, or perineum will be sutured to control bleeding. Occasionally, packing the vagina with sterile gauze is also required to stop bleeding.

Retention of If the placenta or fragments of it are retained in the uterus, *the Placenta* they interfere with contractions, allowing the blood vessels at the placental site to bleed freely. Your caregiver will manually remove the placenta, clots, or fragments—a painful, but necessary procedure—and administer Pitocin. Then you can help by massaging your uterus and by breastfeeding your baby. Ask your caregiver for instructions in uterine or fundal massage.

When a Baby Dies or Has a Birth Defect

All parents worry about the well-being of their baby at some time during pregnancy and the early postpartum period. You may have fears about your baby being stillborn, being handicapped, or dying soon after birth. These fears sometimes remain unspoken, surfacing only in dreams. If possible, share your fears with a supportive partner, midwife, childbirth educator, physician, or friend.

The vast majority of babies survive pregnancy, birth, and the early postpartum period. Stillbirth and death resulting from birth trauma, infection, and handicaps are relatively uncommon. But if you are faced with a birth defect or the death of your baby, your agony, sadness, and loneliness are very real. Being prepared by deciding what you will do if your baby dies or is deformed can be helpful in the first painful days.

You will have some decisions to make about the management of your own and your baby's care. If the baby dies while you are still pregnant and before labor, you will need to consider how you would like your labor managed. Will labor be induced and, if so, when? Do you want to be awake and participate in the birth? If the baby is stillborn, would you like to see and hold her? More than once? Do you want your baby baptized? Would you like a picture of your baby, her blanket, a footprint, or a lock of hair? Will you name the baby? Do you want to recover on the postpartum floor where there are mothers and babies or somewhere else in the hospital, or take an early discharge? Whom can you turn to for support? Do you want a priest, rabbi, or minister to visit? Who will notify your friends and family? Would you like the support of other parents who have experienced a similar loss? Do you want an autopsy performed and do you want to know the results? Will you have a funeral or memorial service?

If the baby has a birth defect, you will have other choices to make. Can you participate in the care of your infant? Do you want to be involved in the baby's care? Do you want to provide your baby with breast milk? If your baby is transferred to another hospital, who will visit? Is early discharge a possibility for you? Would you like the support of other parents who have had similar experiences? How serious is the birth defect? Is it treatable? What are the long-term chances for your child? What are the choices regarding care and treatment? Your baby's doctor and nurses can give you some of the information you need to make these choices. Many communities have organizations that provide support for parents trying to deal with the death or deformity of their baby.

In the event of a stillbirth, death of the newborn, or birth defect, you need time to review, reflect, and understand your labor and birth. This will help you to grieve or care for your baby. Writing a labor and birth report or reviewing your birth experience with your partner, childbirth educator, and physician or midwife can help you immensely. Find out about resources in your community that can help you cope. Lean on these resources; use their support and guidance. Be gentle to yourself. Give yourself time to heal emotionally and physically. Grieving is painful but must be experienced. The process takes a long time. There are some excellent books, such as *When Hello Means Good-Bye*, that can help you through the early stages of grief. (See Recommended Reading.)

Medical Interventions in Labor and Birth

Medical interventions in labor are various procedures carried out by birth attendants to alter the course of labor, provide diagnostic information, or prevent complications. All medical interventions carry some degree of risk (just as medications do), and they should not be used unless they are necessary. There is disagreement within the obstetrical community over how routine these interventions should be. You will want to know what your caregiver considers a desirable routine intervention (and why), and if he or she will encourage you to solve problems of labor and birth using your resources, such as changing positions, comfort measures, relaxation, breathing techniques, and time. Your Birth Plan should include your preferences regarding the use of interventions. Chart 8a on the following pages describes and outlines the benefits and risks of various interventions.

Chart 8a		INTERVENTIONS	
Intervention	Description	Benefits/Purposes	Risks/Disadvantages
Intravenous (IV) fluids	Fluids are administered through a small plastic tube or needle inserted into a vein in the back of the hand or in the arm. The fluid drips continuously from an IV bottle or bag.	• Maintains hydration (fluid intake) when you are unable to drink liquids. • Needed to maintain blood pressure if regional anesthesia is used. • Allows immediate access to a vein if medications are necessary. • Needed for administration of Pitocin (to augment or induce labor). • Provides calories for energy.	• Restricts easy movement during labor, walking is more difficult. • Unnecessary if you are drinking sufficient fluids, receiving no medication or anesthesia, and progressing normally. • May result in infiltration (fluids leaking into tissues surrounding vein, causing tenderness and swelling).
Induction (starting) and augmentation (speeding) of labor A. *"Stripping" the Membranes*	The examiner inserts a finger between the membranes and your cervix, and frees the membranes from the lower part of the uterus. Usually performed in the doctor's or midwife's office before labor begins.	• May start labor by allowing the amniotic sac to slip down into the cervix, further dilating it. • If unsuccessful, pregnancy can continue without danger of infection.	• May not induce labor. • Causes light bloody vaginal discharge, often mistaken for bloody show. • Is sometimes done during a vaginal exam without your knowledge. • May cause ruptured membranes.
B. *Prostaglandin*	A gel or tablet of prostaglandin is placed in or near the cervix for 24 hours or overnight. Sometimes used in combination with Pitocin induction.	• May ripen and soften the cervix. • May start labor by causing uterine contractions.	• May not induce labor. • Not often used in the United States.
C. *Artificial Rupture of Membranes (AROM)*	Either before or during labor, the examiner makes a small hole in the membranes using a specially designed instrument called an "amniohook." AROM is usually done in the hospital during a vaginal examination. There is no pain associated with this procedure other than the discomfort of a vaginal exam.	• May start labor. • May speed the progress of labor by allowing the presenting part to fit snugly against the cervix, stimulating contractions and enhancing dilatation. • Enables examiner to see consistency and color of the amniotic fluid to help assess fetal well-being. • Necessary for application of an internal electronic fetal monitoring device.	• Does not always start labor, and subsequent increased risk of infection requires use of other interventions (usually Pitocin). Most caregivers want the birth to occur within 24 hours of ROM. • May increase discomfort of uterine contractions. • Associated with more compression and molding of fetal head and a drop in fetal heart rate during contractions.

Chart 8a		INTERVENTIONS	
Intervention	Description	Benefits/Purposes	Risks/Disadvantages
D. Pitocin or Other Synthetic Oxytocin	Usually is given in an IV when you are in the hospital. The drip is usually electronically regulated by a special machine.	• Causes uterine contractions. • Used to induce labor when the membranes have ruptured and contractions have not begun or when there is a medical reason to deliver the baby before labor has begun (preeclampsia, maternal diabetes, postmaturity). • May increase the intensity and frequency of contractions when labor progress is stopped or slowed.	• Requires close observation of you and the baby to avoid undesirable effects (see page 196). • Increases intensity of contractions requiring more concentration and use of relaxation and breathing techniques or pain medication. • May be associated with an increased incidence of newborn jaundice. • May result in a premature birth if performed without knowledge of fetal maturity.
Fetal heart rate monitoring A. Fetal Stethoscope	Caregiver (usually a nurse) listens to the baby's heart beat through your abdominal wall using a fetal stethoscope. The fetal heart rate (FHR) may be counted before, during, and after a contraction about every 15 to 30 minutes during the first stage of labor, and more frequently during the second stage.	• Noninvasive. • Allows you to be mobile and active. • Encourages more attention from your caregiver.	• Assessing the relationship between the FHR and the contraction is difficult. • Heart tones may be difficult to hear. • There is no permanent record of FHR and contraction pattern other than staff records. • Pressure of stethoscope on abdomen may be uncomfortable for mother.
B. Hand-held Ultrasonic Fetal Stethoscope	Often called the "Doppler," this device is placed on your abdomen and audibly or visually transmits the fetal heart tones.	• Is the most comfortable method of FHR monitoring. • Encourages more attention from your caregiver. • Allows you to be mobile and active. • Is more sensitive in picking up fetal heart tones than fetal stethoscope. • Volume can be increased so others in the room may hear.	• Assessing the relationship between the FHR and the contraction is difficult. • There is no permanent record of FHR and contraction pattern other than staff records. • Exposes fetus to ultrasound.

Chart 8a		INTERVENTIONS	
Intervention	Description	Benefits/Purposes	Risks/Disadvantages
C. External Electronic Fetal Monitor	An ultrasound device, contained in a belt around your abdomen, sends and receives soundwaves to detect fetal heart rate. Another belt with a pressure-sensitive device can be used to detect uterine contractions. These devices are attached to a monitor that records FHR and uterine contractions. Monitoring can be intermittent (10 to 20 minutes every hour) or continuous.	• Enables assessment of how contractions affect FHR. • Enables assessment of fetal well-being when complications arise and pitocin or other medical interventions are used. • Provides information needed to determine if further medical intervention is warranted. • Provides information on the frequency of uterine contractions. • Provides a permanent record of FHR and contraction pattern. • Helps labor partner know when contractions begin so he or she can help you start a breathing pattern. • Used to observe mother and baby when there is a shortage of nurses. • Does not require artificial rupture of membranes.	• Not always accurate, requiring further assessments with more accurate techniques before changing medical management. • Needs frequent readjustment when you or the baby move. • May be uncomfortable and restrict your movement and ability to use effleurage. Immobility may slow labor. • May tempt your labor partner to watch the monitor instead of you. • Exposes fetus to ultrasound.
D. Internal Fetal Heart Rate Monitor	The fetal heart rate (FHR) is measured by an electrode attached to the fetus. Wires from the electrode transmit the baby's heart rate to the monitor and record it. A pressure-sensitive device in a fluid-filled catheter is placed into the uterus. During contractions, the increase in intrauterine pressure is measured and recorded. Sometimes a combination of internal and external electronic monitoring is used; for example; the internal fetal electrode and the external uterine pressure device.	• Enables assessment of how contractions affect FHR. • Enables assessment of fetal well-being when complications arise and pitocin or other medical interventions are used. • Provides information needed to determine if further medical intervention is warranted. • Provides information on the quality and frequency of uterine contractions. • Provides a permanent record of FHR and contraction pattern. • Helps labor partner know when contractions begin so he or she can help you start a breathing pattern. • Used to observe mother and baby when there is a shortage of nurses. • Is more accurate than the external monitor. • Is less restrictive of your movements in bed than the external monitor.	• Requires rupture of the membranes. • Restricts free movement, especially walking during labor. • May cause uterine infection and/or scalp infection of your baby. • Interpretation of FHR patterns varies among practitioners; fetal distress could be diagnosed when not actually present. • Fluid in pressure catheter may need frequent adjustment.

Chart 8a	INTERVENTIONS		
Intervention	Description	Benefits/Purposes	Risks/Disadvantages
Fetal blood sampling	A small sample of the baby's blood is removed and tested for its oxygen and carbon dioxide levels, acid-base balance (pH), and other factors.	• Enables further assessment of fetal well-being if the FHR monitor indicates problems. • Could prevent an unnecessary cesarean birth if fetal blood samples are normal.	• Invasive • May cause infection in the baby at the sampling site. • Not all hospitals have the necessary facilities on a 24-hour basis that are required to perform these tests.
Episiotomy	A surgical incision is made into the perineum from the vagina toward the rectum (midline or medio lateral) just before the birth of the baby's head. 	• Enlarges the birth canal. • May speed the delivery of the baby. • Provides a straight incision which is easier to repair than a serious tear. • Provides more space for application of forceps or vacuum extractor. • Reduces compression from vaginal tissues on the head of premature baby.	• Causes discomfort in the early postpartum period. • Sometimes performed routinely when not necessary. • May delay mother-infant interaction (holding or nursing) as episiotomy is repaired. • Site of incision may become infected or bleed. • May cause pain with intercourse for several months after the birth. • Could extend and tear further into the perineum.
Forceps	A two-part stainless steel instrument is inserted into the vagina and applied to each side of the baby's head to aid rotation and descent. 	• Helps rotate the baby's head to an anterior position. • Helps bring the baby down when anesthesia is used or your ability to push is reduced. • Helps protect the premature baby's head from prolonged pressure in the birth canal. • Facilitates birth of the head with a breech vaginal birth. • Allows a rapid delivery if necessary.	• Usually requires an episiotomy. • May bruise the soft tissues of the baby's head or face. • Usually requires regional anesthesia. • May bruise vaginal tissues.
Vacuum extractor	A caplike device is applied to the fetal head. A rubber tube extends from the cap to a vacuum pump that creates suction on the baby's head. Pulling on the cap during contractions assists the baby's descent.	• Helps descent of the fetal head. • Can be applied when the fetus is at a higher station than is safe for use of forceps. • Requires less space in the vagina than forceps.	• May cause bruising or swelling of soft scalp tissues. • Not as helpful with rotation as forceps. • Requires 5 to 10 minutes for suction to be created.

Chapter Nine   Medications

Drugs have been used to remedy a variety of human conditions since ancient times. Our ancestors discovered numerous herbs and other substances to treat a host of disorders—opium relieved pain, wild cherry calmed coughs, and digitalis aided the heart. Today, although we possess an enormous assortment of drugs to treat all kinds of ailments, we must keep in mind that all medications, whether ancient herbs or modern complex chemical compounds, can be harmful or helpful, depending on how they are used. For the pregnant woman, drugs are most beneficial when they are used as intended, in the proper amount, and when their benefits outweigh their risks.

General Considerations

Drugs may be obtained by prescription, over-the-counter, from herbs, or from illegal sources. When you choose to take an over-the-counter medication or it is prescribed by your caregiver, you must consider the following, whether you are pregnant or not:

- What benefits will you receive from taking the drug?

- What are the risks of taking the drug?

- Is this the best treatment for your ailment? What are your other options? What happens if you choose not to take it?

- Have you told your physician and pharmacist about your drug allergies and other medications you are taking?

- If the drug is self-chosen, have you read the label carefully?

- What dosage should you take?

• Do you know when or how often to take the drug? Before or after meals?

• Do you know how to store the drug? In a special place—the refrigerator, a dark place?

• What are the side effects of this drug? Which side effects should be reported to your physician?

• How long will you need to take the drug?

During pregnancy, childbirth, and while nursing, you will want answers to the following additional questions since the well-being of your baby, the progress of your labor, and the production of safe breast milk may be affected by the drugs you take.

• What effect will this medication have *on you* during pregnancy and labor, after birth, and while you are breastfeeding? How will this medication affect the progress of your labor?

• What effect will this medication have *on your baby* during pregnancy, labor, after the birth, and while breastfeeding? If you choose not to take this medication, how will your baby be affected?

Once you have the answers to all these questions, you will be able to make an informed decision, one that contributes positively to your health care and to the well-being of your baby.

Pain in Childbirth

When asked to describe labor contractions and the sensations of birth, women say the experience is exhilarating, uncomfortable, frightening, powerful, overwhelming, beautiful, and painful. The pain of childbirth, which is in the forefront of most women's minds when they think about labor and delivery, has been attributed to several factors:*

• Insufficient oxygen supply to the uterine muscle. This pain is more intense if the interval between contractions is short, preventing full replenishment of oxygen to the uterine muscle.

• The stretching of the cervix (effacement and dilatation).

• Pressure by the baby on the nerves lying near the cervix and vagina.

• Tension on and stretching of the supporting ligaments of the uterus and surrounding structures during contractions and descent of the baby.

• Pressure on the urethra, bladder, and rectum.

• Distention of the pelvic floor muscles.

• Fear and anxiety, which can cause the release of excessive stress hormones (epinephrine and norepinephrine), resulting in a longer labor.*

The perception of pain in labor, though it varies greatly from one woman to another, may be increased by the length of pre-labor, fatigue, fear and anxiety, feeling alone, lack of mobility, or a full bladder. At the same time, the presence of a supportive person, the upright position, and other comfort measures can noticeably reduce the perception of pain during labor.

For each woman, the pain of childbirth will be influenced by her past experiences, her cultural background, her beliefs about and her expectations of birth. Often just knowing the reason for the pain may help you cope with childbirth pain. Also, when childbirth is normal, the pain is not a sign of harm or disease; it is, as Sheila Kitzinger says, "pain with a purpose." If you acknowledge the pain, work with your body during childbirth, and remember that the pain will soon end, you will be able to put it into perspective.

This book emphasizes coping techniques and comfort measures that, whether used exclusively or in combination with medication, help reduce the pain of labor and birth. (See chapter 6 for a discussion of these techniques and comfort measures.)

An Unmedicated Birth

If you want to avoid pain medications during labor and birth, you will need to plan and prepare yourself in advance. Here are some suggestions (many of which are explained fully in other chapters) that will reduce the likelihood of your needing medication.

Before Labor
- Prepare yourself thoroughly. Know and master the relaxation skills, breathing techniques, and comfort measures.

- Have one or more supportive partners—husband/lover, friend, relative—prepare with you. Be sure you understand and share each other's priorities and wishes for the birth experience.

- Find a doctor or midwife who is supportive of your wishes. Discuss medications and your feelings about them before labor begins. Ask that your Birth Plan, which includes your wish to avoid medication, be placed on your medical chart.

- Select a setting for birth in which natural childbirth is a common event, where the staff encourages pain-relieving techniques other than drugs (such as massage, showers, or position changes), and, most importantly, offers encouragement and emotional support.

During Labor
- Be sure the staff knows your wishes. Ask them to help you have an unmedicated childbirth. Ask them not to offer you medication, even if you appear to be in pain. Ask them instead to offer you encouragement, advice about your labor progress,

and ideas for helpful measures. This does not mean that you cannot receive medication if you decide you need it.

● Remember the "graph of labor" from chapter 7, page 133.

● If at five to six centimeters you are relaxing between contractions (if not throughout) and using patterned breathing during the contractions, you will probably be able to handle the rest of the labor. Remember that as labor intensifies it also speeds up. Labor's intensity is an encouraging sign of progress.

● If difficulties arise or you become exhausted during labor and want pain medication, get answers to the following questions: How far are you dilated? How is labor progressing? Is it likely to last much longer? Would more coping and comforting techniques help? Have you changed breathing levels or tried other comfort measures (described in chapter 6)? Can you postpone medication for three to five more contractions?

Medications for Pain Relief

Keep in mind the following factors regarding medications for pain relief during childbirth to help you with your decision-making.

● Medications can relieve some or all of your labor pain.

● Labor often hurts more than you may have anticipated.

● "Many new techniques have been evolved, but the perfect method of abolishing the pain of childbirth has not been achieved."* Therefore, you should not expect total relief from pain from the beginning to the end of your labor even if medications are used.

● Drugs and anesthetics may affect your labor. For instance, while some drugs promote relaxation and hasten the progress of labor, others impede its progress and increase the need for other medical interventions.

● Since "no drug has been proven safe for the unborn child,"* most physicians and midwives discourage heavy or unlimited use of medications during childbirth.

● To some degree the fetus will be directly or indirectly affected by any medication you receive. The specific effects will depend on the particular drug, the amount received, how and when it was given, and other factors. When you receive medication, the medical staff watches for negative effects and initiates corrective measures if necessary.

● Because the immature liver and kidneys of the newborn are unable to rapidly detoxify, metabolize, or excrete medications, the effects of some drugs last longer for the baby than they do for the mother.

• Drugs or anesthetics are often used when babies require manual or surgical assistance (such as forceps or an episiotomy) and are always used for cesarean births.

Weigh the Benefits and Risks

The choice is not always an easy one. With the help of your caregiver, you must weigh the expected physical or psychological benefits of a particular medication against its possible risks. If the possible benefits outweigh the possible risks, then you should consider using the medication in labor. Some labors are exceptionally long, difficult, or complicated and the benefits of medication or intervention are likely to outweigh the risks. In straightforward, uncomplicated labors, however, the risks of medication or intervention may outweigh the benefits. In this instance, the decision is really up to you. You should become as informed as possible and consider your options carefully. Look over the following list of possible risks and benefits for a better idea of how to handle the decision.

Since you cannot foresee the type of labor you will have, it is wise to maintain a flexible attitude when considering the possibility of using medication in labor. Keep yourself informed, discuss the options with your doctor or midwife and with your partner, and come to a general understanding before labor begins.

One factor that really cannot be predicted or controlled is the quality of the labor itself. Most labors are uncomplicated and, if desired, can be handled without pain medications. Other

BENEFITS AND RISKS OF PAIN MEDICATIONS		
	Possible Benefits	*Possible Risks*
Effects on you	Medications may reduce your pain, promote relaxation, reduce anxiety, or increase comfort.	Medications may affect your blood pressure, cause dizziness, disorientation, or loss of control, cause nausea, or have little effect on pain.
Effects on labor and birth	Medications may enhance the progress of labor or reduce the pain of surgical or medical intervention.	Medications may slow labor, diminish the urge to push, or increase your need for further intervention.
Effects on the baby	Medication may hasten the progress of labor to benefit a distressed fetus.	Medication may cause an abnormal fetal heart rate, inhibit sucking responses, cause difficulty with breathing, or cause drowsiness.
Individual feelings and perceptions	Fear of pain, belief that medication will be more effective than other techniques.	Fear of "needles," poor experience with medication in the past, or strong desire to avoid risks to baby and self.

labors are far more difficult—some are very long and exhausting, some are extremely short and painful, and some require medical or surgical procedures that may increase pain. Since a difficult labor may require pain medications, your birth preparations should include an understanding of such medications and the circumstances under which they might be used. Then, if you need medication, you can choose wisely and appropriately. Later, when you look back on your labor, you will feel satisfied that you handled a difficult situation well.

Medications Used for Labor and Birth

Certain drugs and anesthetics are appropriate only during particular phases and stages of labor. For example, some medications interfere with the progress of labor if given too early. Others are given early to give time for most of the drug to be excreted from the baby's system by birth. As a result, you may be offered one medication during the latent phase of labor and a different medication during transition or birth. When used appropriately, medications relieve some or all of the your pain while not seriously compromising the well-being of your baby or the progress of labor.

Medications used in labor and birth can be classified in three general categories—systemic medications, regional anesthetics, and general anesthetics.

SYSTEMIC MEDICATIONS			
Systemic medications may be given intravenously, orally, rectally, vaginally, or by injection. These drugs enter the blood stream, affecting the whole body, and readily pass to the fetus through the placenta. The timing of the administration of these drugs in relation to the time of birth influences the degree of risk of side effects to the baby.			
Type	*Examples*	*Benefits/Purposes*	*Risks/Disadvantages*
Sedatives and hypnotics	Barbiturates (Seconal, Luminal, Nembutal), Chloral hydrate, Dalmane	Sedatives or hypnotics are usually administered early in labor. They do not relieve pain, but are used to promote rest, relaxation or sleep, and to reduce anxiety, thereby increasing comfort.	• *To the mother.* Barbiturates can prolong labor by impairing uterine activity. They often cause drowsiness and disorientation. • *To the baby.* Barbiturates may accumulate in fetal tissue, predispose the infant to respiratory depression, and decrease responsiveness and sucking ability.
Amnesics *(anticholinergics)*	Scopolamine	Sedation and amnesia are accomplished when Scopolamine is combined with morphine or Demerol, producing "twilight sleep." A generation ago this technique was commonly used. It is rarely used today. Scopolamine is also administered before surgery to reduce salivation, bronchial secretions and gastrointestinal spasms.	• *To the mother.* Anticholinergics produce dry mouth, blurred vision, heart palpitations, dizziness, depression, disorientation, agitated behavior, and respiratory depression. • *To the baby.* This drug delays newborn reaction time and changes the fetal heart rate.

Type	Examples	Benefits/Purposes	Risks/Disadvantages
Tranquilizers	Atarax or Vistaril, Valium, Librium, Equanil or Miltown, Thorazine, Compazine, Sparine, Phenergan, Largon	Tranquilizers are usually administered before late labor to reduce tension and anxiety. They may raise the pain threshold by altering the mother's attitude toward pain. Vistaril, Sparine, Compazine and Phenergan are also antiemetics that reduce nausea and vomiting.	• *To the mother.* Tranquilizers may cause drowsiness, dizziness, blurred vision, confusion, dry mouth, changes in maternal blood pressure and heart rate. • *To the baby.* Tranquilizers may cause variation in fetal heart tones (Valium), lowered body temperature, jaundice (Valium, Thorazine, Compazine, Sparine), poor muscle tone (Valium, Compazine, Thorazine, Sparine), decreased attentiveness, and slow adaptation to feeding (all but Largon, the side effects of which are unknown).
Analgesics ("narcotics")	Demerol, Nisentil, Morphine, Talwin, Sublimaze, Stadol, Dilaudid, Codeine	Analgesics are administered to reduce, abolish, or alter the mother's perception of pain without loss of consciousness. These drugs may promote relaxation between contractions and help the laboring mother to feel more comfortable and "in control" during contractions. Analgesics are most frequently administered during the active phase of labor. They may also be used during a cesarean or postpartum.	• *To the mother.* Analgesics may cause dizziness, euphoria, and nausea, and they may lower maternal blood pressure. They often make it difficult to focus on breathing patterns. If used too soon, analgesics may slow labor. • *To the baby.* Analgesics may depress the newborn's respiration and may alter the infant's behavioral responses for several days or weeks.
Narcotic antagonists	Nalline, Lorfan, Narcan	The mother or baby receives narcotic antagonists to reverse respiratory depression and other side effects caused by narcotics or related analgesics.	• Little is known about the long-term effects of narcotic antagonists on the newborn.

REGIONAL ANESTHETIC AGENTS

Regional anesthetic agents, given by injection, produce loss of sensation (numbness) in the area injected (a local) or in the region of the body supplied by the nerves affected (a nerve block). See the chart on page 194 for a description of each local and nerve block.

Type	Examples	Benefits/Purposes	Risks/Disadvantages
Caudal, epidural, spinal, saddle, pudendal, paracervical, local.	Nesacaine, Xylocaine or Lidocaine, Marcaine or Bupivacaine, Carbocaine	Regional anesthetics are given to relieve pain during active labor or birth. They block pain impulses and are accompanied by a loss of feeling. They do not affect the mind or make the mother drowsy.	Risks vary widely with area injected, anesthesia, and dosage. • *To the mother.* A regional anesthetic may lower blood pressure, inhibit bearing-down reflex, or cause post-spinal headache. • *To the baby.* If present in the fetal blood stream, anesthetics may change fetal heart rate, depress body functions, and alter neurological behavior in the newborn period. The fetus may be indirectly affected by the maternal response to anesthetics.

REGIONAL ANESTHESIA

The placement of the anesthetic agent determines the area where sensation is abolished and pain is relieved.

Type	Placement of Anesthetic	Area Affected	May Be Given At	Takes Effect In	Effect May Last For	Comments
Paracervical block	Into nerve trunks at both sides of cervix via the vagina.	Cervix and uterus	4 – 9+ centimeters	3 – 4 minutes	1 – 2 hours	Given by physician and may be repeated as needed with 70 percent receiving good anesthesia and 10 to 15 percent some anesthesia.* May cause slowing of fetal heart rate because anesthesia enters maternal circulation and crosses to the fetus. There may be a transient decrease in intensity and/or frequency of uterine contractions. Additional medication (usually "local" or pudendal) is required for episiotomy and its repair.
Caudal block *(extradural anesthesia)*	Caudal canal at base of sacrum: given while you lie on your side or in knee-chest position.	Below ribs to knees	After 5 centimeters	15 – 20 minutes	45 minutes to 1-1/2 hours for single dose	Given by anesthesiologist. 95 percent receive good anesthesia.* May cause drop in maternal blood pressure causing drop in fetal heart rate; diminishes urge to push and bearing-down reflex and impairs normal rotation and descent of baby, increasing need for forceps or vacuum extractor. May be given as a single dose for birth or continuously for labor by catheter left in the caudal canal. May slow labor.
Lumbar epidural block *(extradural anesthesia)*	Between lumbar vertebrae, given while you lie on your side or sit up.	Waist to knees	After 4 – 5 centimeters	5 – 20 minutes	1-1/2 – 2 hours	Much the same as caudal except there is less incidence of drop in maternal blood pressure. Less medication is required for epidural as compared to caudal.* It may be given as a single dose or continuously through a catheter. May slow labor. Often used for cesarean birth.
Spinal block *(subarachnoid block)*	Usually between third and fourth lumbar vertebrae, while you lie on your side.	From breast level down	Late first stage and second stage	3 – 5 minutes	1-1/2 – 2 hours	Often used for cesarean birth; given by anesthesiologist; possible "spinal headache" afterwards; possible drop in maternal blood pressure—greater than with caudal or epidural; may have difficulty with urination later. May slow labor. Nearly 100 percent receive good anesthesia.
Saddle block *(subarachnoid block)*	Same as spinal except given while you sit up.	Inner thighs, perineum, and buttocks	Second stage	3 – 5 minutes	1-1/2 – 2 hours	Used when forceps are indicated; given by physician or anesthesiologist; possible "spinal headache" and drop in maternal blood pressure; may have difficulty urinating later.
Pudendal block	Into pudendal nerve trunks near ischial spines via vagina.	Vagina and perineum	Second stage	2 – 3 minutes	1 hour	Given by physician; not 100 percent effective; fetal risks unknown, excessive amounts may cause fetal depression; used for discomfort during delivery or when forceps are indicated, or for episiotomy or its repair; may inhibit bearing-down reflex by relaxing muscle tone of perineum.
"Local" infiltration	Perineum	Perineum	Second or third stage	5 minutes	20 minutes	Given by physician for episiotomy or repair of tears.

*Reference: John J. Bonica. *Obstetric Analgesia and Anesthesia* (World Federation Societies of Anaesthesiologists, 1980).

Here are other facts important to your understanding of regional anesthesia.

- Midwives administer only local anesthetics.

- Family physicians and obstetricians administer drugs for paracervical, pudendal, and local anesthesia.

- An anesthesiologist usually administers caudal, epidural, spinal, and saddle anesthesia. Nurse anesthetists may administer some of these. There is an additional fee for services of these specialists.

- Drugs for caudal and epidural anesthesia may be given in a single dose or continuously throughout active labor and birth. Continuous anesthesia is achieved by administering the drug through a catheter (thin plastic tube), which is placed in the caudal canal or epidural space.

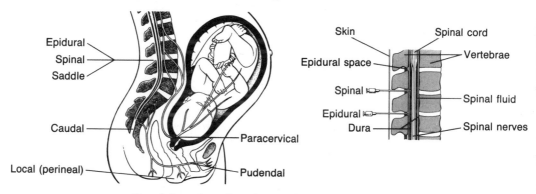

- Caudal and epidural anesthesia are classified as *extradural anesthesia*, which means that the anesthetic is injected outside the dura—the tough covering surrounding the spinal cord. A "spinal headache" rarely accompanies this type of injection and only if the dura was penetrated inadvertently.

- Spinal and saddle anesthesia are classified as *subarachnoid blocks*, which means that the dura must be penetrated. A spinal headache may result from this type of anesthesia. If a headache occurs when the mother's head is elevated but is relieved when she lies flat, it is called a spinal headache. Whether mild or severe, the pain is caused by a loss of cerebrospinal fluid (the fluid surrounding the spinal cord and brain) through the puncture site in the dura. The headache usually disappears within a few days as the dura heals and closes the puncture site. If the headache lingers, a "blood patch" may be made by injecting a small amount of the mother's blood into the epidural space at the puncture site. A clot then forms and seals the puncture. This technique is over 98 percent effective for the immediate and permanent relief of spinal headache.*

GENERAL ANESTHETICS

General anesthetics are usually inhaled in gaseous form and produce a loss of sensation and consciousness. They are rarely used electively for childbirth, even for cesarean section, because they eliminate a woman's awareness and ability to participate in her birth and adversely affect the baby. General anesthetics are administered only when an emergency requires a rapid loss of sensation. At such times, the benefits outweigh the risks of general anesthetic. Normally, regional anesthetics are considered the drug of choice because they have fewer side effects, are less risky, and allow the woman to be fully conscious.

Type	Examples	Benefits/Purposes	Risks/Disadvantages
Induction agents	Pentothal, Brevital	Induction agents are usually very short-acting barbiturates that produce drowsiness. They are given intravenously to aid the induction of inhalation agents.	• *To the mother.* Induction agents cause respiratory depression, lower the blood pressure, and may change her heart rate. Large doses may reduce uterine activity. • *To the baby.* Large doses may result in respiratory depression and poor muscle tone.
Inhalation agents	Penthrane, Nitrous Oxide, Trilene (TCE, Trimar)	Inhalation agents produce rapid loss of sensation and consciousness. They are often used for emergency cesarean section.	• *To the mother.* Inhalation agents may cause respiratory depression, changes in blood pressure and heart rate, and increase the incidence of postpartum hemorrhage. • *To the baby.* Inhalation agents may cause respiratory depression, poor muscle tone, and low Apgar scores.

OTHER KINDS OF MEDICATION

Type	Examples	Benefits/Purposes	Risks/Disadvantages
Drugs used to inhibit premature labor *(labor suppressants)*	Ritodrine, Albuterol, Terbutaline	These drugs, given intravenously or orally, are used during prelabor or early labor before the thirty-fifth week of gestation. They inhibit uterine contractions and give the baby a chance to mature and grow. (They are usually not used if gestation is greater than 35 weeks, and the baby is thought to weigh over 5 1/2 pounds; if the mother has high blood pressure, preeclampsia or diabetes; if there is evidence of placenta previa or abruptio placenta; or if there is evidence that infection has resulted from ruptured membranes.*) Drugs such as Ritodrine, Albuterol, and Terbutaline may be used alone or in combination to stop uterine contractions. Ritrodrine is the most commonly used drug.	• *To the mother.* Labor suppressing drugs are ineffective if active labor is established, the cervix is dilated, or the membranes have ruptured. Side effects from use of Ritodrine include rapid heart rate, anxiety, fluctuations in blood pressures, and pulmonary edema (fluid in the lungs). Terbutaline lowers potassium levels and blood pressure, causes tremors, and may cause pulmonary edema. • *To the baby.* Long-term effects of labor suppressing drugs are unknown. They may cause low blood sugar and rapid heart rate.**
	Ethyl alcohol	Ethyl alcohol was used in the past to attempt to inhibit premature labor contractions.	This drug is rarely used today because its effectiveness is unproven, it can intoxicate mother and baby, and more effective drugs are available.

Type	Examples	Benefits/Purposes	Risks/Disadvantages
Drugs used to stimulate uterine contractions *(Further discussion of these drugs appears in chapter 8 on Interventions.)*	Pitocin and Syntocinon (synthetic oxytocins)	Pitocin or oxytocin-type drugs are used to induce labor contractions, strengthen or augment contractions during labor, or control postpartum bleeding.	• *To the mother.* Pitocin can lower the maternal blood pressure, create anxiety, increase the heart rate, and cause edema and water intoxication. It may cause "tetanic," prolonged contractions of the uterus. • *To the baby.* Pitocin may slow or speed the fetal heart rate and deprive the fetus of oxygen with prolonged contractions. The use of Pitocin may increase the incidence of jaundice in the newborn.
	Ergotrate, Methergine	Ergotrate and Methergine are given by injection or orally; they help control postpartum uterine bleeding.	• The side effects of Ergotrate and Methergine include elevated blood pressure, increased heart rate, headache, and nausea.
	Prostaglandins	Prostaglandins are sometimes used to hasten ripening of the cervix either to start labor or as a prelude to induction with Pitocin.	• Possible side effects of Prostaglandins include tetanic uterine contractions. Other effects of this drug are not yet known.
Drugs used in the management of preeclampsia *(toxemia)*	Magnesium sulfate, Apresoline	Magnesium sulfate is used to prevent seizures when the mother has severe preeclampsia. It may also lower blood pressure. It is given by injection or intravenously. Apresoline dilates blood vessels, lowering blood pressure.	• *To the mother.* Magnesium sulfate may cause flushing, warmth, nervousness, respiratory depression, heart-rate and muscle-reflex changes, and reduced urine output. Apresoline may cause light-headedness, nasal congestion, and urination difficulties. A sedative possibly causing drowsiness may also be prescribed with this type of drug. After receiving any of these drugs, the mother's heart rate, urine output, respiratory rate, and muscle reflexes will be closely monitored.
Drugs used to prevent eye infection in the newborn *(eye prophylaxis)*	Silver nitrate, Erythromycin ointment, Tetracycline ointment	Drops or ointments are placed in the newborn's eyes within the first hour after birth to prevent gonococcal infection, which can cause blindness. Erythromycin is the only drug that also combats chlamydia, an infection which can also cause blindness in newborns.	• *To the baby.* Silver nitrate causes the eyes to become red and swollen, and possibly have a discharge. If instilled immediately after birth, it decreases the newborn's ability to look at his parents. Antibiotic ointments may temporarily blur the infant's vision, but these ointments do not irritate the eyes. Parents may ask that this treatment be delayed for up to one hour so they may have eye contact with the baby.

Type	Examples	Benefits/Purposes	Risks/Disadvantages
Drugs used to prevent milk production *(lactation suppressants)*	Deladumone OB, TACE, Parlodel, Diethylstilbestrol (DES)	Lactation suppressants may inhibit lactation and prevent breast engorgement. Deladumone OB and DES are given by injection following delivery. TACE and Parlodel are given orally in a series of doses.	• *To the mother.* These medications are not significantly more effective in preventing engorgement and milk production than breast binding. Occasionally, after receiving the lactation suppressant, rebound milk production occurs. Obviously lactation suppressants should not be given to women who plan to breastfeed. Deladumone OB may cause pain at the injection site. DES occasionally causes nausea and diarrhea, while TACE may cause nausea. Parlodel is expensive and may stimulate ovulation after delivery sooner than is usual.

*Harry Oxorn, *Human Labor and Birth,* 4th ed. (New York: Appleton-Century-Crofts, 1980), 613.
**M. F. Epstein, et al, "Neonatal Hypoglycemia after Beta-Sympathomimetic Tocolytic Therapy," *Journal of Pediatrics* 94 (1979): 449-53.

Chapter Ten Postpartum Period

The postpartum period, the first six to eight weeks after childbirth, is a time of physical and emotional readjustment. The reproductive organs return to their prepregnant state. The family incorporates and accepts a new person into the home. Each parent changes his or her role within the family to cope with the demands of the new baby.

Each family's adjustment is unique. Some families find a comfortable new balance within weeks, while others take months or longer. Many variables affect the family's experience, including the temperament of the baby, medical complications for the mother or the baby, the amount of available help, economic resources, experiences with infant feeding and care, expectations of parenthood, single parenthood, blended families, and the flexibility of the parents. If you understand the common problems associated with the postpartum period, you can put the experience in perspective and plan to get the help you need.

Physical Adjustments

Your body makes numerous physical adjustments in the first days and weeks after childbirth. You may feel uplifted and energetic immediately after the birth and for the next few weeks. Or you may feel exhausted and let down. Most women are aware of sudden changes in their moods and all new mothers feel tired and need rest. After birth, your body undergoes rapid physical and hormonal changes. These changes are "normal," but can be complicated by fatigue, which undermines your sense of well-being and confidence in your ability to cope with a new infant and a new family life. Fathers often experience similar problems of adjustment, their moods fluctuate and they need extra rest. If your baby is on a very irregular schedule (and many are!), you may need outside help. Plan ahead for this possibility.

Early Recovery Period

After your baby is born, your physical condition will be closely observed to assess your recovery. Your caregivers will frequently check your temperature, pulse, respiratory rate, and blood pressure. They will also monitor the amount and character of your lochia, the size and position of your fundus, and the functioning of your bladder and bowel.

Uterus

In an amazing process called *involution*, the uterus returns to its prepregnant size five or six weeks after birth. Immediately following the birth of the placenta, the uterus weighs between two and three pounds and the fundus can be felt midway between the navel and the pubic bone. During the next two days, it remains approximately the same size and feels like a tight muscle the size of a grapefruit. To maintain the firmness of the uterus, preventing heavy blood loss from the placental site, you or your caregiver will massage the uterus, stimulating it to contract. Nursing your baby will also help contract your uterus.

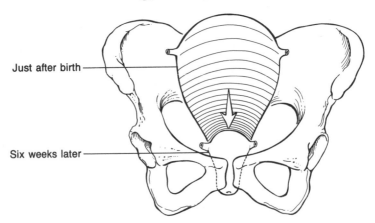

Just after birth

Six weeks later

A week after the baby's birth, the uterus weighs from one to one and one-half pounds. After two weeks, the uterus lies within the pelvis and weighs about a half-pound. By the end of five or six weeks, it weighs two to three and one-half ounces, and it has returned to its previous size.

During involution, lochia is discharged from the uterus. For the first days after birth, the red-colored discharge flows heavily. The amount of flow may change with your activity or body position. Lochia is generally heavier when you change positions (standing or sitting up after lying down), and during breastfeeding, and it normally has a faint, "fleshy" odor. After three or four days, the lochia diminishes and becomes pale pink in color. During the next several weeks, it becomes yellowish white, white, or brown. It may continue for as long as six to eight weeks.

You should report any of the following changes to your midwife or physician: a foul odor, a return to the bright red color after the discharge has paled or turned brown, a sudden increase of discharge, or the presence of large, bloody clots. These changes could be a sign of infection, overexertion, or excessive bleeding.

Afterpains

Afterpains, the uncomfortable and sometimes painful contractions of the uterus after birth, often occur while you are nursing and are more common if you have had a child before. To cope with the pain, relax and use the slow-breathing pattern. Remember that afterpains usually disappear after the first week.

Cervix and Vagina

By the end of involution, the cervix has shrunk almost to its prepregnant size. The outer opening of the cervix does not completely regain its original appearance but remains somewhat wider.

The vagina gradually regains its tone, but the labia remain somewhat looser, larger, and darker than they were before pregnancy.

Breasts

Breastfeeding mothers: For the first twenty-four to seventy-two hours after birth, your breasts secrete colostrum, a yellow fluid that precedes breast milk. Milk production begins between the second and fifth day. At this time your breasts may feel tense, hard to the touch, and painful (engorgement). With frequent nursing for at least ten minutes on each breast, this initial engorgement may not occur or will subside. From this point on, your baby's demands will control your milk production. (See chapter 12 for more information on breastfeeding.)

Nonbreastfeeding mothers: You may be given medication immediately after delivery or during the next few days to suppress lactation. (See page 197.) Even so, you may still produce milk. Breastbinding, ice packs, and the avoidance of breast stimulation help diminish milk production and decrease your discomfort. Do not express milk from your breasts since this will stimulate your breasts to produce more milk.

Circulatory Changes

Some blood loss is a natural result of birth. Average blood loss during an uncomplicated vaginal birth amounts to about seven ounces (or almost one cup). If you have an episiotomy, you may lose ten ounces of blood or more. But do not be alarmed. In pregnancy, you accumulated extra blood and fluid so that a slight loss during birth is not harmful. In the early postpartum period, you will urinate large quantities of fluid and you may also perspire heavily. As a result, you will probably lose as much as five pounds during the first five days afer birth.

Abdominal and Skin Changes

After birth, your abdominal muscles remain soft for about six weeks before they regain their tone, and your stretch marks will fade but not completely disappear. If you have had an increase in skin pigmentation, it will fade. There will also be a gradual reversal of any increase in hair growth.

Hormonal Changes

After delivery, your body undergoes sudden and dramatic changes in hormonal production. When the placenta is delivered, estrogen and progesterone levels drop abruptly and remain low until your ovaries begin producing these hormones again. You will probably begin menstruating again four to eight weeks after delivery if you are not breastfeeding. If you are breastfeeding, you may not menstruate for several months, though ovulation can occur during this time. Your first few menstrual periods following delivery may be heavier than usual, but will soon return to normal.

Care Following Birth

Rest and Activity

• Adequate rest is essential to recovery. Try to rest an extra two hours each day, and go to bed early whenever possible, especially while you are waking up for night feedings.

• If you conscientiously perform the pelvic floor contraction exercise (Kegel), you encourage the healing of your episiotomy or any tears, reduce the swelling in the area, and restore the muscle tone in the pelvic floor.

• Try to begin postpartum exercises within a day or two. (See page 206.)

• Gauge your activity by how you feel. It is wise to establish priorities about working inside and outside the home, to follow your caregiver's guidelines about activity, and to take advantage of all offers of help.

Perineal Care

The basic goals of perineal care are twofold: to prevent infection and to promote healing by avoiding contamination of the vagina and perineum. If an episiotomy was performed or a tear occurred during delivery, you have had stitches which will dissolve of their own accord. Usually complete healing takes place within four weeks, though you may feel discomfort for some time. Discomfort during intercourse may persist for several months.

• After you urinate, clean yourself by pouring warm water over your perineum from the front toward your rectum.

• Always wipe yourself from front to back.

• To relieve soreness, try sitting in a warm tub of water for twenty minutes. Then lie down for fifteen to twenty minutes. Hot or cold packs, a heat lamp or light, or witch hazel may help relieve soreness.

• Lie down and rest as often as you can. Try pelvic floor contraction (Kegel) exercises in a reclining position.

• Do not use tampons before your postpartum checkup.

• Do not douche.

Elimination

• At first, urination may be difficult because of slack abdominal tone, swelling of your urethra, or other factors. If you have difficulty urinating, relax, drink lots of liquids, and pour warm water over your perineum to start your flow. Trying to urinate in the shower or bathtub sometimes alleviates the difficulty. If you are unable to urinate, a catheter may be inserted to empty your bladder.

• You may become constipated after delivery because of lax abdominal muscles or the soreness of the perineum, episiotomy, or hemorrhoids. You can avoid constipation by eating fresh fruits, vegetables, and whole-grain cereals and drinking plenty of water. Walking, exercising your abdominal muscles, and responding to the urge to move your bowels will help restore normal bowel function.

• Supporting the perineal area by gently pressing toilet tissue at the episiotomy site can help relieve soreness when you are bearing down for a bowel movement; doing this will decrease the fear you may have of hurting yourself while straining.

If these suggestions do not help you, your physician or midwife may prescribe stool softeners, suppositories, or an enema.

Hemorrhoids

There are several ways to reduce the discomfort of hemorrhoids and promote healing.

• Avoid constipation.

• Try the pelvic floor contraction exercise, with emphasis on the muscles around the anus.

• Modify for home use any hospital procedure that helped, such as witch hazel and sitz baths.

• Your physician or midwife may prescribe medication.

Bathing

You will find that attitudes and advice about tub baths and showers vary. Showers are used in most hospitals. Ask your physician or midwife about what to do at home.

Diet

• Do not go on a slimming diet. Follow a diet similar to the one you used during pregnancy.

• If you are breastfeeding, drink additional fluids, including milk, and add 200 calories to your daily pregnancy diet.

• Make sure your diet contains plenty of roughage so you will not become constipated.

• Some physicians and midwives will tell you to continue to take your prenatal vitamins and iron.

Early Discharge

If you and your baby are doing well, you may have the option of leaving the hospital within twenty-four hours after the birth. Birthing clinics always discharge mothers and babies within hours after birth. This "short stay" or early discharge option has the following advantages: financial savings; for those who are uncomfortable in hospitals, a chance to return home in a short time; short separation from other children; home cooking; your own bed; and so on. Disadvantages include little time to learn from the nurses; the need for a rested, capable person to watch you and the baby for possible complications; the need for help with your care and your baby's care, and household help.

If you choose an early discharge, you will need help at home during the first few days. You will need to be taught how to observe yourself and your newborn in order to detect problems that need medical care. It will be important for you to have resources to call upon if you have any concerns. And you should schedule an appointment with your caregiver or a public health nurse within a few days after you come home to check for problems and to ask questions. A helpful pamphlet on early discharge is *The First Days after Birth: Care of Mother and Baby.* See Recommended Reading.

Practical Help

Since getting enough rest is essential, but also very difficult, think of ways to minimize your work. You can accept help from others and direct it to meet your needs: "Mother, what I really need is someone to cook a meal or two, someone to do the grocery shopping, and someone to keep an eye on the baby while I get some uninterrupted sleep."

Think in advance about what kind of help you will need. Do

you need someone to cook or clean? Have you checked the neighborhood for babysitters? Do your friends have babysitters they can recommend? Are there mothers in the neighborhood who might want to trade with you? Make arrangements in advance. To keep your perspective, you may occasionally need to get away from the day-and-night responsibility of parenthood.

Postpartum Examinations

It is important that you have a postpartum checkup within three to eight weeks of delivery. A general physical examination, which includes a pelvic exam, will assess your recovery and give you a chance to discuss your recovery problems, your out-of-the-home work schedule, and your plans for contraception.

Your physician will recommend Pap tests on a regular schedule. This test is painless and effectively detects the early symptoms of cervical cancer. Your caregiver will also recommend monthly breast self-examination. The best time to check your breasts is right after your menstrual period. While only a small percentage of breast changes indicate cancer, you should report any thickening, lumps or nonmilk discharge to your physician.

Here is how to conduct a breast self-examination.

1. *You can examine your breasts while bathing or showering. Wet skin allows your fingers to slip easily over your skin. Flatten your fingers and move them gently over every part of each breast, feeling for any lump or thickening.*

2. *Standing in front of a mirror, look at your breasts with your arms at your sides, then with your arms raised over your head. Look for changes in contour, swelling, dimpling of the skin, or changes in the nipple.*

3. *You should also examine your breasts while lying down. To check your right breast, put a pillow under your right shoulder and place your right hand under your head. With your left hand (fingers flat), press gently around your breast in a circular motion. Making smaller circles, gradually move in toward the nipple, until you have examined your entire breast (including the nipple). Repeat this procedure on your left breast after switching the pillow and placing your left hand behind your head.*

Breast self-examination is less reliable during breastfeeding because changes in size and shape occur every day. If you are breastfeeding, it is best to check your breasts right after a feeding. Until your periods resume, mark a calendar as a monthly reminder. While you are weaning and your milk supply is diminishing, you may find lumps in your breasts. This is common, but if you feel unsure about the condition, call your physician or midwife.

Sexual Adjustments

Some women and men want to resume intercourse as soon as possible after the birth. Others feel constrained or afraid. Obviously, a sore perineum, a demanding baby, lack of help, and extreme fatigue will affect your ability to relax and enjoy making love. If you are not ready to resume intercourse, "pleasuring" (touching and enjoying each other's bodies sensually with or without orgasm and without pressure to have intercourse) can help you relax and show your love. Keep your sense of humor and be honest with each other about your feelings.

Doctors often recommend that you refrain from intercourse for six weeks, but this is a somewhat arbitrary and outdated suggestion. It is probably safe to have intercourse when your stitches heal, your vaginal discharge stops, and you feel like it. But be gentle. You will probably be sore at first. After birth, you will have a decrease in vaginal lubrication because of hormonal changes; if you are breastfeeding, this will continue. Any sterile, water-soluble lubricant, such as K-Y Jelly or a contraceptive cream, can alleviate this problem during intercourse. Keep in mind that conception can occur whether or not menstruation has resumed. While there are restrictions on certain contraceptives, your physician or midwife can help you choose a satisfactory method. The condom in combination with spermicidal foam, cream, or jelly is safe and effective soon after birth.

Postpartum Conditioning

The conditioning exercises you practiced during pregnancy will also help you recover your former contours and strength during the postpartum period. With your doctor's or midwife's approval, you can start the first three exercises described below as early as one hour after delivery. If you have had a cesarean birth, however, you should begin with different exercises. (See pages 174 to 177.)

In addition to gentle conditioning, many new mothers want to resume more vigorous exercises. Check first with your caregiver. Before or instead of exercising strenuously, you can begin taking walks. You will often be amazed at how getting out of the house lifts your spirits and, sometimes, calms the baby.

Postpartum Exercises

At first, two areas of your body need special attention—your abdominal muscles and your pelvic floor. You can see that your abdomen is not as flat as it was. After months of stretching, it needs toning and conditioning. At the same time, the pelvic floor muscles need exercise to increase circulation, to reduce swelling and promote healing in the perineum, and to restore vaginal muscle tone. The pelvic floor muscles need support while you exercise your abdominal muscles, so when you are doing abdominal exercises, first contract the pelvic floor muscles.

After the birth of your baby, you may think you do not have time to exercise. Luckily, these exercises can be done while you go about your daily tasks. For instance, each time you change a diaper you can contract the pelvic floor muscles or do several pelvic tilts. Before a feeding you can do wide arm circles. During a shower or bath, you can practice the abdominal tightening exercise. Once every day or two, sit on the floor and perform the exercises requiring this position. You can also combine baby play with the last four exercises. By consciously exercising as part of your daily routine, you will rapidly regain your muscle tone and feel better at the same time. Remember, if you experience any pain, discontinue that exercise for a while. You did many of the following exercises during your pregnancy. Refer to the pages indicated to review the complete descriptions.

1. Pelvic Floor Contraction (page 84)

Starting right after birth, gently tighten and then relax the muscles of your perineum. You may hardly feel the contractions of these muscles at first, but if you did this exercise before delivery, you will benefit from your efforts now. Start by doing two to three contractions each hour for the first few hours, then progress to five contractions several times a day.

After a few days, hold the pelvic floor contraction for a count of two or three. Gradually work up to a slow count of five. Try this exercise while you are urinating by partially emptying your bladder, then stopping the flow. Do not be discouraged if this is difficult at first.

As you progress with this exercise, you will be able to do the "elevator" variation. You can test the strength of your perineal muscles during sexual intercourse. You can perform this exercise when you are lying down, sitting, or standing.

2. Abdominal Tightening (page 86)

This exercise is designed to tone up the abdominal muscles. You will feel the muscles tightening if you keep your hands on your abdomen. Remember to exhale while performing this exercise. Try five and progress slowly to ten each day.

3. Pelvic Tilt (page 86)

This exercise will help tone and strengthen abdominal muscles, relieve backache, and aid the return of your prepregnant posture. Soon after the birth, lie flat in bed with your knees bent, tighten your abdominal muscles to tilt your pelvis, and press your low back into the bed for a count of two or three. Increase gradually to a count of five. After a few days, do pelvic tilts while standing, sitting, or on hands and knees.

CHECKING FOR SEPARATION OF THE RECTUS MUSCLES

Before you begin any abdominal muscle exercises (other than the pelvic tilt), check for separation of the rectus muscles. Like a zipper opening under stress, these vertical abdominal muscles may have separated painlessly and without bleeding during pregnancy. This separation protects the abdominal muscles from stretching excessively around the growing uterus.

To test for separation of the rectus muscles, lie on your back with knees bent, press the fingers of one hand into the area just above your navel (fingers should be together and horizontal). Slowly raise your head and shoulders off the bed

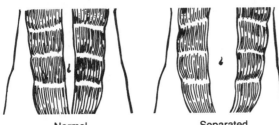

Normal   Separated

or floor. The rectus muscles will tense, pressing on your fingers allowing you to detect any gap. A slight gap (one or two fingers wide, side by side) indicates normal muscle weakness after pregnancy. An extreme gap, three or four fingers wide, between the muscles indicates a need for some preliminary work to reduce the gap before you begin strenuous abdominal exercises. Strenuous exercise in the presence of a wide separation only increases the separation and defeats the purpose of the exercise.

To reduce the separation, begin with the following exercise. When the gap narrows to the width of one or two fingers, proceed to exercises 4, 5, and 6.

Head Lift Exercise

Lie on your back with your knees bent; cross your hands over your abdomen, placing them on either side of your waist. Breathe in. As you exhale, raise your head off the floor or bed; at the same time, pull the rectus muscles toward the midline with your hands. Slowly lower your head back down.

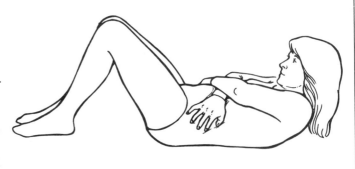

4. Leg Sliding (page 88)

This exercise helps strengthen the lower abdominal muscles. Remember to maintain a pelvic tilt and only lower your legs as far as you can while keeping your low back on the floor. Go slowly, progressing from five to ten a day.

5. Sit Back

A week or two after the birth, begin this exercise, which strengthens the abdominal muscles. It is easier than a sit up or central lift (and equally effective) because you do not have to overcome the force of gravity at the beginning of the exercise

Sit with your knees bent and your arms out in front of you. Lean back, but only as far as you can without losing control of the position. If you feel unsteady or weak, sit back up. Gradually increase the distance you lean back as you build strength. Soon you will be able to touch the floor. Folding your arms across your chest makes the exercise more difficult. Later try it with hands clasped behind your head.

6. Diagonal/Central Lift (page 88)

During pregnancy, you did the diagonal lift (reaching toward the right and left). Now you can add the central lift (reaching straight toward your knees). By adding the central lift, you strenghten both the rectus and the diagonal abdominal muscles.

Follow the same procedure you used with the diagonal lift, and remember to exhale as you raise your head and shoulders. You still need to come up only as far as you can with your waist still on the floor—about eight inches. Your movements should be smooth, not jerky.

First twist and reach to the left and hold for a count of five. Relax back slowly. Next reach toward the center and hold. Relax back to original position. Finally, twist and reach to the right and hold. Relax back.

As you strengthen your abdominal muscles, you can do this exercise with arms folded across your chest and later clasped behind your head. Gradually increase the number of repetitions from five to ten per day. Work up to holding the lift for a slow count of five.

7. Wide Arm Circles

This exercise helps increase circulation in the breasts and may help prevent and relieve clogged milk ducts (page 254).

Stand, kneel, or sit with arms straight and extended to the side. Move both arms in large, wide circles, first in one direction, then in the other. Try this exercise without a bra on. Do five to ten rotations in each direction.

8. Relaxation and Slow Breathing (chapter 6)

Because the postpartum period is stressful, it is wise to practice the helpful relaxation techniques you used during pregnancy and childbirth. Try five minutes of slow breathing on a hectic day and see how it relaxes and refreshes you.

Exercising with Your Baby

Shaping up can be fun for both you and your baby. These exercises, which combine conditioning for you with play for your baby, are designed as all-around toners for the abdomen, arms, legs, and buttocks.

1. Up, Up, and Away (Arm Toning)

Starting Position: Lie on your back with your knees bent and feet flat. Place your baby face down on your chest, holding her under her arms.

Exercise: Slowly and gently raise the baby off your chest. Gently lower the baby back onto your chest.

Repetition: Repeat five times.

2. The Twist (Hip Walking)

Starting Position: Sit on the floor with legs extended. Hold your baby on your thighs, with her head and shoulders cradled in your hands.

Exercise: "Walk" forward on your buttocks, twisting as you go. Then "walk" backwards.

Repetition: Repeat four or five times.

3. Rocking (Central Lift)

Starting Position: Lie on your back with hips and knees bent and lower legs parallel to the floor. Place your baby face down on your shins, with her eyes peeking over your knees. Hold her under the arms.

Exercise: Tuck your chin, slowly raise your head and shoulders, and rock forward. (This is like a gentle central lift.) Then gently rock back, lowering your head to the floor. Avoid holding your breath.

Repetition: Repeat five times.

4. Rolling (Sit Back)

Starting Position: Sitting on the floor with knees bent, feet flat on the floor, hold your baby against your chest or resting the baby on your thighs.

Exercise: Gently lean back as you would in the sit-back exercise (page 209). Roll back about halfway, then return to an upright position.

Repetition: Work gradually up to five repetitions.

Emotional and Psychological Adjustments

*"The postpartal period is the most vulnerable period today for the mother, for the infant, for the beginning mother-child relationships, for the continuity of husband-wife relationships, and for the nuclear family's survival."**

After childbirth, you will experience in various degrees the emotional ups and downs associated with post partum. These emotional fluctuations may be partly due to the drastic change in hormone levels, to fatigue, to inexperience or lack of confidence with newborn babies, and to the constant full-time demands made by the baby. For some women, these emotional fluctuations decrease within a few weeks and are a minor aspect of motherhood. For others, they are overwhelming and long-lasting, creating feelings of anxiety, depression or inability to cope. If you have such feelings, even with adequate rest, you might benefit from counseling by a professional who has expertise in postpartum emotions. Below are listed some signs that may indicate a need for counseling:

- Excessive talking or worrying
- Depression
- Extreme changes in appetite
- Crying spells
- Inability to sleep

Parenting You should be aware that each parent needs to develop a comfortable relationship with a new baby. Try not to interfere with each other or protect each other from the realities of the baby (like diapers and crying). Support each other. You do not have to do things the same way to appreciate each other as parents. Distinguish between small problems and large ones. Let the small problems (diapers on backwards, pajamas inside out) go so you can work out the large ones together. If you have different approaches to the baby's crying, try to talk about your views and arrive at a comfortable compromise. The price paid for one parent always getting his or her way ("Well, I figured she was the mother," as one father put it) is that the other parent begins to feel discouraged, incompetent, and less involved. Parents need to become aware of their goals and feelings about parenthood, and it does not happen overnight. It is an on-going process.

A supportive pediatrician, family practice physician, or pediatric nurse practitioner can help alleviate some of the anxieties of early parenthood. Choose a doctor before the birth. Shop around. Interview several physicians to determine who supports your views on bottle- or breastfeeding, circumcision, and child-rearing. Do not be afraid to ask how much an appointment costs, what hospital the doctor uses, who his or her colleagues are, and how large the practice is. Before making a decision, consider how close the doctor's office is to your home. Once you have chosen a physician, feel free to ask questions of either the doctor or the office nurse. They are there to help you.

Unfortunately, parenting is not an instinctive skill. No one is born with the ability to parent. But you can learn. The ability to parent depends on how your parents treated you; experiences you have had with young children (younger sisters, brothers, or other children you have cared for or taught); your knowledge of the physical, emotional, and intellectual needs of infants and children; and the examples of parenting you see around you. Even if you have not had past experiences with children, you can still learn about your infant's needs and development by reading or attending parenting classes. You can also observe other parents with their children. You will like some of the relationships you see; you will not like others. Try to figure out the differences so you can develop your own parenting style.

A Baby Changes Your Life

How will this new family member affect your relationship as a couple? How will he affect your roles at home and away from home? How will you share the housework and baby care? Your feelings about these questions will change and need to be re-negotiated periodically. How will the two of you find time to relax and make love? How will you arrange to get away from home? At some point you may have to figure out which of your commitments are important and which can be dropped. You do not need a lot of external pressures when you begin your family life. Support from relatives, friends, and babysitters can help you work out your priorities.

In addition to the overnight changes that occur when you become a parent, there are also changes occurring in our society, transitions in family roles, both inside and outside the home. This may mean that your expectations of yourselves as mother or father have changed in recent years and that your actual feelings about being a mother or father may not mesh very comfortably with the reality. This may be particularly true if you are exploring new arrangements in your family and do not have any role models for guidance and reassurance.

The challenges of parenting increase for the single parent. The time, energy, and emotions are much greater. The wise single parent takes advantage of parent support groups and parent-infant classes. Other single parents may also be a source of support and help.

Parenting is a time of disequilibrium. To keep things in perspective, take a look at the "pie of life" chart on the next page. You may be a parent the rest of your life, but this time with your infant represents only a small portion of your life. Enjoy it!

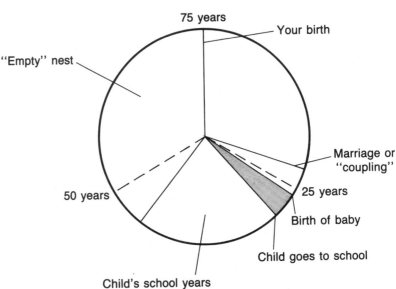

Pie of Life

The "pie of life," illustrated above, graphs the phases in your life. Roughly one third of your life is spent before you have a child; one third is spent bearing, rearing, and launching a child or children. The last third is spent with an "empty nest." In addition, it is possible that a woman will spend the last years of her life a widow, since women usually live longer than men.

Notice how small a "slice of pie" is the time you spend bearing children and caring for them before they enter school. This time in your life is very short, although it is probably the most demanding and stressful for both individuals and couples. It is during this period that many couples, so caught up in caring for the children and possibly pursuing one or two careers, neglect the little things that keep them close to each other. Make time for conversation and shared activities.

In addition, it is important not to neglect your individual interests, even though they have to take a lower priority when the baby and young child need so much of your attention. Later in your life you will find that what you did during this brief childbearing period played an important part in your development as a couple and as individuals.

Chapter Eleven Caring for Your Baby

N ew parents are often surprised at the physical appearance of their newborn. The size and shape of the head, the baby's initial dusky color, the presence of vernix and streaks of blood, and the baby's size often make the strongest immediate impression. You will probably find that you are captivated and cannot take your eyes off your new baby.

Your Newborn's Appearance

Body

The average full-term baby weighs seven to seven and one-half pounds and measures about twenty inches. A newborn's shoulders are narrow and sloping, her abdomen protrudes, her hips are small, and her arms and legs are relatively short and flexed.

Head

Size. A newborn's head is large in proportion to the rest of her body.

Molding. Your baby's head may be temporarily elongated or molded from pressures during labor and birth. It will regain its normal shape within a few days. Occasionally there is also some bruising and swelling of the scalp, but that condition will disappear in time.

Soft spots. Babies are born with two "soft spots" or fontanels—areas where the bones of the skull have not completely fused. A large, diamond-shaped soft spot is on the top front portion of the head, while a smaller, triangle-shaped spot lies at the back. The larger one usually closes by eighteen months, the smaller one by two to six months. The membrane covering the fontanels is thick and tough, so brushing or washing the scalp will not hurt the baby.

Hair

Some babies are born with full heads of hair, while others are virtually bald. Fine, downy body hair, called *lanugo*, is more noticeable on the newborn's back, shoulders, forehead, ears, and face. It is more pronounced in premature babies. Lanugo disappears during the first few weeks.

Eyes

Fair-skinned babies usually have blue-gray eyes; dark-skinned babies have brown or dark gray eyes. If her eye color is going to change, it usually does so by six months. The tear glands of many newborns do not produce many tears until about three weeks.

Blister on the Lip

Intense sucking may often cause a painless blister on the center of the upper lip. Sometimes the sucking blister peels. It disappears gradually, as the lip toughens.

Skin

Color. At birth, your baby's skin may be gray-blue in color, wet, and streaked with blood and varying amounts of vernix, a white creamy substance. After your baby begins breathing, normal skin tones develop, beginning on her face and trunk and eventually reaching her fingers and toes.

Milia. Obstructed sweat and oil glands cause small white spots on your baby's nose, cheeks, and chin. When the glands begin functioning, after several weeks, the milia will disappear. You do not need to treat the condition or try to remove the whiteheads; simply wash her face with water and a washcloth.

Mottled skin. A newborn's skin often remains slightly transparent for several weeks. Fair-skinned babies particularly look blotchy, with areas of redness and paleness.

Peeling skin. Many babies have peeling skin, particularly at the wrists, hands, ankles, and feet. Overdue babies seem to peel more than term babies. This is normal and no treatment is necessary.

Vernix caseosa. This white creamy substance, which protected your baby's skin before birth, often remains in skin creases even after bathing. There is no need to remove the vernix. Gently rub it into the creases and folds of your baby's body.

Stork bites. A collection of superficial blood vessels, "stork bites," often appear on the back of the baby's neck, eyelids, nose, or forehead. They redden when the baby cries. They are not permanent birthmarks and are not caused by injury during birth. Although they usually fade or disappear within nine months, some, especially those on the neck, remain longer.

Mongolian spots. Mongolian spots, areas of dark pigment, commonly appear on the lower back and buttocks of some dark-skinned babies. The spots look like "black and blue" marks or bruises. They gradually fade and usually disappear by age four.

Breasts

Due to maternal hormones, both male and female babies may have swollen breasts. Some babies even leak milk from their nipples. This is normal and needs no treatment. Do not express milk from your baby's nipples; the condition will disappear.

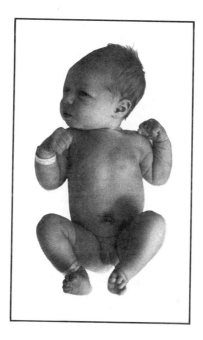
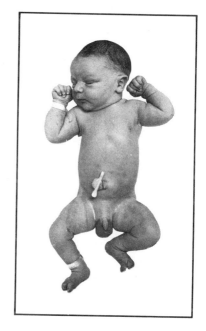

Umbilical Cord

A newborn's umbilical cord is a bluish-white color immediately after delivery. The umbilical cord dries up, darkens, and falls off spontaneously between the first and third weeks. Since it is important to keep the cord clean, do not cover the stump with diapers or plastic pants. Wipe around the base of the cord daily with a cotton swab dipped in water. Try to keep the cord dry at other times. Traditional advice for cord care includes keeping the cord dry by using alcohol swabs and giving sponge baths until the cord has fallen off. Alcohol, however, is potentially irritating and may be no more effective than water; sponge baths are more chilling than tub baths and are of questionable benefit.* Many physicians now recommend swabbing with water and giving tub baths from the beginning.

Genitals

Exposure to maternal hormones may cause swollen genitals in both male and female newborns. Female infants may even discharge a milky or bloody substance from the vagina. Male infants may have unusually large testicles. These conditions are normal and temporary and do not require treatment.

Your Newborn's Senses

For years, baby-care specialists believed that new babies were extremely limited in their range of responses. It was thought that a wet diaper, hunger, or colic would cause a new baby to respond, but not much else. It was believed that babies could not see at birth, and, when they finally did, they could not discern color. It was also believed that babies could not hear because their ears were full of mucus and fluid. And it was thought that babies could be spoiled if they were picked up every time they cried.

After years of study, however, we now recognize some of the newborn's amazing capabilities. Consider the following:

Seeing. When she is quiet and alert, your baby can focus on objects seven to eighteen inches away. She prefers to look at human faces, complex patterns, and slowly moving objects— particularly shiny objects with sharply contrasting colors. Your newborn will follow a slowly moving object in a 180-degree arc above her head (if the object catches her attention). She can stare at you until she satisfies her need for stimulation, then turn away from you. In this way, your baby has some control over her world.

Hearing. Infants hear from birth and react to sound. They respond to human voices (especially female, which is why people often unconsciously raise the pitch of their voices when talking to babies). Your baby heard your heartbeat, your voice, and other internal and external noises when she was inside your body, and she will sometimes calm down or become alert when she hears these familiar sounds (when you hold her close or talk to her) or when she hears repetitious, droning sounds (such as a dishwasher, a washing machine, or certain music). She will also startle at sudden, loud noises.

Smell. Your baby has a refined sense of smell. She recognizes differences in smells and can even tell the difference in smell between her own mother's milk and another mother's milk.

Taste. Babies may react to sweet, sour, salty, and bitter tastes, probably preferring sweet substances.

Touch. Your baby enjoys being stroked, rocked, caressed, gently jiggled, and allowed to nestle and mold to your body while being held. She also likes comfort and warmth—not too hot or cold. She enjoys swaddling when she is young and freedom of movement as she grows older.

Your Newborn's Reflexes

Much of a newborn's physical behavior is reflexive in nature—she cannot consciously control most of her movements—so, awake or asleep, she yawns, quivers, hiccups, stretches, and cries out without apparent reason. Rooting, sucking, and swallowing are survival reflexes that enable the baby to eat. Other reflexes, such as coughing, relieve irritation or help her avoid unpleasant stimuli. A new baby sneezes when her nose is irritated or a bright light shines in her eyes. She blinks if her eyelashes are stimulated. She pulls away from a painful stimulus, like a pinprick in the heel.

A newborn is not helpless. If she is lying on her stomach, she will lift her head and turn it to the side to avoid smothering. If you place an object over her nose and mouth, she will twist away from it, mouth it vigorously, or attempt to knock it off with her arms.

NEWBORN REFLEXES	
The following list summarizes common newborn reflexes. The descriptions refer to the full-term infant, since reflexes in premature infants often last longer and are more exaggerated.	
Moro ("startle") reflex	When startled, your newborn will stretch out her limbs and straighten her body, then rapidly curl up. By the fourth month, the baby is less easily startled and her response is less marked. By the sixth month the reflex disappears, except in cases of extreme fright.
Galant reaction	If you stroke your baby's back on one side while she is lying on her stomach, she will bend her trunk toward that side. This reaction fades by the end of the second month.
Automatic walking *(dance reflex)*	When your baby is supported upright with her feet bearing some weight, she will alternately move her feet as if she were walking. This reflex disappears at the end of the second month.
Placing reaction	Put your baby's shins against an edge and she will step up onto the top of the surface. This reflex disappears at the same time as the automatic walking reaction by the end of the second month.
Grasp reflex	*Hands:* When you touch the baby's palms, she will grasp your fingers firmly and support some or all of her body weight. By the fifth month, the strength of her grasp diminishes, and the reflex disappears. *Feet:* The soles of the feet exhibit the same reflex. Here, however, the reflex does not disappear until the eighth month.
Sucking reflex	With her mouth, your newborn can grasp and suckle the nipple and areola (the pigmented area) if you are breastfeeding her or suck on the nipple of a bottle if she is formula-fed. This reflex will continue until you wean your child.
Rooting reflex	When you touch your baby's cheek, she will open her mouth and turn her head in that direction and search for the nipple. This reflex also continues as long as she nurses.
Tonic neck reflex *(fencing position)*	When your baby lies on her back and turns her head to the right, she will extend her right arm and leg to the right while flexing her left arm and leg. When she looks to the left, her movements are reversed. The tonic neck reflex may not appear until several days after birth, and it disappears by the end of the third month.

Special Babies

Premature Infants

If your infant is born early and weighs less than five and one-half pounds, he is considered *premature*. Developmentally immature, a premature infant looks different from a full-term infant—he is small, limp, and frail; his skin is reddish and appears tissue-paper thin; and he has little or no fatty tissue. His head appears disproportionately large, while his musculature is slight. Lanugo is abundant, finger and toenails have not grown out, and his tiny ears are soft and hug his head. His cry is more feeble, and he is more difficult to soothe than a full-term infant.

An immature infant is physically disadvantaged until he grows older. You will notice that a premature baby sucks weakly, and his swallow and gag reflexes are unreliable. Tube feeding is sometimes necessary. Because the premature's body temperature is unstable, often below normal, he is usually kept in the controlled environment of an isolette. His respirations are irregular, rapid, and often shallow because his lungs are immature. His breathing requires close observation. He may need oxygen and help with breathing. His ability to absorb food is less efficient than that of a full-term infant, although his need for nutrients, especially calories, protein, iron, calcium, zinc, and vitamin E, may be greater.

Giving birth to a premature infant may be upsetting and frightening. Your premature baby needs special attention that may separate him from you, but he also needs to be touched, stroked, and talked to, even while inside the isolette. Today, most modern hospitals want you to visit and care for your premature infant. If he cannot suck at your breast, you can express milk, which can be fed to him in a bottle with a special nipple or via a stomach tube. Your milk is different from the milk of a mother of a full-term baby, and is especially suited to the nutritional needs of your premature infant. By feeding and touching him, you help your baby through this difficult time. Parents often feel guilty or responsible for the premature birth of their baby, even though no specific cause of prematurity can be found in over 50 percent of premature births. In the majority of the remaining cases, where the cause is known, the parents could have done nothing to prevent an early birth.

Parent support groups provide valuable information and assistance to parents coping with a premature infant. In addition to listening with understanding and giving practical suggestions, members of a support group may even supply you with clothing or patterns for clothing small enough for your baby. If you would like more information about premature babies, check with your local childbirth education group, caregiver, or hospital, or write to Parents of Prematures, 13613 Northeast Twenty-sixth Place, Bellevue, WA 98005.

Infants Small for Gestational Age

In the past, some full-term babies who weighed less than five and one-half pounds were wrongly called premature. Babies who are small in size and weight for the length of pregnancy are more properly called *small for gestational age*. This condition has three general causes: an inadequate transfer of nutrients across the placenta to the baby; some congenital and genetic malformations; and certain infections of the fetus, such as rubella and toxoplasmosis.

Postmature Infants

A baby is considered *postmature* if he is born well after the anticipated due date and exhibits the following characteristics: the absence of lanugo; little vernix caseosa; long fingernails and toenails; pale, peeling skin; and unusual alertness. In postmaturity, the amniotic fluid may be scant or stained with meconium. Postmaturity is rare. If your caregiver suspects a postmature fetus, he or she will test for fetal well-being (see chapter 3). Depending on the test results, your caregiver may deliver the baby before spontaneous labor begins.

Common Concerns about Newborns

Physiological Jaundice

Jaundice, a yellow tinge of the baby's skin and in the whites of the eyes, is caused by large amounts of bilirubin in the blood. (Bilirubin forms normally as red blood cells break down.) Mild jaundice is found in about 50 percent of full-term and 80 percent of premature babies. It usually appears during the second or third day after birth and disappears before the end of the second week. If jaundice appears, your baby's doctor may call for a blood test to measure the level of bilirubin in the blood. Blood is drawn from the heel.

If there are high levels of bilirubin in the baby's blood, the baby may be treated with phototherapy. The naked baby, with his eyes covered, is placed under bright lights (bililights), which help break down the bilirubin in the skin. Jaundice is rarely serious or harmful, but doctors often prescribe phototherapy in case the jaundice is the rare, harmful (not physiological) type. If you notice a yellow tinge to your baby's skin or the whites of his eyes, notify your midwife or doctor. (See "Recommended Reading" for further information.)

Circumcision

Circumcision, the removal of the foreskin covering the head (glans) of the penis, is probably the oldest surgical operation known, dating back some 6,000 years. It is a covenant of the Jewish religion and part of the puberty ceremonies of some Islamic, African, and New Guinean cultures. It is also commonly performed in North America for nonreligious reasons as a matter of parental choice. Performed by physicians (usually the obstetrician), circumcision is a surgical procedure for which prior, written parental permission is needed. Since the decision about circumcision is up to you and your partner, discuss the subject during pregnancy when there is time to gather information. Although most American newborn males are routinely circumcised, the trend has been declining over the past few years.

While you are making this decision, you may think about whether other males in the family, school, and community have been circumcised, feeling that your son should look the same. In reality, however, the implications of circumcision or noncircumcision are no greater than the other physical differences that naturally exist between unique individuals.

Facts to Consider:

• There are no medical or legal reasons for circumcising the newborn. The American Academy of Pediatrics officially opposes routine, non-religious circumcision of the newborn.

• The procedure does not take long. Healing takes seven to ten days.

• The newborn will feel pain, because anesthesia is not often used.

• Complications, though rare, occur in 0.5 to 2 percent of the cases. Complications range from the minor to the serious and include infection, bleeding, and irritation of the head of the penis from the friction of wet diapers, sometimes followed by pain on urination and scarring of the urinary outlet.

• There is a fee.

• Contrary to previous reports, there is no evidence that circumcision prevents cancer of the penis or the prostate gland in the male, or cancer of the cervix in female partners. Neither does it prevent transmission of venereal diseases.

• There is no evidence that circumcision or noncircumcision affects sexual performance.

Care of the Circumcised Penis

If you choose to have your son circumcised, ask the staff about care of the penis. The staff often suggests frequent diaper changes, gentle washing with soap and water, and application of vaseline or petroleum jelly to aid healing and prevent irritation. You can expect very slight bleeding, but report any excessive bleeding or swelling to your doctor. Some babies sleep more comfortably on their sides until the area has healed.

Care of the Uncircumcised Penis

The foreskin of an uncircumcised newborn does not usually retract (pull back). It is normally joined to the glans, so avoid forcing it back over the end of the penis. It will gradually become looser, and between three and five years of age, most boys' foreskins are fully retractable. Normal bathing provides adequate cleansing during infancy.

Spitting Up

Many babies spit up milk during or after a feeding. Some spit up more than others because they cry hard before a feeding, eat too much, or swallow air during the feeding; some babies have an immature sphincter muscle at the top of their stomachs, which allows milk to come up with air bubbles. You can reduce spitting up, which is usually not harmful, by burping your baby during and after feedings (burp newborns after each breast or after each two ounces of formula), not overfeeding her, and handling her gently and positioning her properly after feedings (lay her on her side or sit her in an infant or car seat with her head elevated 20 to 30 degrees).

Continuous or frequent forceful (projectile) vomiting is more serious and can lead to dehydration. If your infant vomits following two or three consecutive feedings, consult your physician.

Bowel Movements

A newborn's stool pattern is different from an adult's. Your baby's first bowel movements will consist of *meconium*, a sticky, green-black substance present in the intestine before birth. For two to six days following birth, her stools will be a mixture of meconium and milk by-products, spinach-green or yellow in color. Later, your baby will have yellow, green, or brown stools with or without curds. The frequency and consistency of stools depend on the individual baby and on the food she is fed. Some newborns have one stool every few days; others have ten stools a day.

Constipation—hard, dry stools that are difficult to pass—is rarely found in breastfed babies. Some older breastfed babies have only one bowel movement per week. These babies are not constipated; their more mature digestive systems are efficiently using more of their mothers' milk. Call your doctor, however, if your baby seems constipated.

Your baby probably has *diarrhea* if her stools are mucusy, foul smelling, more frequent than usual, blood-tinged, or watery (the diaper shows a water ring around the stool). When in doubt, note the color, consistency, and frequency of your baby's stool; then call your doctor.

Diaper Rash

Many substances can irritate your baby's skin, including urine and stool, some laundry products, inadequate diaper washing, or chemicals used in some disposable diapers. To prevent or treat diaper rash caused by urine, change diapers frequently, rinse the diaper area with water at each change, and avoid plastic pants, which retain moisture. You can reduce irritation from laundry detergents by running the diapers through an extra rinse cycle or by changing to a milder product, such as Dreft or Ivory.

To reduce the amount of ammonia retained in the diapers, add half a cup of vinegar to the diaper pail or the rinse water. Other treatments for diaper rash include exposing the rash to fresh air for a few hours each day, blow-drying your baby's bottom with a hair dryer set at medium heat, or applying a commercial ointment to the dry, irritated skin. (You can remove the heavy white ointment with a cotton ball moistened with baby oil.) If diaper rash persists, consult your physician.

Facial Rashes

Mild rashes on the face commonly occur in the first months of life. The rashes—smooth pimples, small red spots, or rough red spots—come and go, and rarely require treatment.

Prickly Heat

This common, warm-weather rash appears on overdressed or overwrapped babies. Found most often in the shoulder and neck regions, prickly heat looks like clusters of tiny pink pimples surrounded by pink skin. As it dries, the rash becomes slightly tan. Prickly heat may look worse than it apparently feels to your baby. To avoid this rash, keep her cool and dry. Cornstarch applied over the area may help.

Cradle Cap

Cradle cap is a yellowish, scaly, patchy condition found on the scalp or sometimes behind the ears. Daily washing or brushing of the scalp may prevent cradle cap and will help treat it if it does appear. Comb or brush out the scales, using a baby comb, fingernail brush, or soft toothbrush; wash with mild soap. Continue this procedure until the scales are gone. Neither baby oil nor vegetable oil helps.

Newborn Breathing Pattern

Periods of irregular breathing are normal in newborns, but may be frightening to new parents. When your baby is sleeping, she will snort, gasp, groan, and even occasionally pause in her breathing. These irregularities disappear in a month or two.

Sleeping and Waking

Your baby's sleep cycle is closely related to how often he eats. After adjusting to his new environment, a baby will sleep anywhere from twelve to twenty hours in a twenty-four-hour period. Early on, his sleeping periods may be short but frequent.

When your baby is older, he may awaken at night and then settle back to sleep. However, a newborn may need to be fed, walked, rocked, changed, sung to, massaged, or otherwise soothed before going back to sleep. Many new parents wonder when to get up and feed the baby. When your infant is awake and hungry, he will cry hard, wave his arms and legs vigorously, and root and suck at anything close by.

Where your baby sleeps will depend on your personal preference. A newborn should sleep on a firm surface and in a safety-approved crib, bassinet, or similar piece of furniture. Many babies sleep some of the time in their parents' bed.

Six states of sleep and wakefulness have been identified in the infant: deep sleep, light sleep, drowsy, quiet alert, active alert, and crying. While each state has specific characteristics, movement from state to state varies with the individual infant. Some move gradually from one state to another, while others make abrupt transitions.

Properly identifying the state can help you determine how best to care for your infant. The following paragraphs define each state and examine their implications for parenting.*

Sleep States **Deep Sleep.** In this state your baby is very still; his breathing is rhythmic. He occasionally jerks or makes sucking movements with his lips, but rarely awakens. You cannot feed or play with your baby in this state. If you rouse him, he will stay awake only for a moment, then resume a state of deep sleep. Take this opportunity to rest, make a phone call, take a bath, or spend some time with your partner.

Light Sleep. This state of sleep is the most common in newborns. Your baby's eyes are closed, but they may move behind his lids. In light sleep, he moves, makes momentary crying sounds, sucks, grimaces, or smiles. He breathes irregularly. He responds to noises and efforts to arouse or stimulate him. Sometimes he awakens to a drowsy state or remains in this state and falls into a deep sleep.

Many parents rush to care for a baby who moves and makes mewing or crying sounds. Often, however, the baby is not ready to awaken. The wise parent waits a few moments to see if the baby is entering the drowsy state and needs care, or is falling back to sleep.

Awake States **Drowsy.** In this state your baby appears sleepy, his activity level varies, and he may startle occasionally. His heavy-lidded eyes, opening and closing for brief periods, lose focus or appear cross-eyed. He breathes irregularly and reacts to sensory stimuli in a drowsy way. He either returns to sleep or becomes more alert. If you want your baby to return to sleep, avoid stimulating him. If you want to rouse him, talk to him, pick him up, massage him, or give him something to suck or look at.

Quiet Alert. This state, which usually precedes a long sleeping period, is pleasing and rewarding for parents. Your baby lies still, looks at you calmly with bright, wide eyes. He breathes with regularity, and he focuses attentively on what he sees and hears. By providing something for him to look at, listen to, or suck on, you will encourage him to stay in this state. You can sing and talk to your baby, or try some of the infant exercises described on pages 229 to 231. Take time to enjoy these moments of eye contact, alertness, and calm.

Active Alert. In this state your baby is readily affected by hunger, fatigue, noises, and too much handling. He cannot lie still; he may be fussy. His eyes are open but do not appear as bright and attentive as in the quiet-alert state. He breathes irregularly and makes a lot of faces.

When your baby reaches the active alert state, it is time to either feed or comfort him. He probably needs less stimulation. If you act immediately, you may bring him to a lower, calmer state before he enters the crying state.

Crying. A crying baby is difficult for every parent. Keep in mind that your baby has only one way of telling you he cannot cope any more. If he is tired, sick, hungry, frustrated, wet, or lonely, he says so by crying. He also moves his body actively, opens or closes his eyes, makes unhappy faces, and breathes irregularly. Sometimes crying is a release, a self-comforting mechanism that enables him to enter another state. At other times, he needs you to comfort him.

Recording Your Baby's Sleep and Activity

You can make a chart like the one below to record your baby's activities and sleep for a week. This chart, which was adapted from the Sleep-Activity Record of the University of Washington School of Nursing, will show you how much time your baby spends sleeping, awake and content, or awake and crying. You will also see the large amount of time you spend diapering, feeding, and caring for your baby. After using the chart for a week, you can often see that your baby does follow a fairly consistent pattern. As your baby matures, the sleep and activity patterns will undergo further changes.

SLEEP AND ACTIVITY CHART

Symbols

Sleep ————
Awake and crying or fussy ∿∿∿
Awake and content ₴₴₴₴₴₴

Feeding—breast [HOW LONG]
Feeding—bottle [OUNCES]
Parent-baby interaction (bath, car ride, play, etc.) (ACTIVITY)
Diaper change X

Day	a.m. 1	2	3	4	5	6	7	8	9	10	11	Noon	p.m. 1	2
4/5			∿X [45 min.] X				[60 min.]	X₴₴₴₴(Bath)X [40 min.]					∿[45 min.]	₴₴₴
4/6	[50 min.] X∿∿(Rock)				[60 min.] X		₴₴₴[15 min.]₴₴₴(Bath)X [30 min.]						
4/7	∿[40 min.]X					∿[45 min.] X₴₴₴₴₴₴₴(Bath)X₴₴[40 min.]							∿[30 min.]

Crying

A newborn who is not eating or sleeping may spend a lot of time crying, and most parents feel frustrated when they cannot understand why their baby cries. This is a natural reaction. Remember to stay as calm as possible. Your tension is contagious, move slowly and calmly around a crying infant.

After you have ruled out hunger, consider whether the baby is overdressed, underdressed, sick, or bored. Does she have diaper rash or colic? Does she need cuddling or attention? Is she just plain tired? Exhaustion commonly causes crying. She may simply need to be put to bed and allowed to cry awhile to settle herself. (Set the timer between five to fifteen minutes or it may seem like an eternity.) Patting or stroking her bottom or back, or gentle rocking may also help her relax.

Many infants have a regular fussy time every day. Unfortunately this period often occurs in the late afternoon or evening, when everyone else in the house is tired and wants peace. You might find that attention and cuddling quiet her down. If not, consider these suggestions.

• Babies love motion: try a swing, rocker, front pack, or sling, or a walk in a stroller. You can even go for a ride in the car.

• Play music, turn on the radio or television, or sing. The dishwasher, washing machine, clothes dryer, or vacuum cleaner may provide soothing noises.

• Your baby may be bored; put her in the center of family activity. Keep in mind, however, that some babies get overstimulated and need quieter surroundings.

• Wrap your infant snugly in a receiving blanket. Many newborns love the security this provides.

• Once breastfeeding is well established, try giving your baby a pacifier. The breast or bottle may not satisfy her need to suck. Wet the pacifier first in water.

• Plan and prepare dinner ahead of time; eating will be a more relaxing time for everyone.

Some parents fear that if they give their babies too much attention, they will spoil them. A newborn, however, cannot be spoiled. She needs attention, cuddling, and handling. Enjoying and responding to your baby is not spoiling her. When your infant cries, she needs more care, not less. Your newborn infant is not manipulating you when she cries for attention; she simply has no other way to tell you she needs something. You might have trouble figuring out exactly what she wants, but pick her up, cuddle her, and trust your instincts and feelings.

Colic   Colic is another reason that babies cry. No one knows the exact cause of colic, so it is sometimes difficult to recognize. You may suspect colic, however, if your baby cries inconsolably at about the same time every day—often between 6 and 10 p.m. The infant draws her knees up in pain and screams loudly for two to twenty minutes; then the crying stops, only to resume later. She may pass gas from the rectum. Despite the apparent discomfort, colicky babies seem to thrive.

You can comfort your baby by:

• Lying her on her abdomen across your lap or on a hot water bottle wrapped in a towel, and gently rubbing her back.

• Letting her suck on your breast, pacifier, or finger.

• Holding her face down, draped over your arms or hands, which provides pressure against her abdomen.

• Walking or rocking her.

• Maintaining a tension-free atmosphere as much as possible. This may mean taking turns getting away from a colicky baby.

• Swaddling her, holding her close, or putting her in a front pack.

• Using a special medication prescribed by your doctor.

The colicky period is very stressful for parents, and maintaining a calm atmosphere may seem impossible at times. Try to keep in mind that colic does not produce any lasting harmful effects, and that it usually disappears by the third or fourth month. Consult your doctor if constant crying is associated with vomiting, a cold, a fever, or hard stools.

Development and Growth

Each baby is an individual with a unique temperament and personality. Your newborn differs from others in his appearance; activity level; response to pain, hunger, or boredom; and sleeping and eating patterns. Your child is like a puzzle; it will take time for you to figure him out. If you remember that your child is an individual, not a reflection of you, it will make the job of parenting easier. Some babies are more difficult to live with than others. An infant who has a combination of intense reactions, irregularity, slow adaptability, and a high activity level can be difficult to care for; you will need to be more patient and flexible parents. As you get to know your baby, you will discover his temperament and care for him in a more effective or satisfying way.

While your baby's temperament tends to change little over time, his abilities and size will change rapidly. Remember that normal development patterns vary widely from one baby to the next.

Do not feel anxious if your baby takes a developmental step later or earlier than someone else's infant. His developmental pattern is uniquely his own.

DEVELOPMENTAL MILESTONES	
Here is a list of developmental characteristics and behaviors, and the ages at which your baby is most likely to begin to show them.	
Developmental Characteristic	*Approximate Age*
Looks at your face.	Birth to 4 weeks
Follows an object with his eyes for a short distance.	Birth to 6 weeks
Holds his head off bed for a few moments while on stomach.	Birth to 4 weeks
Pays attention to sound, becomes alert, or turns toward it.	Birth to 6 weeks
Smiles or coos when you smile, talk, or play with him.	3 weeks to 2 months
Holds head upright while lying on stomach.	5 weeks to 3 months
Holds head steady when upright.	6 weeks to 4 months
Brings his hands together in front of himself.	6 weeks to 3-1/2 months
Laughs and squeals.	6 weeks to 4-1/2 months
Rolls over from front to back or back to front.	2 months to 5 months
Grasps a rattle placed in his hand.	2-1/2 months to 4-1/2 months

Playing with Your Baby

Play is more important to babies than it is to adults. For an adult, play is usually a form of recreation; for a baby, it is a means of learning about herself and the world around her. When she grabs and shakes a rattle, gums and chews a teething ring, squashes and squeaks a rubber duck, she is learning that she can make things happen. She learns about herself, as well as about the objects she is playing with.

When you talk, coo, laugh, hug, and kiss your baby, she learns that certain things she does make an impact on you. Learning activities (play) for a baby during an average day might include singing and talking; caressing, touching, cuddling when changing or feeding her; a massage after a bath; baby exercises; moving to different rooms; games such as peek-a-boo; and playing with appropriate toys.

Baby Exercise   Much has been written about baby exercise, and some community centers feature classes in infant stimulation and parent-baby exercises. The purpose is twofold: to educate parents about their infants' growth and development, and to teach parents some appropriate and fun ways to play with their babies. By using these simple exercises, you not only play with your baby, but you learn her limitations and capabilities.

These exercises will probably not speed up your baby's development, since growth and development normally occur in an orderly and predictable fashion, even without infant exercise. But you can enhance your baby's development by giving her the chance to use the muscles she is already learning to control.

The exercises discussed in this section are designed for babies one week to three months old. (Exercises for mother *and* baby are described on pages 210 to 211.) A young baby (one to six weeks) may have tightly flexed legs and arms. If you gently jiggle or pat her hands, arms, or legs, you may help relax her muscles and they will move more easily. Keep your movements slow, gentle, and rhythmic. After a few sessions, she will relax and seem to anticipate the movements.

Exercise or play with your baby when she is in the quiet alert state—wide awake, calm, and attentive. If she is fussy, hungry, upset, or sleepy, chances are you will not enjoy yourselves. Unless otherwise noted, do the following exercises on the floor. As your baby grows older, you may want to try other exercises.

1. The Grasp
Aim: To elicit the grasp reflex.

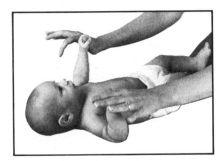

Exercise: Put your thumbs in your baby's palms. She will grasp them. If her hands are closed tightly, pat and bounce them in yours to get them open. Gently pull her hands toward you; she will pull back on your fingers. Do *not* attempt to pull her head and shoulders up.

2. Arm Cross
Aim: To relax chest and upper back muscles.

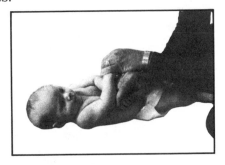

Exercise: Place your thumbs in your baby's palms. When she grasps them, open her arms wide to the side. Bring them together and cross her arms over her chest. Repeat slowly and gently, using rhythmic movements in time to your song.

3. Arm Raising

Aim: To facilitate flexibility of the shoulders.

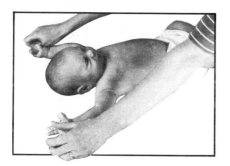

Exercise: Grasp your baby's forearms or hands. Raise them over her head, then lower them to her sides. Repeat slowly and gently, using rhythmic movements. Alternate arms—while one goes up, the other goes down.

4. Leg Bending

Aim: To facilitate flexibility of hips; may help baby pass gas.

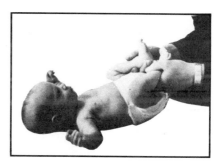

Exercise: With your baby on her back, grasp lower legs and gently bend her knees up toward her abdomen and chest. Gently lower her legs until they are straight. Repeat several times. Alternate, bending one leg while straightening the other.

5. Inchworm

Aim: To bring about extension of legs and back.

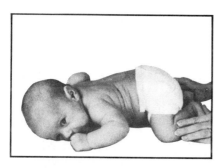

Exercise: With your baby on her tummy, bend her knees under her, holding her feet with your thumbs against the soles. Thumb pressure on her soles will cause her to straighten her legs and move forward like an inchworm.

6. Baby Bounce

Aim: To comfort baby or ready the baby for play.

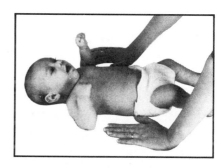

Exercise: Place your baby on her back or tummy on a foam rubber pad, bed, your lap, or any soft, bouncy surface. Slowly and gently press the bouncy area around the baby (or bounce baby on your lap) so the baby rocks up and down. Use a gentle, rhythmic up-and-down motion, and she will relax. You may also try patting your baby rhythmically on her chest, back, arms, and legs.

Baby Massage   Massage is the language of touch. With a massage, you can calm and soothe your baby and communicate your love and care. During massage, keep these points in mind: A nice way to start is with a bath. Then, after making sure the room is warm, remove the towel or receiving blanket, and put your baby on the floor. (You can also sit with the baby on your lap or kneel in front of her.) Baby lotion and baby oil soak into the skin too fast, so use vegetable oil or cornstarch. Put the oil or powder on your hands first, then rub your hands together to warm them. Tell your baby what you are doing or sing a song. Be gentle during the first month; as the baby gets older, you can exert more pressure. Once you have touched the baby, keep at least one hand in contact with her until the massage is over. Do not massage your baby's trunk if her stomach is full. Be sensitive and responsive to her reactions; stop if she is not enjoying herself.

If she is enjoying herself, and she probably will, here are some motions you can try:*

- Stroking with your open palms
- Stroking with the thumbs or fingers
- "Raking" with the tips of the fingers
- Tapping lightly with the tips of the fingers
- Massaging arms or legs with a wringing motion

Do whatever feels good to you and makes the baby happy. For further instruction in massage, see Recommended Reading, pages 273 to 275.

Babysitters

Childrearing is physically and emotionally demanding. You may need some time to maintain your sense of self and your relationship as a couple. When you go out, you need someone to babysit—a grandparent, friend, relative, member of a babysitting cooperative, or hired babysitter. Unless you have confidence in the sitter, however, you probably will not enjoy your time away from your baby.

What are the characteristics of a good sitter? If he or she is an older person, make sure the sitter's strength, hearing, and alertness are adequate to handle an emergency. If the sitter is a teenager, consider his or her past experience, age, rapport and confidence with babies, and familiarity with emergency measures. For more information about babysitters, see Recommended Reading, pages 273 to 275.

Car Safety

Be sure that your baby is restrained in a dynamically tested car seat whenever riding in a car. Your baby is safest when his car seat is attached to the center of the rear seat. A child accustomed to a safety device from an early age gets used to it and only occasionally protests. Never leave your baby alone in a car. Remember that everyone in the car should "buckle up," since other passengers are endangered if even one person is not restrained.

Medical Care

Immunizations

Immunizations protect your child from certain potentially serious diseases. Since many of these illnesses occur in the first years, it is important to immunize your child early and keep to a regular schedule. Immunizations are given at your doctor's office or, for a minimal fee, at public health clinics.

The first vaccination, an injection called DPT, combines immunization against diphtheria, whooping cough (pertussis), and tetanus. A polio vaccine is also given at this time. Later, measles, mumps, and rubella vaccines may be given, either alone or in combination.

IMMUNIZATION SCHEDULE	
Birth-2 months	DPT and Polio
3-4 months	DPT (Polio optional)
4-6 months	DPT and Polio
15 months	Measles, Mumps, and Rubella
16-24 months	DPT and Polio
4-6 years	DPT and Polio
12-16 years	TD (Tetanus-Diphtheria)
Every 10 years thereafter	TD

Keep a record of your child's immunizations. These records will be required by schools and camps throughout her life. If the immunization schedule is interrupted, resume it where you left off in the series, rather than beginning again.

Possible Reactions

Your baby may have one or more reactions to these vaccines. Common reactions include local pain and tenderness at the injection site, fever, irritability, and loss of energy and appetite. A rash may occur six to twelve days after the measles immunization. Your doctor will recommend treatment if it is required. *Note:* If your child has a severe reaction, such as inconsolable crying or high fever, be sure to notify your doctor immediately.

When to Call the Doctor

If you are worried about your baby's health and cannot rest until the question is settled, then call your doctor. Before you call, however, give careful thought to, and then note on paper, all the symptoms that worry you. Here are some things your doctor may wish to know:

Physical symptoms. Abnormal temperature, breathing difficulties, coughing, vomiting, diarrhea, constipation, fewer wet diapers, rash.

Behavioral symptoms. Loss of appetite, listlessness, unusual fussiness or irritability, change in typical behavior and activity level.

Home treatment. What have you done and how has your child responded? Have you given your child any medications? What and when?

General considerations. Has there been recent exposure to illness? Is anyone at home or day care sick?

Have a paper and pencil handy to write down your doctor's suggestions. Also, know your pharmacist's phone number, as the doctor may want to call in a prescription.

Colds

It is normal for babies to have a slight, stuffy, rattly noise in their noses. Your infant probably has a cold, however, if she has a very runny nose, is fussier than usual, has trouble eating and sleeping, and has a slight fever.

To lessen the chance of a cold, minimize the number of visitors (adults and children) when the baby is very young. People with colds should stay away. You will probably want to consult your physician for your baby's first cold. He or she may suggest a cool-mist vaporizer, sleeping in a semireclined position (place a folded blanket or pillow under the head end of the mattress), clearing the nostrils gently with a bulb syringe, using nose drops, or giving medication.

Medications

How to Give Medications or Vitamins

• Put medicine between the baby's cheek and gum—let infant suck medication.

• Insert a dropper of medicine next to a pacifier on which your baby is sucking.

• Pour medication into an empty bottle nipple; flush emptied nipple with water to ensure that the baby has received a full dose.

Note: Do not put medication in formula, juice, or water. You will be unsure how much your baby has received if she refuses to finish it.

Chapter Twelve Feeding Your Baby

W|hile she is inside her mother, a baby grows rapidly from a small cell to a mature baby weighing around seven pounds. All her nutritional needs are met by her mother's body. For the newborn, growth also continues at a rather rapid rate, but now she is dependent on milk and other foods to supply the nutrients necessary for the extraordinary growth occurring in her first year. Amazingly, the full-term infant will generally double her birth weight by five months and triple it by one year, and she will grow ten to twelve inches longer than she was at birth!

Two important organ systems not fully developed at birth are the skeletal system and the central nervous system, which includes the brain. Because the most rapid growth of the skeleton occurs in fetal life and during the first year of life, malnutrition at these times can cause a delay in its growth and maturation. There are two rapid periods of brain growth—between fifteen and twenty weeks of fetal life and from thirty weeks of fetal life until one year of age. In fact, by one year, the brain has grown to 82 percent of its adult size. It is not surprising, then, that malnutrition, especially before six months of age, can permanently impair brain development and function.*

Parents have the very important responsibilities of providing their baby with foods to promote her healthy growth, and of feeding their baby in a caring and loving way to foster the development of a sense of trust. "No other aspect of the infant's life can exert greater influence on the infant's physical health and emotional well-being than the way her parents meet her nutritional needs."*

Feeding Guidelines

Knowing how infants were fed in the past will help you better understand infant nutrition today. With this perspective, you will know why you were fed cereal so soon in your babyhood and why your baby's doctor now encourages you to delay solid foods for your baby for several months.

In the early 1900s, most babies were breastfed or fed modified cow's milk for the first year of life. Solid foods were seldom offered, except cod liver oil to prevent rickets and orange juice to prevent scurvy. From about 1920 through the next half-century, solid foods were offered earlier and earlier (even in the first week of life) to supply the baby with iron, vitamins, and a more varied diet. Parents of this era believed that introducing solid foods early would help their baby sleep through the night sooner (a myth). And they hoped that their baby would grow chubby and round. Also at this time, the practice of breastfeeding declined because it was thought to be old-fashioned, and bottlefeeding, seemingly more scientific, became highly popular. By 1940, fewer than half of all babies in the United States were breastfed; and by the late 1960s, fewer than a quarter of all babies in the United States were breastfed.

By 1975 a change had taken place. Breastfeeding was becoming increasingly more popular because it was now considered to be more natural and was recognized to have distinct emotional and health benefits to baby and mother that had not previously been known. The trend toward breastfeeding was led by La Leche League International. By 1979, over 50 percent of American mothers were choosing to breastfeed their babies.

Today, over 60 percent of mothers breastfeed. In addition, nutritionists had begun to advise mothers to delay introducing solid foods until their infant was at least four to six months old. They recognized that infants are not developmentally or socially ready to handle solids before this age; introducing solids early may contribute to allergic reactions and may also interfere with a child's developing good eating habits; and, finally, offering a child solid foods too early may contribute to overfeeding.*

In 1980, the American Academy of Pediatrics Committee on Nutrition published its guidelines for infant feeding for the first year of life.* Three overlapping feeding periods were defined: the nursing period, during which breast milk or an acceptable formula is the only food in the infant's diet; the transitional period, during which solid foods are offered in addition to breastmilk or formula; and the modified adult period, during which most of the infant's food comes from the family table. This chapter will focus on the first feeding period—the nursing period—and will discuss the parents' and infant's role in feeding when milk is the only food in the baby's diet.

Breast or Bottle?

The decision whether to breastfeed or bottlefeed is a personal one that should not be made lightly. Before making up your mind, try to become informed about each method of feeding. What are the advantages and disadvantages? Under what circumstances is breastfeeding superior to bottlefeeding and vice versa? Do you have support and commitment from loved ones, friends, and your baby's doctor for your decision? After gathering the facts, it might be helpful for both you and your partner to list all the reasons for, and drawbacks to, each feeding method.

Why Breast Milk Is Recommended

Breastfeeding is recommended for many reasons:

- Breast milk is the ideal food for human babies.
- Breast milk is easily digested.
- Breast milk contains antibodies that protect the baby from many infections.
- Breastfeeding reduces the possibility of allergic reactions.
- Breastfeeding aids involution (the return of the uterus to its normal size).
- Breastfeeding allows the mother and baby to have a special, intimate relationship for feeding.
- Breastfeeding is convenient and economical.

To be successful, though, breastfeeding must appeal to you and your partner. You will need the support of those close to you and of the medical professionals overseeing your baby's care. Also, you will need to be committed to the value of breastfeeding to persist in spite of common problems such as sore nipples, fatigue, or returning to work.

When Breast Milk Is Not Recommended

There are certain rare instances, however, when breastfeeding may not be recommended or possible:

- If the mother has had extensive breast-reduction surgery.
- If the mother has hepatitis.
- If the mother's breasts are infected with beta streptococcus or active herpes.
- If the mother receives significant amounts of certain drugs (such as chemotherapeutic drugs for cancer), certain seizure-preventing drugs (such as dilantin), and radioactive materials for certain diagnostic tests.
- If you would be uncomfortable, resentful, or unhappy breastfeeding.
- If circumstances cause you to be separated from your baby for days or weeks at a time.

Prenatal Preparation for Feeding

Before your baby is born, you have time to prepare your nipples for breastfeeding or to explore the variety of equipment available for bottlefeeding. If you choose to bottlefeed, learn about the bottles and nipples you will use. Purchase the equipment before the baby arrives and practice using it so that you become familiar and comfortable with it. Your baby's doctor will suggest a formula and tell you how to prepare it and how much to feed your baby. Check with stores and pharmacies to find the best prices.

If you have chosen to breastfeed, you do not need as much equipment as the bottlefeeding mother, but you still need to prepare. Prenatal preparation is important and helpful in readying you physically and emotionally for breastfeeding.

1. The first step is to become familiar with your breasts. Look at yourself in the mirror, keeping in mind that while size and shape of breasts and nipples vary from woman to woman, this has virtually no effect on your ability to produce enough milk for your baby. You may notice that your breasts are larger now and possibly more tender than they were before you became pregnant. The veins are more visible. The Montgomery glands (the small bumps on the areolae) are also larger. In addition, you may have noticed that colostrum (a yellowish fluid) leaks from the nipples from time to time.

Normal protracted   Inverted

2. Next, check that your nipples are suitable for feeding. Gently press the areola just behind the nipple between your forefinger and thumb. This simulates the compression of your baby's mouth on your nipple during feeding. The nipple should protrude or stick out. If it adheres to the underlying tissue, it cannot protrude into the baby's mouth, but stays flat or inverts (dips inward), making feeding difficult or impossible. This condition of flat or inverted nipples can be successfully treated and corrected prenatally. Use the following equipment or techniques:

Breast cups and shields. These plastic dome-shape cups are placed over the areola and help draw out the nipple. These cups are sold under such names as Woolwich, Swedish Milk Cup, Eschman, Netsy, and Hobbit. They work by exerting a continuous, gentle pressure over the areola, causing the nipple to be pushed through the opening in the inner plastic ring. Wear these cups in the last two trimesters of your pregnancy, starting with an hour each day and gradually working up to several hours. Because the skin may become moist under the plastic, be sure to dry your nipples each time after you wear the shields.

Nipple stretching. Stretching the nipple tissue several times a day during the last six weeks of pregnancy can correct flat or inverted nipples. Try the following stretching exercises:

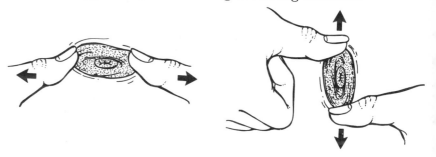

• *Place your thumbs at three and nine o'clock positions at the base of your nipples. Gradually stretch the nipple tissue by pressing and moving your thumbs away from each other. Repeat at twelve and six o'clock positions.*

• *Support your breasts with your fingers and grasp the areola just behind the nipple with your thumb and forefinger. Draw the nipple out to the point of discomfort, hold several seconds, and release. You may also pull the nipple out in this same manner, rolling the nipple between your thumb and forefinger while the tissue is stretched.*

• *Oral suction on the nipples during lovemaking stretches the nipples and can be helpful, too. However, if you are at risk for preterm labor, avoid this technique.*

3. The next step in preparing for breastfeeding is to condition your nipples. Try nipple rolling for several minutes each day, rubbing your nipples with a terry towel, and then airing them for two hours by removing your bra and letting your outer clothes rub against your nipples. Avoid using soap, tincture of benzoin, or alcohol on your areolae and nipples. These products dry the skin. Just these few measures have been proven to significantly reduce total nipple pain in the first few days of breastfeeding.* You might also try exposing your nipples to sunshine or sunlamp at a safe distance for several minutes daily. In regions of the world where women's breasts are always exposed, problems with sore nipples are rare.*

Women are sometimes advised to express colostrum from their breasts as another way to prepare for breastfeeding. The benefits of this practice probably do not outweigh the possible risk of causing preterm labor by stimulating the breasts. Use other methods instead.

Besides the benefits of correcting flat or inverted nipples and preventing or reducing some later nipple soreness, prenatal nipple preparation provides an important emotional benefit. Until pregnancy, the breasts are perceived by most people primarily as sexual objects, and a change in attitude toward them is helpful for successful breastfeeding. Handling the breasts, as with breast preparation, helps you and your partner make this important transition to thinking of the breasts in terms of their function—nourishing a baby.

Breastfeeding

Anatomy of the Breast

The breasts are well designed to make milk. The internal structures change gradually during pregnancy, enabling your breasts to make milk by the time the baby is born. Once you are pregnant, the duct system inside your breasts develops and enlarges in response to estrogen, and the lobes, lobules, and alveoli increase in size in response to progesterone.

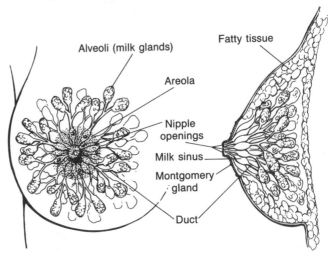

The illustration on the right shows a cross section of the breast. It is divided into fifteen to twenty lobes (milk-producing units), with alveoli in each lobe containing milk-producing cells that release milk into the ductule. Each ductule then leads to a larger duct, which empties into a milk sinus, located behind the areola. As the infant compresses the sinus with his lips, gums, and tongue, he massages milk out of the nipple. The Montgomery glands, the small sebaceous glands on the areola, secrete a lubricating substance that keeps the nipple supple and also helps prevent infection.

Milk Production

Two hormones, prolactin and oxytocin, play a significant role in milk production and milk ejection (flow). The infant suckling at your breast stimulates the anterior pituitary gland (in your brain) to release prolactin. The prolactin in your bloodstream in turn causes the cells in the alveoli to combine water and nutrients from your blood to make milk. In like manner, oxytocin is released into your bloodstream by the posterior pituitary gland in response to the infant's suckling (or sometimes just by thinking about the baby or hearing a cry). Oxytocin causes the small muscles around the milk-producing cells to contract and release milk. This process is called the *let-down reflex*. You may feel the let-down as a tingling, itching, or burning sensation in your breasts.

The amount of milk you produce is controlled by a mechanism called the "supply and demand response." The more your baby suckles at your breast, the more milk you produce. Delaying feedings by using a pacifier, offering supplements of water or milk, or attempting to place your baby on a three- to four-hour feeding schedule will decrease your milk production. Feeding frequently, on demand, and for at least ten minutes at each breast will increase your milk production.

Composition of Breast Milk

The first milk produced by the breasts, colostrum, is a yellowish fluid that is higher in protein and lower in fat than mature milk. It is ideally suited to the newborn's needs: it provides a laxative effect that helps the newborn to expel meconium; it helps establish the proper balance of bacteria in the infant's digestive tract; and, rich in antibodies, it protects the infant from infection. Transitional milk is produced next. It is higher in fat and calories and lower in protein and antibodies than colostrum. Finally, the mature milk comes in, containing more calories than both the transition milk and colostrum. However, water is still the largest constituent of mature milk. Its other components include the following:

Fats. Fats present in human milk account for most of the calories. Cholesterol, a fat in human milk, is thought to be necessary to trigger the enzyme systems which later help the adult to safely utilize cholesterol. Other fats in human milk aid digestion by helping to form a soft curd in the infant's stomach.

Carbohydrates. Lactose (milk sugar), the primary form of carbohydrate in human milk, is present in human milk in greater

241

quantities than in cow's milk. It helps the infant absorb calcium and is easily metabolized into two simple sugars that are necessary for the rapid brain growth occurring in infancy.

Proteins. Whey and casein constitute the proteins in milk. Whey is the primary protein in human milk. It is easily digested and becomes a soft curd from which nutrients are easily absorbed. By contrast, casein is the primary protein in cow's milk. When fed to a human baby, it forms a rubbery curd, which is less easily digested. Other components of the milk proteins have an important role in protecting the infant from disease and infection. This helps to explain why breastfed infants have a significantly lower incidence of respiratory infections and diarrhea than formula-fed infants.*

Vitamins and minerals. Some of the vitamins and minerals present in breast milk deserve special attention. Iron is present in human milk in small quantities. However, it is in a highly absorbable form. A full-term, healthy, breastfed baby rarely needs iron supplementation before six months of age.*

Though rare, rickets has been seen in breastfed infants. As a result, the American Academy of Pediatrics recommends that when breastfed babies and their mothers have little exposure to sunlight due to climate or clothing, the baby should be supplemented with vitamin D.*

Fluoride in the drinking water has a minimal effect on the fluoride levels in breast milk. Some experts believe that breastfed infants should be supplemented with fluoride. Others question the necessity of supplementing, while still others feel it may be unnecessary, citing the better dental health record and fewer cavities of breastfed babies when compared to bottlefed babies.* Discuss fluoride supplementation with your baby's doctor or your dentist.

Changing Composition of Breast Milk

Milk varies in composition during a single feeding. The first milk early in the feeding, called the *foremilk*, is continuously secreted into the lactiferous ducts between nursings. It represents a third of the milk volume in each feeding. The *hindmilk* constitutes the remaining two-thirds of the feeding. It is released with the let-down reflex, contains more fat and protein than foremilk, and provides the calories infants need to thrive. As your infant grows, his requirements for nutrients change and your breast milk responds to his changing needs.

Diet for Breastfeeding

By the time your baby is one month old, you will be producing about twenty ounces of milk each day. By three months, you will produce about twenty-three to twenty-five ounces a day, and by six months, you will produce about twenty-five to twenty-

Foods to Avoid

The best policy on avoiding foods is to observe your baby. If you notice that certain foods cause an apparent digestive upset or an allergic reaction (rash, stuffy nose, diarrhea), eliminate those foods from your diet. The most common offending foods are cow's milk and milk products. Be sure to check with your doctor or midwife about your calcium intake if you eliminate dairy products from your diet while nursing. Other common offending foods include food dyes and additives, certain spices, eggs, chocolate, cola, corn, citrus fruits, peas, broccoli, cabbage, beans, wheat, nuts, tomatoes, shellfish, certain meats, onions, garlic, and any foods to which you are allergic.

Drug Use

The alcohol content in breast milk is approximately equal to the concentration in your blood. Therefore, the effects on the baby correspond to the amount you have consumed. Too much alcohol can inhibit the let-down reflex, reducing the amount of hindmilk available to the baby. Though an occasional drink has not been proven harmful, it is probably wise to limit or eliminate alcohol consumption during lactation. The recent findings on alcohol raise questions about the advice given in some older books on breastfeeding that recommended alcohol to stimulate the let-down reflex. They did not take into account potential effects on the baby and the inhibiting effects of excessive alcohol on milk production.

Heavy smoking has been shown to reduce milk production,* reduce the vitamin C content of milk, and increase the incidence of nausea, colic, and diarrhea in infants.* Smoking near the baby increases the incidence of pneumonia and bronchitis in the baby.* As in pregnancy, it is wise to abstain from smoking or to limit smoking during lactation and to avoid smoking in the presence of the baby.

Maternal consumption of large quantities of caffeine, found in beverages such as coffee and cola, has been related to hyperactivity, fussiness, and colic in infants. If you suspect your baby's fussiness is aggravated by your caffeine intake, try reducing or eliminating caffeine from your diet.

Another substance, vitamin B_6, has received some attention for its relationship to lowered milk production. When taken in large doses (more than the amount in a prenatal vitamin), it may inhibit lactation.*

With a few exceptions, any medication you take will be present to some degree in your breast milk. Some medications do not present a problem for your baby, while others do. Check with your doctor, midwife, baby's doctor, or pharmacist before taking any drug, prescribed or over-the-counter, while you are breastfeeding. If you need medication, remind your doctor you are breastfeeding so he or she will choose the medication that is best suited for you and your baby.

seven ounces a day. When you introduc
of milk you produce may decline.

How will you manage to produce so mu
an important part. A good prenatal
addition to plenty of liquids, adequate 1
lation of your breasts by your baby's s
duce all the milk your baby needs. In
prevents your body from being deplet
need to feel well and remain healthy.

During pregnancy, your body prepare
storing five to seven pounds of extra we
extra calories necessary for milk produc
For the first months of breastfeeding,
pregnant stores and will need about 5C
more than when pregnant) a day. Once
above your normal weight (allowing ab
for the weight of your lactating breast
you in deciding if you need more (or fe
a day to maintain your weight. Some w
have a large baby, or are nursing more tl
need to consume a thousand or more
to maintain their weight.

Foods to Eat

Your diet while nursing should incluc
calcium-containing foods, more vitamins
your normal diet. (See chapter 4 for la
But you can easily get the foods you nee
diet similar to your pregnancy diet. In adc
more milk, continue to take your prena
special attention to your fluid intake. T
fluids a day are helpful for milk producti
this much liquid, try drinking an eight
milk, or water each time you nurse your

Fatigue resulting from lack of sleep anc
whelming responsibility of caring for a n
to feel too tired to eat or drink. Loss of a
are your body's ways of telling you that you
on rest and on caring for yourself. Re
adequate intake of fluids and calories, i
can decrease your milk supply.

To replenish a declining milk supply, try
baby for a whole day. Pick a day when you
household chores, telephone calls, and o
the day nursing your baby as often as possi
sleeping, and nurturing yourself. In addit
milk supply and catching up on needed res
way to learn more about your baby.

Breastfeeding Basics

First Feeding You can help ensure your success in establishing your milk supply and avoid some early breastfeeding problems by nursing your baby as soon after birth as possible and by allowing your baby to suckle frequently. When mothers breastfeed within an hour after birth and feed their babies frequently on demand, their milk comes in sooner (within twenty-four to forty-eight hours after birth) and engorgement is less of a problem than when they wait to begin breastfeeding.*

The first feeding is special. You and your baby get to know each other better and begin the beautiful, synchronous interaction that characterizes breastfeeding. If you have never breastfed before, the technique of feeding may seem awkward and cumbersome at first. But be reassured that breastfeeding is a skill that improves with experience. Here are some suggestions:

• Breastfeed your baby as soon as possible after birth. Babies are often more alert and interested in feeding in the first hour following birth than later that day.

• Use the help of experienced staff or request privacy if you feel confident about initiating feeding without help.

Sitting

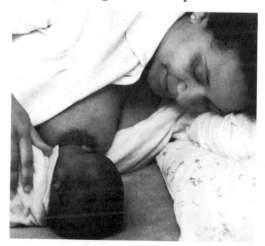

Lying on your side

• Get into a comfortable position. If you nurse right after delivery, sit comfortably supported or lie on your side. If your perineum is sore, ask for an ice bag to ease the pain and help you relax. If you have just had a cesarean, sitting in bed with the baby across your lap on a pillow or positioned beside you in a "football hold" may be most comfortable. (See page 249.)

• Nurse your newborn in an atmosphere of calm and tranquility, if possible; this will help you relax and allow you and your baby to concentrate on feeding.

What to Do

1. Make yourself comfortable with your baby's body tipped toward you.

2. Grasp your breast with your free hand behind the areola and compress the nipple with your thumb and forefinger, aligning your nipple with the baby's mouth.

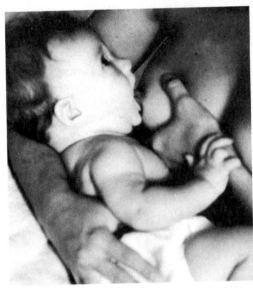

Tickling her lips   Correct nipple grasp

3. Stroke your baby's cheek and tickle her lips with your nipple to stimulate her rooting reflex. Bring your baby to your breast rather than bringing your breast to your baby.

4. Make sure as much of the areola as possible is in the baby's mouth to ensure a good latch.

5. Let your baby suckle at each breast for at least ten minutes. This advice is contrary to the common instructions to limit feedings to five minutes or fewer in the hopes of preventing sore nipples. Five minutes is hardly time to get started. "In early feedings after birth, the let-down reflex may not occur for as long as three or more minutes after feeding begins; following the 'learning' period, the let-down usually begins within the first thirty seconds after the baby is put to the breast or sometimes even sooner."* Further research has shown that limiting the amount of time your infant spends at the breast merely delays rather than prevents the onset of sore nipples.

6. After nursing at one breast, release the baby's suction by placing a finger in the corner of her mouth.

7. Allow your baby to nurse from the other breast.

Some babies seem to know how to feed right from the beginning, while others seem uninterested, sleepy, or have difficulty latching on to the nipple. If you have a tough time getting started, the following suggestions may help.

• Arouse your baby's sense of taste and smell by expressing a few drops of colostrum and rubbing the nipple on her lips.

• Hold your baby close enough to you that she can get the whole areola in her mouth, and compress the milk sinuses with her lips, gums, and tongue.

• Tilt her head slightly backward and guide your nipple toward the roof of her mouth, making sure your nipple is above rather than under her tongue. You might need to depress her tongue with one finger and stroke the roof of her mouth with the soft side of another finger before placing your nipple in her mouth. For this you might need the help of a supportive partner or nurse.

• If your baby is sleepy, make sure she is not swaddled too snugly. Talk to her, stroke her arms and legs, and wiggle her toes. Make her a little uncomfortable.

• Make use of the help from breastfeeding counselors, experienced nurses, your doctor, or your midwife.

• Do not despair if your baby does not nurse on the first try. Whether she suckles or not, the stimulation of her nuzzling, licking, and being close to your body encourage milk production. Sometimes babies are too tired from being born or too drowsy from the effects of some medications to nurse. Perhaps you also are too tired following a long, difficult labor to try nursing. Rest and nourishment may relieve your fatigue, just as rest and time will help your baby. Later, with your patience and perseverence, she will undoubtedly learn to nurse quite efficiently.

The initial nursing may seem different than you expected. Your baby may be tentative, licking, and mouthing your breast; she may struggle to get your whole nipple in her mouth. Or she might seem experienced, immediately latching on to your nipple, tugging, and sucking vigorously. Those energetic nursers sometimes grasp and pull on the nipple so firmly that they cause pain. You may experience afterpains with the let-down reflex, especially if this is not your first baby. Relaxation and slow breathing may help in either case.

Frequency of Feeding

Breastfeeding on demand (every one to three hours or eight to eighteen times a day) during the day is the best way to establish an adequate milk supply. Begin each successive feeding with the breast your baby last nursed from, since babies usually nurse most vigorously at the first breast, and this will make sure that both breasts get an equal amount of stimulation. You might use a safety pin in your bra strap to remind you which side to begin with. Feed ten minutes from the first breast and for as long as the baby is interested from the second.

If your baby is rooming-in with you, you will know when she needs to be fed. But if she spends some or all of her time in the nursery, you will want to ask the nursing staff to bring your baby to you when she is hungry, day or night. Also keep in mind that full-term, healthy babies do not need supplementary bottles of milk, sugar water, or water if they are breastfed frequently on demand from both breasts. Only when breastfeeding is limited in frequency or duration (or both) are the baby's requirements for nourishment and fluids not met. Policies restricting feeding time are often based on requirements for formula-fed babies and cannot be applied to breastfed babies. In addition, supplementary bottles of milk and water have several disadvantages. Milk and sugar water contain calories that diminish your baby's hunger and interfere with her desire to nurse. Furthermore, sucking on a bottle nipple is entirely different from sucking on your breast, and it often results in "nipple confusion" and the development of faulty sucking patterns. If this occurs, it can be corrected by persistently depressing your baby's tongue with your finger before your nipple is placed in her mouth and also by avoiding the use of bottle nipples until nursing is well established. If for some reason your baby must receive supplements of water and milk in the first several weeks, offer them by a medicine dropper to avoid nipple confusion.

Your Milk Comes In

You will know your milk has come in when your baby begins to gulp and swallow rapidly while nursing. You may see some milk in the corners of her mouth; your breasts may be heavy, hard, and tender, and you may feel the tingling sensation of your milk letting down.

First Weeks

In the early weeks following birth, your baby will nurse every one to three hours. If your baby sleeps five to six hours at a stretch at night, be sure to feed her frequently during the day so she will get all the nourishment she needs. Babies who sleep a great deal during the day and awaken frequently at night to feed may need to be awakened every two to four hours during the day to be fed to change the night-feeding pattern. Avoid pacifiers in the early weeks. Besides causing nipple confusion, they may satisfy your baby's sucking needs and interfere with nursing and adequate nutrition. Over time, your baby will consume more at each feeding, reducing the total number of feedings each day.

Growth Spurts

At about three weeks and six weeks, three months and six months, your baby may return to more frequent nursing. She may be fretful, irritable, more sensitive to stimuli during this time, and seem to need to nurse constantly. She is experiencing a growth and developmental spurt, and nursing frequently is her way of stimulating you to make more milk to meet her needs. If you are troubled by the increased demands, do not worry. Within about a week, your baby's needs will level off once again.

Involving the Family

Although you produce milk and feed your baby, your husband's and family's support and encouragement are absolutely necessary for successful breastfeeding and are often the key factors in keeping you going in the face of difficulty. Your family can help you eat and drink well, and allow you to rest by caring for the baby and by shielding you from unnecessary stress. If they can relieve you of some or all of your day-to-day chores, you will be free to devote yourself to caring for yourself and establishing breastfeeding.

"Football hold"

Some Early Breastfeeding Problems

Certain predictable and normal problems with breastfeeding occur for most women in the first weeks after birth. These include the following:

Is the Baby Getting Enough Milk?

A number of signs can tell you if your baby is getting enough milk. A baby who feeds adequately every two or so hours with occasional shorter or longer periods between feedings will have six to eight wet diapers each day. After passing his meconium stool, a breastfed baby may have a loose stool with each feeding. Later, as he matures, he may have a bowel movement every other day or even once a week. Your baby's elimination patterns along with his contentment after being fed are good indications that he has received enough milk. Your baby's doctor will watch your baby's weight gain and growth as a way to determine if he is getting enough milk. If his weight gain seems to be slow, it could be the result of several factors:

Limited sucking time. The let-down may not occur with limited sucking. The baby does not get the hindmilk and as a result does not gain as expected. Your baby may need more time at the breast—at least ten minutes at each breast.

Gas bubbles. Swallowed air can make the baby feel full. Be sure to burp your baby between breasts or during the feeding.

Scheduled feedings. A breastfed baby needs to be fed more frequently than every three or four hours. Allowing your infant to nurse on demand (ranging from eight to eighteen times a day) will correct this. Wake a sleepy baby during the daytime to feed him, especially if he sleeps for long stretches at night.

Limiting feedings to one breast. Feeding from one breast at each feeding may result in inadequate milk production.

Nonnutritive sucking. Some infants satisfy their sucking needs by sucking on their own fists, tongues, lips, or pacifiers or by chewing and sucking on the tips of their mother's nipples. Once their sucking needs are satisfied, they may not indicate a need for milk.

Difficulty with the let-down reflex. Anxiety, fatigue, inadequate nipple stimulation, excessive amounts of alcohol, caffeine, and smoking—especially during the hour before feeding—all may inhibit the let-down reflex.

Fatigue, insufficient intake of fluids and calories, or poor diet. These may reduce your milk supply. Spend a day in bed with the baby as described previously. Then over the long term, pay attention to the amount of fluids and calories you consume and the quality of your diet.

Poor latch. If the baby has not positioned his mouth properly on the nipple, he will not be able to compress the areola well, and will not stimulate a let-down reflex. The baby's mouth making a "clicking" sound during sucking indicates that the suction is breaking with each sucking effort.

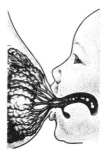 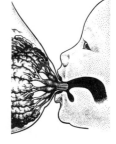

Correct latch   Incorrect latch

Treatment

If your nursing patterns show any of the above problems, make the necessary changes. Feed longer, more often, and from both breasts. Throw out the pacifiers, at least for a while. Do not try to postpone feedings. Help the baby get a good grasp with his mouth on your areola. Get more rest and adequate fluids. Eat well. Get help from a knowledgeable person—a La Leche League leader (they are listed in the phone book), your childbirth educator, your doctor, an experienced breastfeeding mother. A poor newborn weight gain is usually possible to improve if you can figure out the problem.

Engorgement

Engorgement results from two causes: increased blood supply and the accumulation of milk in the breasts. It occurs when the milk comes in, usually the second or third postpartum day, and its severity is often greater in first-time mothers. The breasts swell, become hard to the touch, and painful. Keep in mind that engorgement is less pronounced when the baby has been encouraged to nurse frequently for an adequate time and with proper latch.

Treatment

• Wear a well-fitting bra day and night for support. Check to make sure no areas are compressed.

• Apply cold packs at first to reduce blood flow to breasts and to provide comfort.

• Use warmth later to help the milk flow.

• Express milk while standing in a warm shower; cover your breasts with warm, moist towels; or immerse your breasts while in the bathtub.

• Express milk right before a feeding to soften a hard, swollen areola that could make it difficult for the baby to grasp the nipple. Breast massage stimulates the milk flow. (Expression of milk is described on pages 255 to 256.)

• Nurse frequently and for sufficient periods to allow the milk to flow and your breasts to empty.

• Use an electric or mechanical breast pump to relieve the fullness in your breasts.

Sore Nipples

This temporary condition occurs most commonly in the first weeks of nursing. Sore nipples are usually due to improper positioning of the baby's mouth on the areola (or poor latch). Soreness may range from pain only when the baby first grasps the nipple to continual soreness. The nipples may even crack and bleed. Limiting the frequency and duration of feedings does not cure the problem. It only delays the onset of sore nipples, allows the breasts to become engorged, and impairs milk production.

Treatment

• Make sure the baby's mouth is correctly positioned on your nipple.

• Feed your baby frequently, and begin by nursing on the less-sore side.

• Vary the feeding position. Try sitting, lying, or using a football hold. As a result, the pressure from your baby's sucking will not be in the same place all the time.

• Dry the nipples well after feeding. Let them air dry with your bra flaps down or use a hair dryer set at medium heat.

• Express a small amount of breast milk and rub it over the sore area. Breast milk has healing properties that can help remedy sore nipples.

• Breast creams and ointments are often recommended but may cause problems such as irritation of the breasts, clogging of pores, and inhibiting healing.

• Apply a warm, moist tea bag to the sore area. Leave it on for five to ten minutes. Dry your breasts well after removing the bag. Tea contains tannic acid, a soothing toughening agent.

• Expose your breasts to sunshine or a sunlamp (at a distance of four feet for one-half to one minute). But take care not to sunburn the skin.

• Use breast cups or shields to keep the nipples dry. A paper breast pad with a hole in the center for your nipple will help absorb perspiration.

• Apply an ice pack to the sore area before feeding at that breast.

Breast Pain on Letdown

Some women experience a sharp, deep pain behind the areola at the beginning of each feeding. The pain, which subsides when the milk is flowing, does not indicate a problem and will subside in time without treatment.

Newborn Jaundice (Physiologic Jaundice)

Physiologic jaundice, beginning usually on the second or third day after birth, should not be a deterrent to breastfeeding, nor an indication for water and formula supplements. Frequent nursing on demand is recommended to establish milk flow, provide calories, encourage elimination of the bilirubin-laden meconium stool, and prevent dehydration. There is no scientific evidence that water supplements have any effect on the bilirubin levels;* in fact, insufficient calories due to scheduled restricted feedings or too much water can cause jaundice in the newborn.*

Treatment

• Breastfeed frequently, at least every two to three hours for ten or more minutes on each breast.

• Request that your baby not be given water supplements.

• Once at home, expose your baby to sunlight to help bring down bilirubin levels.

• Medical treatment sometimes is begun if bilirubin reaches high levels.

Breast Milk Jaundice

Breast milk jaundice, a rare condition, does not occur until five to seven days after birth and is caused by a substance sometimes found in breast milk that interferes with the normal metabolism of bilirubin. The bilirubin accumulates, causing the jaundice. To slow the rise in bilirubin or reverse a high bilirubin level, the mother may be asked to stop breastfeeding for one or two days. This is usually enough to lower bilirubin levels. If there is another rise, interrupting feedings once again is suggested. Repeating this pattern until the bilirubin levels fall or stay down is usually all that is necessary to treat this problem. The mother will want to pump her breasts during the periods she is not nursing her baby to maintain her milk supply and her comfort.*

Interrupting breastfeeding in this way is very stressful for the parents, especially the mother, who is trying to establish her milk supply. She should be reassured that her milk is not defective and the baby is unlikely to be hurt by this bilirubin. Sometimes babies with jaundice determined to be caused by breast milk are also treated with phototherapy.

Treatment

• Continue nursing your baby unless your baby's doctor indicates the bilirubin levels are dangerously high.

• If you are asked to interrupt breastfeeding, pump your breasts to maintain your milk supply.

Leaking

Milk often leaks from the breasts early in nursing. It subsides as the breasts become more finely tuned and they "learn" how much milk to make and when to let it down. Leaking often occurs when your breasts are very full, when you are feeding from the other breast, when you hear a baby cry, or in response to orgasm with sexual arousal.

Treatment

• Press your hands or forearms firmly against your nipples to slow the flow of milk.

• Compress your nipple between your thumb and forefinger to stop the flow of milk.

• Wear cotton or disposable breast pads, and then discard them when they become damp. Avoid breast pads with plastic liners.

• Wear plastic breast cups, such as the Nesty cup, for short periods of time when you want to keep your clothing dry. Because these cups actually stimulate milk production, avoid using them for long periods. Discard any milk collecting in the cups and allow the nipples to dry well between wearings.

Clogged Ducts and Mastitis

Redness, pain, or swelling can mean either a clogged duct or mastitis (an infection). If these symptoms occur in an area in one breast, but you do not have other flulike symptoms, you may have a caked, clogged, or plugged duct. If untreated, this could lead to mastitis, but it should not have to because the condition can be easily treated.

Treatment of Clogged Ducts

• Apply a warm, moist pack to the area.

• Massage the area toward the nipple.

• Perform wide arm circle exercise, page 209.

• Express milk.

• Nurse frequently, emptying the breasts.

Mastitis is an infection of the breast that occurs most often in the first five postpartum weeks, but can occur at any time while you are nursing. Symptoms include a tender, reddened, hot breast, nausea, fatigue, and perhaps a fever. If you suspect mastitis, call your caregiver.

Treatment of Mastitis

• Continue to nurse from both breasts. The milk is unaffected. Make sure the mastitic breast is as empty as possible after feeding.

• Take antibiotics if prescribed.

• Apply a warm, wet towel over the painful area.

• Drink lots of water, juice, and other fluids.

• Perform wide arm circles (see page 209) to help increase the circulation to the breast, aiding healing.

• Rest and stay in bed as much as possible.

If both breasts are mastitic, it could indicate a B-streptococcal infection which means you may have to interrupt breastfeeding.* Your doctor or midwife can help you decide if you should stop breastfeeding until this type of mastitis is resolved.

Expressing and Storing Breast Milk

Expressing your breast milk and storing it safely allows you to leave your baby for a while without altering her usual diet. Collect the milk in plastic rather than glass containers since some of the immunological (disease-preventing) components of breast milk cling to the walls of glass containers, and also because plastic containers seem to better maintain the stability of all the constituents of human milk.*

Any method of expressing or pumping milk from your breasts requires clean hands, clean equipment, plastic storage containers, and practice. Pumping and expressing milk is most effective following a let-down reflex. To stimulate your let-down reflex, try the following:

• Nurse your baby and take advantage of the let-down reflex that comes during a regular feeding time. As your baby suckles, collect any milk that drips from the other breast, or pump that breast. It may take another person or a specialized one-hand breast pump (the Ora' Lac pump and Evenflo with a bottle are such pumps) to pump during a feeding.

• Massage your breasts with your fingertips. Imagine the round shape as the face of a clock—massaging at twelve o'clock, one o'clock, and so on. Start way back under your arms and at the outer boundaries of your breasts, and massage toward your nipples.

• Apply warm, wet towels to your breast.

• Relax and imagine your baby nursing.

• Some mothers use a prescribed nasal pitocin spray. If the other methods do not work, you might discuss this option with your doctor.

Expressing Breast Milk

There are many ways to express or pump milk.

1. *Expressing by hand is effective for many, and also inexpensive and convenient. Once milk is flowing, grasp your breast at the back of the areola and press toward your chest as you compress the areola. Your milk may drip or spurt into a collect-*

ing bottle. At first you may obtain only several drops or a half-ounce. With practice, you will be able to collect more.

2. You can also buy or rent effective equipment designed for pumping your breasts. Your childbirth educator, La Leche League leader, breastfeeding counselor, midwife, or physician may suggest a method. Several especially efficient pumps include the Lloyd B pump, Egnell Cannister, Ora' Lac, Marshall Expressing Unit (Kaneson, Comfort Plus, and Happy Family Breast Milking-Feeding Unit), and electric pumps (Egnel and Medela).

Using Expressed Breast Milk

Fresh: use within thirty minutes or refrigerate.

Refrigerated: use within twenty-four hours if kept at 40 degrees F.

Frozen: use within one to two weeks if kept in freezer compartments within a refrigerator or for one or two months if kept at 0 degrees F. in a freezer compartment separate from the refrigerator. Keep in mind that freezing destroys some of the immune properties.

To thaw frozen breast milk, hold it under cold water first, then under warm water until it is liquified; or let it thaw slowly, six to eight hours, in the refrigerator. Shake the milk once thawed. Do not heat the milk since this destroys more of the immune properties. There is no data on the effects on milk defrosted by microwave.*

Special Situations

Under certain special circumstances, breastfeeding mothers and their babies need more support and persistence than usual to establish lactation.

Premature Infants

Mothers who give birth to premature infants produce a milk different from the milk produced by the mother of a full-term infant. It is especially well suited to the unique nutritional needs of the premature baby—it is higher in protein, nitrogen, sodium, calcium, fat, and calories. In 1980, the American Academy of Pediatrics Committee on Nutrition issued the following statement: "At this time the Committee considers it optimal for mothers of low birth weight newborn infants to collect milk for feeding their own infants fresh milk."*

It is possible and highly desirable to breastfeed when your baby is born early. If you choose to breastfeed and your baby is unable to suckle well, express your colostrum for your baby by using hand expression or a pump. This expressed colostrum and milk can be fed to your baby until he is able to suckle at your breast. Contact your hospital's nursing staff, a Parents of Prematures support group, or La Leche League for help in establishing lactation and in overcoming some of the obstacles you may encounter in the process.

Working Outside the Home

It is possible to breastfeed exclusively and work outside the home, if you wish, by expressing and storing milk to be fed to your baby while you are away. The more flexibility your job has, the easier it will be for you to combine breastfeeding and work. You might consider finding part-time work, establishing a work schedule of longer days with a feeding break midday, or choosing a day-care setting near your work so you can nurse your infant during your breaks and at lunch time. But if feeding your baby during the work day is not an option, make arrangements for time and privacy to hand express or pump milk at work. The milk then needs to be stored in a refrigerator or an ice chest and fed to the baby the next day unless it is frozen.

The age of your baby is a factor. If you are able to delay returning to work until your baby feeds less frequently and is on a more predictable schedule, breastfeeding will be easier.

Some working mothers decide to breastfeed while at home and supplement with formula while they are away. The breasts are amazingly cooperative in producing adequate milk as long as you nurse on a regular schedule for an adequate period of time. If your supply seems to dwindle, nurse frequently during the evening and on days off to stimulate your milk production.

Relactation

It is possible to reestablish or initiate lactation after you have stopped nursing or after you have been separated from your baby. However, it does require persistence and a commitment to succeed on your part, as well as an interested baby. Frequent, round-the-clock nipple stimulation by massaging and suckling have been most effective. You may use a Lact-Aid Nursing Trainer during your early nursing efforts. This device encourages the baby to suckle at an empty or near-empty breast while receiving supplemental milk through a plastic tube that you place by your nipple. It is helpful in causing you to produce milk in response to the baby's sucking and in providing enough milk for a feeding. La Leche League and others knowledgeable about relactation would be especially helpful in supporting and counseling you if you decide to reestablish breastfeeding.

Breastfeeding and Fertility

Breastfeeding usually suppresses or delays ovulation and menstruation, especially if breast milk is the only food your baby receives and you nurse frequently around the clock. There is, however, wide variation among nursing women. Some ovulate as early as several months post partum, while others do not ovulate until twelve to eighteen months. Because you can ovulate before menstruating, you should not assume that breastfeeding is a failproof method of contraception.

Your midwife or physician can counsel you about the most appropriate methods of contraception while you are lactating. Oral contraceptives, estrogen-progestin, or progestin only are not recommended for nursing mothers. The use of oral contraceptives has been associated with reduced milk production and potential long-term, harmful effects for the infant exposed to the steroidal hormones present in the breast milk.*

Bottlefeeding

If you have chosen to bottlefeed from birth or to discontinue breastfeeding before your baby is one year old, a commercially prepared formula is the milk of choice; evaporated milk formulas are not well suited to your baby's nutritional needs and two percent, skim, whole, and goat's milk are not appropriate choices in the first year. Your baby's doctor can recommend a formula for your baby and tell you how much to feed your baby each day. Because these commercial formulas are fortified with vitamins and minerals, your baby will not require a vitamin supplement. So if you change from breastfeeding to bottlefeeding, discontinue giving your baby any vitamins he received while nursing. The only exception might be a fluoride supplement if your water supply does not contain fluoride.

Infant Formulas

Infant formulas are available in ready-to-feed preparations, canned liquid concentrates, and powdered form. The powdered formula is the least expensive; ready-to-feed is the most expensive, but it might be especially useful for trips where the water supply is questionable.

When reconstituting formula, carefully follow the directions on the can or package. An overconcentrated mixture can cause diarrhea, dehydration, and other problems for your baby. Over-diluting the formula is particularly hazardous since your baby will not receive the calories and nutrients he needs to thrive.

Equipment

While your baby's doctor or your friends might offer suggestions about purchasing bottles and nipples, many recommend using an orthodontic nipple (Nuk) to promote good mouth and facial development. Your baby's doctor can advise you about whether to sterilize or simply to wash your baby's bottles and nipples with the family dishes. Thorough hand-washing before handling the equipment is advisable with either method.

Check the equipment before feeding your baby. It is working correctly if drops of milk drip out in quick succession when you hold the bottle upside-down. If milk comes out in a stream, the nipple hole is too big—your baby will feed too fast and his sucking needs will not be satisfied. If the milk drips too slowly or not at all, your baby will swallow too much air, tire, and perhaps not get enough during a feeding. If the nipple hole is too large, discard the nipple. If it is too small, pierce the hole with a hot, clean needle and check it again.

Tips for Bottlefeeding

You can make your baby's feedings consistently successful and happy by remembering to do a few simple things:

• Hold him with his head higher than his body during feedings so that the milk will go down his throat, not pool around his eustachian tubes (which go from the back of the throat to the ears). This has been associated with middle-ear infections.

• Hold the baby sometimes in your right arm, sometimes in your left arm for feeding to promote normal eye muscle development.

• Burp your baby every one to two ounces when he is little, and about halfway through a feeding as he matures.

• Make feeding your baby a special time. Be sure to cuddle him. Never prop his bottle and leave him alone for feedings. Do not cut off the tip of the nipple so he feeds more rapidly. Do not add solid foods to his milk. Interacting with a loving person during feedings helps him thrive emotionally and develop trust in you and those who care for him.

Cautions

Feeding water to your baby may be helpful during hot weather or if he seems constipated. But do not mix honey in the water; feeding honey (cooked or uncooked) to a baby under one year of age has been associated with infant botulism.

Though it may seem tempting to coat the nipple with sugar or juice to entice your baby to feed, most babies refuse the bottle simply because they are not hungry. Adding additional sugar to formula is not recommended either because it provides your baby with fattening, empty calories, and it may cause diarrhea.

Conclusion

In summary, feeding your baby has far greater significance than simply providing nutrients and calories for physical growth. A baby whose cries are consistently answered develops a sense of trust, security, and well-being. A baby who is smiled at, talked to, and cuddled develops a sense of emotional security. And holding your baby close stimulates the senses of touch, smell, and taste. The continuing requirements of feeding afford many opportunities for your baby to express affection and appreciation by cooing, grinning, patting, and other endearing behaviors. Feeding time becomes an important catalyst for the emotional development of the infant and the strengthening of family ties.

Chapter Thirteen Preparing a Child for Birth and a New Baby

I f you already have a child and are expecting another, you will want to prepare your older child for the birth of a sibling—a baby brother or sister. Sibling preparation includes providing your child with information about pregnancy, birth, and life with a newborn that is realistic and appropriate to her age. This chapter offers a variety of ways to prepare your child. Some suggestions will be more appropriate than others, depending on the age and maturity of your child and your plans and desires. Several books listed in the Recommended Reading section can also help prepare you and your child for another baby. One exceptionally well-written book is *Your Second Child* by Joan Weiss.

Preparations before the Birth

You can begin preparing your older child for the upcoming birth at any time during the pregnancy. You might announce the pregnancy early to explain why you are especially tired or vomiting each morning. The news of a baby's anticipated arrival may be a welcome relief to the child who has been fearful that you are ill. If your child is very young and unable to understand waiting, you may want to put off announcing the pregnancy until later, when your pregnancy becomes obvious and you begin to look "fat." A special calendar is helpful for the child who repeatedly asks when the baby will come.

You may be reluctant to tell your child about the baby because of your own feelings of guilt or worry about displacing her.

Under these circumstances, the longer you wait, the more likely it is that your child will feel displaced. You can ease your child's adjustments if you include her in the preparations and provide time and an opportunity for building positive but realistic feelings and expectations about the new baby.

Suggestions The following suggestions will help involve and prepare your child before the birth:

• Talk to your child about the pregnancy and birth. Find out what your child already knows, correct misconceptions, fill in the gaps, and answer questions. Use appropriate terms or examples: the baby is in the "uterus," not the "stomach." However, you will want to avoid overwhelming a small child with too much information.

• Read books to your child about pregnancy, birth, new babies, and feelings about being a big brother or sister. See Recommended Reading for suggestions.

• Arrange to bring your child to one or more prenatal visits to meet your doctor or midwife.

• Let your child hear the baby's heart beat and feel the baby move. Talk about fetal development with your child. Tell her what abilities the fetus has.

• Attend a sibling preparation class if one is available in your area. Let your child see films, slides, or pictures of birth and the newborn; a demonstration of a birth with a doll can also be helpful.

• Practice prenatal exercises with your child. Explain that these exercises help you feel better during pregnancy and afterwards.

• Take your child on a hospital tour if possible.

• Help your child make a picture book about pregnancy, birth, babies, big brothers, sisters, and families.

• Show your child photographs of herself as a baby—especially ones showing you caring for her as a newborn.

• Have your child see and interact with a friend's baby. Let her see how small and sometimes unplayful a baby is.

• Have your child help you pack your suitcase or the baby's bag for the hospital. If she will be staying with someone while you are in the hospital, have her pack her bag, including special gifts for those who will care for her.

• Make changes in room or sleeping arrangements several months before the birth to prevent your child from suddenly feeling displaced. Set up the new baby's sleeping area to give your child time to become accustomed to where the new baby will be.

- Safety-proof your home if it is not already done, since accidents can happen when you are busy with the new baby.

- Be sensitive to the possibility of overloading your child with talk of a new baby.

Preparing to Attend a Birth

You may want to consider having your child present at the birth. Although it is not a widespread practice, many family-centered hospitals, birth centers, and homebirths make this option available. Because there is little research on the subject and it is almost an unprecedented practice in most cultures, the issue of children attending birth is as much of an unknown as the issue of fathers attending birth was in the 1960s and earlier. Experience with the large-scale participation by fathers at birth has shown that they are helpful and supportive partners. Today most medical staff see the father as an important contributor to the mother's well-being.

But what about children attending birth? What about the impact on a child's feelings toward his mother, and toward birth? Will a child be disruptive to the parents or caregivers? What about infection? Can children be a positive addition to the birth experience? Can they help? Can their presence at the birth bring them closer to their parents and to the new baby? Why do parents want their children at the birth?

Some parents wish to minimize or avoid separation from the older child and so they choose to give birth where sibling involvement is possible and the child can remain with them throughout the labor and birth—at home, in a birth center, or in a family-centered hospital. These parents feel that if there is no separation, the child will not develop separation anxiety and will not see the new baby as the one who took the mother away. This can enhance bonding between the older child and the new baby—another reason for choosing to have a child attend the birth.

An older child may associate warm and positive feelings with the baby if he is present as an important and welcome participant, if he gets to hold the baby, and if his parents cuddle him together with the baby afterwards. In addition, many parents believe that the sensitive period following birth, when parents form loving and binding attachments with their newborns, can exist for children as well. They believe that the presence of their children, performing various helpful tasks (photographing, playing records, bringing hot cloths, backrubs) and sharing the intensity and excitement of the birth, will enhance bonding with the new baby.

In our culture, fear and anxiety dominate our attitudes toward childbirth. Childbirth preparation classes spend much time and effort dealing with such worries, trying to undo a lifetime's attitudes in a few weeks. But many parents believe that being part of a normal and happy birth experience will positively influence a child's attitudes toward birth. Though it is unproven, it may be that those who have participated in normal birth as children will be freed from such anxieties. One father said, "To hear Julie (age six) describing what was happening during labor made me certain we had made the right decision in having her there. She said, 'Your uterus is hard as a rock, Mommy. That's good.' Later, 'Is your tummy hurting you now? You need to breathe and rub your tummy.' And during birth, 'Oh Mommy! There's the head, I think. Yes, it's the head! Oh, Mommy, can you see? It's our baby!' Julie picked out the baby's clothes and dressed him. She was proud as a peacock." Afterwards, Julie's mother said Julie's reactions and interpretations of her contractions meant a lot to her. "Julie had been prepared through classes, reading, and our discussions, and applied what she learned very well. I'm so glad she was with us."

Guidelines

Because birth is a major life event involving many potentially frightening features, certain requirements need to be met to make it a positive experience for your child. Education for everyone involved is essential in providing understanding, accurate interpretation, and constructive responses. The following are essential for a positive birth experience for your child.

• As parents, you must be prepared. You need to feel comfortable about birth and know how to relax and respond appropriately to contractions.

• You and your child (if he is old enough to make such a decision) must want him to be present.

• You will need to assess your child's physical health and emotional readiness. If your child is ill and feels badly, he may not tolerate the birth experience well. If your child has had a recent painful, traumatic, or frightening experience, involving his own body, doctors, or hospitals, he may not be ready to attend a birth. For example, one couple wanted to have their three-year-old daughter present at the birth of their second child. In the latter part of the pregnancy, however, she developed a urinary tract infection and underwent several painful cystoscopy examinations. She told her parents that she did not want to see any blood or "anyone hurting." Her parents decided that these painful experiences were too fresh in her mind for her to be able to take on a different perspective toward the birth. Now, several months later, she is asking her parents to have a boy and to let her be there.

• You will want to arrange for a support person for your child—someone different from the mother's support person. A relative, a close friend, or sometimes the child's father can be there to look after the child's needs and help interpret and explain what is going on.

• You will want to prepare your child. In some areas, classes are available for children. Many books, films, and teaching aids are available, and family discussions are essential. Familiarize your child with the following:

1. *The birth setting, equipment, and caregivers.*

2. *The sights and sounds of labor and birth: his mother unclothed; her face red with effort; the presence of blood; the baby's initial wetness and dusky color; moaning, grunting, or straining by his mother; the baby's crying; the cutting of the cord; and so on.*

3. *The appearance of a newborn, placenta, and umbilical cord.*

4. *The duties of the mother, father, your child's support person, and your birth attendants.*

5. *The tasks your child can perform: bringing a cool cloth for mother, giving backrubs, walking with mom, bringing fluids, taking pictures, playing music, being quiet when mom asks, and so on.*

6. *What labor and birth is like—long, boring, exciting at times.*

7. *The possible interactions between the older child and the newborn—touching, holding.*

• You will want to provide an environment for the birth that makes your child's participation feasible (room for your child, flexibility to come and go, clear guidelines).

• You will want a supportive labor and delivery staff (nurses, midwives, doctors) who will not be upset at having a child present.

• You will want an alternative plan to use if your child is sick, asleep (and does not want to wake up), bored, or changes his mind, or if labor complications develop requiring transfer from the alternative setting to a standard labor ward or delivery room. Before your labor, explain these possibilities to your child, and prepare a plan for his care under such circumstances.

• Have realistic expectations of your child. One does not expect a two- or four-year-old to be transformed during labor. He will not suddenly become more calm, ask fewer questions, or begin to perceive birth as a transcendental experience. Children still fuss, need to go to the bathroom, say "no," argue, need cuddling, want to know where their Tinkertoys are, and so on. One mother of three boys decided to have the two older children present for the birth of their fourth child (also a boy). The third child was still very dependent on his mother and very physically active. His parents are low-key, patient people, and usually find his behavior easy to tolerate; but they felt it would be a strain on them both during labor. They were realistic in understanding that they would not be able to meet his needs and their own, so he was not present for the birth. They took an early discharge from the hospital, feeling they had found the best way to handle their particular situation. The older boys (ages six and nine) found it exciting to be awakened in the middle of a winter night and go to the hospital, where they helped their parents take photographs, brought fruit juice to their mother, rubbed her back, and cranked up the bed. When the baby was born, the oldest said, "Oh darn, mom; it's another boy." The second said, "That's good. I didn't want any old girl anyway."

The point of all this is that children are children, and will not suddenly step out of character for a labor or birth. An eighteen-month or two-year-old may be preoccupied with a toy at the time of birth, and when her support person says, "Look, Annie. The baby's coming!" she may or may not glance up. She may simply say, "No," and continue with her play. For a child of that age, the principal benefit of being present for the birth may be simply not being separated from her mother and father.

Children take birth in stride, responding as they would to any long-awaited, exciting event. With preparation and good support at the time, the birth of a new sibling can be a positive experience for your child. And with it exists the potential for developing long-term healthy attitudes about birth.

Preparing for Separation from the Mother

If you are planning a hospital birth with a typical three-day stay, you will need to consider the possibility of separation anxiety, which results from a child being separated from one or both parents, in any situation. When you leave to have your baby, your child's ability to tolerate the "separation" will vary, depending on your child's age, how long the separation lasts, how comfortable she is with her caregiver and setting, how well she understands what is happening, and how much contact she has with you during the period of separation. Most children experience some degree of separation anxiety, including such reactions as fretting or crying for mother, sadness, clinging, irritability, sleeping difficulties, and tantrums. When they are reunited with their mothers, some children react in a positive way, others continue to react negatively and may even ignore their mothers. These reactions are the child's way of expressing her dismay at being left.

Suggestions   You can do several things to ease this anxiety:

• At some point during the last weeks of your pregnancy, let your child know you will be leaving to go to the hospital for the birth. Tour the hospital with your child if possible. When labor begins, tell your child when you are leaving and where you are going. Your child will also be less anxious if she is familiar with the person who will care for her during your absence. A close friend, relative, or a favorite babysitter can make the separation less traumatic. Be sure your child knows your plans for her care during your absence.

• Before the birth, increase the father's role as caregiver if he is not already responsible for much of your child's daily care, such as giving baths and putting the child to bed. Try to establish a routine that is not greatly disrupted by your hospitalization or the arrival of the new baby.

• Find out what regulations there are at your hospital or birth setting, and if possible have your child visit you there. May you see your older child in your room, the hallway, or a visitor's lounge? As sibling visitation has become recognized as being valuable to the emotional well-being of the family, more hospitals are allowing children to visit their mothers after the birth of a baby. Some hospitals even allow siblings in the recovery room to see both mother and newborn.

What can you realistically expect when your child visits you in the hospital? She will probably be reassured by seeing you and the baby, responding in a positive way to the opportunity to visit. It is possible, however, that she may ignore you and the baby, and cling excessively or cry uncontrollably when it is time to leave. You may feel that it would have been easier on both of you to avoid the visit entirely. However, as difficult as it is for your child to see you for short periods and not be able to stay with you, it is healthier for a child to see you, even if only briefly, than to be separated for a longer period. The negative reaction shows that the child is under stress; the visit provides her with an opportunity to express her anger or frustration.

What if your child cannot visit you? You might try some of the following options for "long-distance visiting" with your child: talking on the phone, waving to your child outside; or sending polaroid pictures, notes, and gifts home. You might also consider an early discharge from the hospital to minimize the time away from your family.

Adjusting to the New Baby

In addition to the separation from his mother, becoming a sibling involves another traumatic aspect for the older child: the constant presence of a helpless, crying newborn who requires almost continuous care. Life is never the same for the older child after the arrival of a baby. Parents who once provided total attention and care for the older child are suddenly less available—all because of the new baby!

Your child may express his feelings in a variety of ways: temper tantrums, return to outgrown behavior such as thumb-sucking, wanting a pacifier, feeding from bottle or breast, or wetting his pants; excessive preoccupation with the baby; aggression toward parents or baby (hitting, biting, throwing things); and changes in eating and sleeping patterns. Some parents have never seen such behavior in their child before and are caught by surprise.

Suggestions Perhaps the most important way you can help your older child adjust to the newborn is to accept whatever reaction he displays. Try not to be disappointed in him. Accept the behavior as a normal reaction and work from there. The following suggestions may also help ease your child's adjustment to a new baby in the family:

• Before and after the birth, read books to your child about living with a new baby.

• Give your child a doll so he has a "baby" to care for.

• Plan for time alone with your older child to do what he wants to do.

• Use the time when the baby is asleep and you are rested to give special attention to your older child.

• Have a birthday party after the birth with cake for all.

- Give a gift to your older child in the hospital or at home.

- When visitors bring presents for the baby, your older child may feel left out. It may help to have him open them, to have special treats or gifts ready for him, or to delay opening them until he is not around.

- Include your child in baby-care activities that he wants to help with and that are appropriate to his age: holding the baby, helping with diapering, dressing or bathing the baby, helping feed and burp the baby, and entertaining the baby with smiles or talk.

- Allow your child to have nothing to do with the baby if that is what he wants.

- Read or talk to, plan an activity with, or provide a snack for your older child while feeding the baby.

- Avoid statements like "You now have a new playmate" or "You're going to love the baby" when these are not very likely to occur.

- "Tell" the baby about her special older brother while he is with you and listening.

- Take care of yourself. Try to rest when possible. This may not decrease your child's resentment or jealousy, but you will be able to cope better.

The age of the child has much to do with how and when he will react to the baby. Some children, particularly those three or four years old and older, recognize immediately the impact the new baby has on their own relationship with their parents. Younger children tend not to recognize the threat for several months, until the baby begins crawling, interfering in play, and getting into things. Even children eight to ten years old may feel resentment toward the baby, although it is usually accompanied by guilt and may be successfully hidden from the parents.

Remember that although adjusting to a new baby may be difficult, even traumatic, for a child, it is one of life's normal growth experiences. Your goal should not be that your child feel no displacement but that he adjust in a healthy and positive way. With time and your help, your child will find ways to adjust to the baby. A lasting bond between the siblings eventually will develop.

References

The references below refer to the asterisks you will find in the book. Note that some pages will contain more than one reference.

Chapter 1
Page 11 * A. B. Bennetts and R. W. Lubic, "The Free-Standing Birth Centre," *Lancet* 8268 (13 February 1982): 378; C. Reinke,"Outcome of the First 527 Births at the Birthplace in Seattle," *Birth: Issues in Perinatal Care and Education* 9 (Winter 1978): 241; J. L. Epstein,"A Home Birth Service That Works," *Birth and Family Journal* 4 (Summer 1977): 71; and L. E. Mehl,"Complications of Home Birth," *Birth and Family Journal* 2 (Winter 1975): 123.

Page 12 * W.M.O. Moore, "Antenatal Care and the Choice of Place of Birth," in *Place of Birth*, eds. S. Kitzinger and J. A. Davis (New York: Oxford University Press, 1978), 1.

Chapter 2
Page 32 * R. L. Naeye, "Coitus and Associated Amniotic-fluid Infections," *New England Journal of Medicine* 301 (29 November 1979): 1198.

Chapter 3
Page 48 * J. F. Pearson and J. B. Weaver, "Fetal Activity and Fetal Well-Being, an Evaluation," *British Medical Journal* 1 (1976): 1305-07.

Chapter 4
Page 55 * J. Vermeersch, "Physiological Basis of Nutritional Needs," in *Nutrition in Pregnancy and Lactation*, eds. B. Worthington-Roberts, J. Vermeersch, and S.R. Williams (St. Louis: C. V. Mosby Co., 1981), 55.

* H.F. Weeks, "Iron Supplements," *Maternal Child Nursing* 5 (September 1980): 354.

Page 56 * Vermeersch, 53.

Page 59 * Vermeersch, 60.

Page 61 * S. R. Williams, "Nutritional Therapy in Special Conditions of Pregnancy," in *Nutrition in Pregnancy and Lactation*, eds. B. Worthington-Roberts, J. Vermeersch, and S. R. Williams (St. Louis: C. V. Mosby Co., 1981), 114-115.

* Williams, 115.

Page 63 * J. A. Pritchard and P. C. MacDonald, "Prenatal Care," in *Williams Obstetrics*, 16th ed. (New York: Appleton-Century-Crofts, 1980) 309.

* Pritchard and MacDonald, 323.

Page 64 * R. K. Grad, et al., "Bendectin Withdrawn from Market," *APRS Federal Monitor* 6 (30 July 1983): 1.

Page 66 * R. M. Hill, "Drugs Ingested by Pregnant Women," *Clinical Pharmacology and Therapeutics* 14 (1973): 654; A. Oakley, *Becoming a Mother* (New York: Schocken Books, 1979): 46.

Page 68 * M. B. Meyer and J. A. Tunascia, "Maternal Smoking, Pregnancy Complications, and Perinatal Mortality," *American Journal of Obstetrics and Gynecology* 128 (1 July 1977): 494.

Page 69 * American Lung Association, "How Not to Love Your Kids" (nd.)

* N. R. Butler, et al., "Smoking in Pregnancy and Subsequent Child Development," *British Medical Journal* 4 (8 December 1973): 573-75.

* C. Lecos, "Caution Light on Caffeine," *FDA Consumer,* October 1980: 6-9.

* P. S. Weathersbee, et al., "Caffeine and Pregnancy—A Retrospective Study," *Postgraduate Medicine* 62 (1977): 64.

* S. Linn, et al., "No Association Between Coffee Consumption and Adverse Outcomes of Pregnancy," *New England Journal of Medicine* 306 (21 January 1982): 141-45.

* W. Herbert, "Coffee-Linked Birth Problems Premature," *Science News,* 30 (January 1982): 121.

Page 70 * M. B. Morris, et al., "Caffeine and the Fetus: Is Trouble Brewing?", *American Journal of Obstetrics and Gynecology* 140 (15 July 1981): 607-10.

* J. W. Scanlon, "A Cup of Coffee and a Cigarette: Prolonged Caffeine Blood Levels in Healthy Babies," *Perinatal Press* 5 (July-August 1981): 87.

* R. K. Siegel, "Herbal Intoxication," *Journal of the American Medical Association* 236 (2 August 1976): 473-76.

Page 71 * R. L. Berkowitz, et al., *Handbook for Prescribing Medications during Pregnancy* (Boston: Little Brown and Co., 1981), 198-200.

* Berkowitz, 198-200.

* Berkowitz, 198-200.

Page 73 * M. A. S. Harvey, et al., "Suggested Limits to the Use of the Hot Tub and Sauna by Pregnant Women," *Canadian Medical Association Journal* 125 (1 July 1981): 50-53.

* D. W. Smith, *Mothering Your Unborn Baby* (Philadelphia: W. B. Saunders Co., 1978), 65-66.

Page 74 * H. J. Evans, et al., "Sperm Abnormalities and Cigarette Smoking," *Lancet* 8221 (21 March 1981): 627-29.
* J. M. Friedman, "Genetic Disease in the Offspring of Older Fathers," *Obstetrics and Gynecology* 57 (June 1981): 745-49.

* C. D. B. Bryan, "The Veteran's Ordeal," *The New Republic* 188 (27 June 1983): 26.

Chapter 5
Page 83 * L. Sibley, et al., "Swimming and Physical Fitness during Pregnancy," *Journal of Nurse-Midwifery* 26 (November-December 1981): 3; C. A. Collins, et al., "Maternal and Fetal Responses to a Maternal Aerobic Exercise

Program," *American Journal of Obstetrics and Gynecology* 145 (15 March 1983): 702.

Chapter 6

Page 92 * Grantly Dick-Read, *Birth of a Child* (New York: Vanguard Press, 1958), 12.

Page 93 * Sheila Kitzinger, *Complete Book of Pregnancy and Childbirth* (New York: Alfred A. Knopf, 1980), 164.

Page 94 * R. P. Lederman, et al., "The Relationship of Maternal Anxiety, Plasma Catecholamines, and Plasma Cortisol to Progress in Labor," *American Journal of Obstetrics Gynecology* 132 (1 November 1979): 495.

Page 102 * Relaxation countdown adapted from the relaxation ripple in B. Dale and J. Roeber, *Exercises for Childbirth* (London: Century Publishing Co., 1982), 76.

Page 105 * Kathryn Schrag, "Maintenance of Pelvic Floor Integrity during Childbirth," *Journal of Nurse-Midwifery* 24 (March-April 1979): 26.

Chapter 7

Page 123 *A.R. Fuchs, et al., "Oxytocin Receptors and Human Parturition: A Dual Role for Oxytocin in the Initiation of Labor," *Science* 215 (12 March 1982): 1396; D. M. Strickland, et al., "Stimulation of Prostaglandin Biosynthesis by Urine of the Human Fetus May Serve as a Trigger for Parturition," *Science* 220 (29 April 1983): 521.

Page 124 * J. Roberts, "Alternative Positions for Childbirth—Part II: Second Stage of Labor," *Journal of Nurse-Midwifery* 25 (September-October 1980):13; Pritchard and MacDonald, 279-280.

Page 136 * P. Dunn, "Obstetric Delivery Today: For Better or for Worse?" *Lancet* (10 April 1976): 790; A. M. Flynn, et al., "Ambulation in Labor," *British Medical Journal* 6173 (26 August 1978): 591; R. Caldeyro-Barcia, "Physiological and Psychological Bases for the Modern and Humanized Management of Normal Labor," in *Recent Progress in Perinatal Medicine and Prevention of Congenital Anomaly* (Tokyo: Medical Information Services, 1980), 77-96; J. Roberts, et al., "Maternal Positions in Labor: Analysis in Relation to Comfort and Efficiency," in *Perinatal Parental Behavior*, ed. B. S. Roff (White Plains, N. Y.: March of Dimes Birth Defects Foundation, 1981): 97-128.

Page 141 * C. Beynon, "The Normal Second Stage of Labour: A Plea for Reform in its Conduct," *Journal of Obstetrics and Gynecology of the British Commonwealth* 64 (June 1957): 815.

* R. Caldeyro-Barcia, "The Influence of Maternal Bearing-Down Efforts during Second Stage on Fetal Well-Being," in *Kaleidoscope of Childbearing: Preparation, Birth, and Nurturing*, eds. P. Simkin and C. Reinke (Seattle: Pennypress, 1978), 38-42.

Page 144 * P. Simkin, "The Physiologic Second Stage: Preparation, Management, and Support," lecture presented at a conference on "Childbirth Education: Avocation or Vocation," sponsored by the Bay Area branch of the American Society of Psychoprophylaxis in Obstetrics, San Francisco, 19 March 1983.

Chapter 8

Page 158 * J. P. Elliott, et al., "The Use of Breast Stimulation to Ripen the Cervix in Term Pregnancies," *American Journal of Obstetrics and Gynecology* 145 (1 March 1983): 553.

* A. Jhirad, et al., "Induction of Labor by Breast Stimulation," *Obstetrics and Gynecology* 41 (March 1973): 347.

* J. A. Read, et al., "Randomized Trial of Ambulation Versus Oxytocin for Labor Enhancement: A Preliminary Report," *American Journal of Obstetrics and Gynecology* 139 (15 March 1981): 669.

Page 159 * E. Davis, *A Guide to Midwifery: Hearts and Hands* (Santa Fe: John Muir Publications, 1981), 76.

Page 166 * J. G. B. Russell, "The Rationale of Primitive Delivery Positions," *British Journal of Obstetrics and Gynecology* 89 (September 1982): 712.

Page 168 * O. Fall, et al., "External Cephalic Version in Breech Presentation under Tocolysis," *Obstetrics and Gynecology* 53 (June 1979): 713; S. Fianu, et al., "External Cephalic Version in the Management of Breech Presentation with Special Reference to Placental Location," *Acta Obstetrica Gynecologica Scandinavica* 58 (1979): 209.

Page 177 * H. Oxorn, *Human Labor and Birth*, 4th edition (New York: Appleton-Century-Crofts, 1980), 665; American College of Obstetricians and Gynecologists Committee on Obstetrics: Maternal and Fetal Medicine, "Guidelines for Vaginal Delivery after a Cesarean Childbirth," (7 January 1982); D. Young, *Unnecessary Cesareans: Ways to Avoid Them* (Minneapolis: International Childbirth Association, 1980), 15.

Page 178 * K. Keolker, *Vaginal Birth after Cesarean* (Seattle: Pennypress, 1981), 1.

Page 179 * Pritchard and MacDonald, 877.

Chapter 9

Page 188 * Oxorn, 397.

* Lederman et al., 495.

Page 190 * Oxorn, 397.

* American Academy of Pediatrics Committee on Drugs, *Pediatrics* 51 (1973): 297-99.

Page 195 * J. J. Bonica, *Obstetric Analgesia and Anesthesia* (World Federation Societies of Anaesthesiologists, 1980), 94-95.

Chapter 10

Page 212 * Reva Rubin, "Maternity Nursing Stops Too Soon," *American Journal of Nursing* 75 (October 1975): 1684.

Chapter 11

Page 217 * A. Henningsson et al., "Bathing

or Washing Babies After Birth?" *Lancet* 1 (19-26 December 1981): 1401.

Page 225 * Kathryn Barnard et al., "Early Parent-Infant Relationships," from *First Six Hours of Life*, no. 1, mod. 3 (White Plains, N. Y.: National Foundation/March of Dimes, 1978), 21; and adapted from T. Berry Brazelton, *Neonatal Behavior Assessment Scale* (Philadelphia: J.B. Lippincott, Spastics International Medical Publications, 1973).

Page 232 * Gloria Myre, *Massage for Parents and Infants* (Seattle: Central Community College, Health and Human Service Division, 1979), 1.

Chapter 12
Page 235 * D. Smith and R. Marshall, *Introduction to Clinical Pediatrics* (Philadelphia: W.B. Sauders Co., 1972), 52.

* Smith and Marshall, 34.

Page 236 * S. Fomon, et al., "Recommendations for Feeding Normal Infants," *Pediatrics* 63 (June 1979): 52-59.

* American Academy of Pediatrics Committee on Nutrition, "On the Feeding of Supplemental Foods to Infants," *Pediatrics* 65 (June 1980): 1178-79.

Page 239 * L. D. Atkinson, "Prenatal Nipple Conditioning for Breastfeeding," *Nursing Research* 28 (September-October 1979): 267.

Page 240 * J. Riordan and B. A. Countryman, "Basics of Breastfeeding," *Journal of Obstetrics, Gynecologic, and Neonatal Nursing* 9 (September-October 1980): 279.

Page 242 * A. S. Cunningham, "Morbidity in Breastfed and Artificially Fed Infants," *Journal of Pediatrics* 95 (1979): 685-89.

* J. Riordan, *Practical Guide to Breastfeeding* (St. Louis: C. V. Mosby Co., 1983), 31.

* AAP, "On the Feeding of Supplemental Foods to Infants," 1179.

* R. A. Lawrence, *Breastfeeding: A Guide for the Medical Profession* (St. Louis: C. V. Mosby Co., 1983), 66.

Page 244 * A. Hervada, et al., "Drugs in Breastmilk," *Perinatal Care* 2 (1978): 19.

* H. Vorherr, "Drug Excretion in Breastmilk," *Post Graduate Medicine* 56 (1974): 97.

* J. R. Colley, et al., "Influence of Passive Smoking and Perinatal Phlegm on Pneumonia and Bronchitis in Early Childhood," *Lancet* 2 (1974): 1031.

* W.A. Bowes, "Effect of Medications on the Lactating Woman and Her Infant," *Clinical Obstetrics and Gynecology* 23 (1980): 1073.

Page 245 * E. M. Salariya, et al., "Duration of Breastfeeding after Early Initiation and Frequent Feeding," *Lancet* 2 (25 November 1978): 1141-43.

Page 246 * Riordan, *Practical Guide*, 46.

Page 253 * Riordan, *Practical Guide*, 208.

* Ross Roundtable on Critical Approaches to Common Pediatric Problems, *Counseling the Mother on Breastfeeding* (Columbus, Ohio: Ross Laboratories, 1980), 44.

* Riordan, *Practical Guide*, 207.

Page 255 * Lawrence, 107.

* Lawrence, 283.

Page 256 * Riordan, *Practical Guide*, 250; S. C. Shepard and R. E. Yarrow, "Breastfeeding and the Working Mother," *Journal of Nurse-Midwifery* 27 (November-December 1982): 20.

* American Academy of Pediatrics Committee on Nutrition, "Human Milk Banking," *Pediatrics* 65 (1980): 854.

Page 258 * Riordan, *Practical Guide*, 135.

Recommended Reading

Following is a list of books that can provide additional background on many of the subjects covered in this book. Most of these books are available by mail order from the Birth & Life Bookstore, P.O. Box 70625, Seattle, WA, 98107, and the ICEA Bookcenter, P.O. Box 20048, Minneapolis, MN 55420. The descriptions of the following books are from *Imprints*, the catalog of the Birth & Life Bookstore.

Pregnancy, Birth, and Childbirth Preparation

Bean, Constance. *Methods of Childbirth,* rev. 1982. Overview of childbirth preparation options.

Bing, Elisabeth. *Six Practical Lessons for an Easier Childbirth,* 3rd ed. 1982. Step-by-step Lamaze guide. Fully illustrated.

Bing, Elisabeth and Colman, Libby. *Making Love during Pregnancy,* 1977, illustrated guide, created to dispel the myths about having intercourse during pregnancy.

Bradley, Robert. *Husband-coached Childbirth,* 3rd ed., 1981. Basis of the "Bradley method" of childbirth.

Brewer, Gail, editor. *The Pregnancy after 30 Workbook,* 1978. Exercise, self-awareness and diet to help assure a healthy pregnancy, birth and postpartum period.

Brewer, Gail and Greene, Janice. *Right from the Start: Meeting the Challenges of Mothering Your Unborn and Newborn Baby,* 1981. Natural, healthier, more relaxed ways for mothers-to-be to care for themselves and their new babies.

Dale, Barbara and Roeber, Johanna. *The Pregnancy Exercise Book,* 1982. A joyful book about body awareness in pregnancy, nicely illustrated.

Ewy, Donna and Rodger. *Preparation for Childbirth,* 3rd ed. 1982. Popular, well-illustrated Lamaze guide.

Flanagan, Geraldine. *The First Nine Months of Life,* 1962. Baby's development from conception to birth.

Heinowitz, Jack. *Pregnant Fathers: How Fathers Can Enjoy and Share the Experience of Pregnancy and Childbirth,* 1982. Helps parents appreciate the importance of fathers' participation, with a section for childbirth educators.

Kitzinger, Sheila. *The Complete Book of Pregnancy and Childbirth,* 1980. Comprehensive, splendidly illustrated guide.

Kitzinger, Sheila. *The Experience of Childbirth,* 1978. Particular focus on psychological aspects in her "psychosexual" childbirth preparation.

Klaus, Marshall and Kennell, John. *Bonding,* 1983. Early parent-infant attachment, and care of newborn and his family to enhance their relationship; includes unexpected outcomes.

Lansky, Bruce and Vicki. *The Best Baby Name Book in the Whole Wide World,* 1979. Over 10,000 names with meanings, other interesting and useful information.

McKay, Susan. *Assertive Childbirth: The Future Parents' Guide to a Positive Pregnancy,* 1983. Thoughtful survey of birth alternatives during pregnancy.

Nilsson, Linnart. *A Child Is Born,* rev. 1977. Human reproduction from conception to birth with outstanding photographs. New edition has almost all new pictures and an updated text.

Noble, Elizabeth. *Essential Exercises for the Childbearing Year,* rev. 1982. Therapeutic exercises for pregnancy and postpartum restoration.

Noble, Elizabeth. *Having Twins,* 1980. Comprehensive parents' guide on multiple births from conception through early childhood.

Noble, Elizabeth. *Childbirth with Insight,* 1983. How to trust the body and let go during childbirth, allowing labor to take its natural course.

Olkin, Slyvia. *Positive Pregnancy through Yoga,* 1981. Yoga for mental, physical and spiritual adjustment to pregnancy and birth.

Smith, David. *Mothering Your Unborn Baby,* 1979. How to prevent birth defects.

Verney, Thomas. *The Secret Life of the Unborn Child,* 1981. Demonstrates that the unborn child is deeply influenced by his environment well before birth, and explores the significance of that fact.

Alternatives (Home Birth, Etc.)

Anderson, Sandra and Simkin, Penny. *Birth—Through Children's Eyes,* 1981. A complete guide for professionals and parents on children at birth.

Baldwin, Rahima. *Special Delivery: The Complete Guide to Informed Birth,* 1979. Practical guide for couples who want to take greater responsibility for the birth of their babies.

Kitzinger, Sheila. *Birth at Home,* 1979. Risks and advantages of home birth, how to prepare for it, including needs of an older child.

Cesarean Birth

Cohen, Nancy and Estner, Lois. *Silent Knife: Cesarean Prevention and Vaginal Birth After Cesarean (VBAC),* 1983. Powerful, impassioned, thoroughly documented critique of the growing reliance on cesareans, and strategies to prevent unnecessary cesareans.

Hausknecht, Richard and Hellmann. *Having a Cesarean Baby,* 1983. Reasons for cesareans and what to expect.

Meyer, Linda. *The Cesarean (R)evolution,* rev. 1981. Resources and options for family-centered cesareans.

Young, Diony and Mahan, Charles. *Unnecessary Cesareans: Ways to Avoid Them,* 1980. Alternatives to safely avoid a cesarean or make it a better experience.

Women, Health Issues

Boston Women's Health Book Collective. *Our Bodies, Ourselves*, rev. 1976. A comprehensive "course" on the biological and psychological function of women.

Gunn, Terri and Stenzel-Poore, Mary. *The Herpes Handbook*, 1981. Clear, accurate introductory explanation of herpes, with realistic and supportive tone.

Stewart, Felicia, et al. *My Body, My Health*, 1981. A complete guide to gynecology for the concerned woman.

Problem Pregnancies, Grief

Borg, Susan and Lasker, Judith. *When Pregnancy Fails*, 1981. For families coping with miscarriage, stillbirth and infant death, and their support networks.

Friedman, Rochelle and Gradstein, Bonnie. *Surviving Pregnancy Loss*, 1981. Physical and emotional consequences of pregnancy loss, with first person accounts and exploration of future options.

Schwiebert, Patt and Kirk, Paul. *When Hello Means Good-bye*, 1981. Sensitive pamphlet for parents whose child dies at birth or shortly after.

Food, Nutrition

Gazella, Jacqueline. *Nutrition for the Childbearing Year*, 1979. Nutrition guide with menus and recipes, by a nurse-midwife and childbirth educator.

Lansky, Vicki. *Feed Me! I'm Yours*, 1974. Delicious, nutritious and fun recipes for parents.

Lappe, Frances. *Diet for a Small Planet*, rev. 1974. Getting adequate protein in a vegetarian diet.

Williams, Phyllis. *Nourishing Your Unborn Child*, 1982. Nutrition during pregnancy and post partum with menus and recipes.

Worthington, Bonnie. *Nutrition in Pregnancy and Lactation*, 1981. All aspects of maternal nutrition for health professionals.

Breastfeeding

Ewy, Donna. *Preparation for Breastfeeding*, 1975. Clear explanation emphasizing psychological aspects.

Kitzinger, Sheila. *The Experience of Breastfeeding*, 1980. Goes beyond technique to family relationships. A readable, complete guide.

La Leche League. *The Womanly Art of Breastfeeding*, rev. 1981. Enlarged edition of a practical manual by the acknowledged international authorities.

Pryon, Karen. *Nursing Your Baby*, rev. 1973. Informative and stimulating, with discussion of how the breasts function and week-by-week guide.

Riordan, Jan. *A Practical Guide to Breastfeeding*, 1983. Problem solving approach to breastfeeding.

Family Planning

Hatcher, Robert et al.. *It's Your Choice*, 1982. Detailed and practical instructions for choosing a birth control method.

Kass-Annese, Barbara and Danzer, Jan. *Patterns*, 1982. A well-organized explanation of natural family planning and fertility awareness.

Nofziger, Margaret. *A Cooperative Method of Natural Birth Control*, 1976. Combines temperature and mucus methods. Emphasizes responsible cooperation.

Wexler, Jay and Sheila. *Preparing for Conception: A Guide to the Pregnant Year*, 1982. Preconception preparation for the nurturance of optimal conditions.

Parenthood

Boston Women's Health Book Collective. *Ourselves and Our Children*, 1978. Balancing the roles of parent and self.

Colman, Arthur. *Earth Father/Sky Father: The Changing Concept of Fathering*, 1981. Examines fathering models from mythology, literature, contemporary fathers, with emphasis on the nurturing "earth father."

Friedland, Ronnie and Kort, Carol. *The Mother's Book: Shared Experiences*, 1981. Candid personal accounts by mothers on the emotional aspects of mothering.

Galinsky, Ellen. *Between Generations: The Six Stages of Parenthood*, 1981. Parents change and grow in reaction to the demands of the developing child.

Knight, Bryan. *Enjoying Single Parenthood*, 1980. Upbeat guide with worksheets on goals and feelings.

Montagu, Ashley. *Touching: The Human Significance of the Skin*, rev. 1978. Tactile experience is as important as breathing, eating, or resting to the survival of humans.

Rozdilsky, Mary Lou and Banat, Barbara. *What Now?*, 1975. All facets of the adjustment to new parenthood.

Wolfson, Randy and DeLucas, Virginia. *Couples with Children*, 1981. A distillation of couples' experiences in successfully merging parenthood into a marriage.

Child Care and Development

Beck, Joan. *Best Beginnings*, 1983. Guide to a child's optimum care from conception to age 6, and balancing child-raising with career.

Brazelton, Berry. *Infants and Mothers: Differences in Development*, rev. 1983. Variations in normal development in three "typical" infants in their first year.

Brazelton, Berry. *On Becoming a Family: The Growth of Attachment*, 1981. Traces the attachment process as it develops in pregnancy, at birth, and in the early months.

Burtt, Kent and Kalkstein, Karen. *Smart Toys: For Babies from Birth to Two*, 1981. Easy-to-make toys to stimulate your baby's mind.

Caplan, Frank. *The First Twelve Months of Life*, 1973. Each month is separate with text, growth chart, many appealing photos.

Cohen, B. D. *Born at Risk*, 1982. An engrossing look at the care of premature or ill babies in an intensive care nursery.

Fienup-Riordan, Ann. *Shape Up with Baby*, 1981. Postpartum exercises as playtime with baby.

Hagstrom, Julie. *Games Babies Play* and *More Games Babies Play*, 1979. Games to stimulate, relax and entertain babies.

Hart, Terril, M.D., ed. *The Parents' Guide To Baby and Child Medical Care*, 1982. Encyclopedic guide to home treatments for common childhood illnesses, injuries and emergencies.

Hillman, Sheilah. *The Baby Checkup Book*, 1982. A parents' guide to well baby care in the first two years.

Jones, Sandy. *To Love a Baby*, 1981. Combines the art of mothering with recent scientific findings. Outstanding photos.

Lansky, Vicki. *Dear Babysitter*, 1982. General information for babysitters, plus a pad for your instructions.

Lansky, Vicki. *Practical Parenting Tips*, rev. 1982. Over 1000 "it-worked-for-me" ideas.

Leach, Penelope. *Your Baby and Child: From Birth to Age Five*, 1978. Comprehensive and sensitive guide to child care and development. Beautifully illustrated.

Nance, Sherri. *Premature Babies: A Handbook for Parents*, 1982. Written by and for parents of prematures, including how they can handle their fears and anxieties.

Samuels, Mike and Nancy. *The Well Baby Book*, 1979. Holistic approach to pregnancy and child care.

Schneider, Vimala. *Infant Massage: A Handbook for Loving Parents*, 1979. Massage program to enhance infant development, affectional non-verbal communication.

Sears. *Creative Parenting: How to Use the New Continuum Concept to Raise Children Successfully from Birth to Adolescence*, 1982. Comprehensive, well-illustrated child care reference.

Sparling, Joseph and Lewis, Isobel. *Learningames for the First Three Years*, 1981. Combines loving, playing and learning in 100 fully illustrated adult-child games.

Theroux, Rosemary and Tingley, Josephine. *The Care of Twin Children*, 1978. Practical, succinct guide on care of multiples.

Thevenin, Tina. *The Family Bed*, 1976. All aspects of co-family sleeping.

Weiss, Joan. *Your Second Child*, 1981. Theoretical and practical aspects of second-time parenting.

For Children

Baker, Gayle and Montey, Vivian. *Special Delivery: A Book for Kids About Cesarean and Vaginal Birth*, 1981. Conception, birth, mother's recovery, with split text for younger and older children.

Banish, Roslyn. *I Want to Tell You about My Baby*, 1982. A small sibling experiences the family arrival of a new baby. Beguiling text and 45 photos.

Fagerstrom, Grethe. *Our New Baby*, 1982. An expectant family explains the mysteries of sex and birth to their children. Full color cartoon-like illustrations.

Malecki, Maryann. *Mom and Dad and I Are Having a Baby*, 1980. Picture book to prepare children of all ages to be present at birth. Split text.

Malecki, Maryann. *Our Brand New Baby*, 1980. Introduces a child to the joys and frustrations of a new baby in the family. Split text. Ages 3-7.

Nilsson, Lennart. *How Was I Born?*, 1975. Story of reproduction and birth for children. Beautifully illustrated with photos.

Sheffield, Margaret. *Where Do Babies Come From?*, 1973. Beautiful pastel paintings. Explicit without being stark or frightening. Primary ages.

Pamphlets, Posters

Andersen and DelGuidice. *Siblings, Birth and the Newborn*, 1983.

Anderson, Bob. *Pregnancy Stretches*. 17-by-22-inch folded chart.

Edwards, Margot. *A Working Mother Can Breastfeed When . . .*, 1983.

Edwards, Margot. *Childbirth: A Teenager's Guide*, 1978.

Edwards, Margot. *When Food Is Love*, 1977.

Edwards, Margot and Simkin, Penny. *Obstetric Tests and Technology: A Consumer's Guide*, 1980.

Keolker, Kathy. *Cesarean Birth: A Special Delivery*, 1980.

Keolker, Kathy. *Vaginal Birth after Cesarean*, 1981.

Kitzinger, Sheila. *Sex after the Baby Comes*, 1979.

Kitzinger, Sheila. *Sex during Pregnancy*, 1979.

Meadowbrook Press. *Our Baby's First Year*, 1982. Colorful baby record and updated wall calendar.

Myrabo, Jessica. *The First Days after Birth: Care of Mother and Baby*, 1982.

Reinke, Carla. *Herpes in Pregnancy*, 1982.

Simkin, Penny and Edwards, Margot. *When Your Baby Has Jaundice*, 1980.

Simkin, Penny and Reinke, Carla. *Planning Your Baby's Birth*, 1979.

Wallerstein, Edward. *The Circumcision Decision*, 1980.

Wallerstein, Edward. *When Your Baby Boy Is Not Circumcised*, 1981.

White, Rulena. *Fitness during Pregnancy*, 1983.

Young, Diony. *Bonding*, 1978.

Index

Boldface numbers refer to pages on which definitions or descriptions of key terms will be found.

You and Me, Baby

The YMCA's Official Guide To Prenatal, Postpartum, and Infant Exercise

This medically approved exercise program was developed by a national commitee of the YMCA to offer a safe fitness and health plan for expectant mothers. The easy-to-follow step-by-step instructions show you how to exercise to prepare for a healthy delivery, control weight gain and get back into shape after baby is born. There is also instruction on baby massage and how to exercise with your child. **Only $8.75 ppd.**

First-Year Baby Care

Edited by Paula Kelly, M.D.

The practical up-to-date guide for new parents. It's fully illustrated with over 100 step-by-step photographs and illustrations in a handy format. Dr. Paula Kelly includes what you want to know and what you need to know, from bathing and diapering to handling medical emergencies and baby development. It is authoritative yet practical and easy to use. The perfect companion for new parents. **Only $6.75 ppd.**

Baby & Child Medical Care

A first aid and home treatment guide that shows parents how to handle over 150 common childhood illnesses in step-by-step illustrated treatment format. Edited by Terril H. Hart, M.D., it contains: — *index of symptoms — record forms — height and weight charts — accident prevention — childproofing tips.* **Only $8.75 ppd.**

The Best Baby Name Book In The Whole Wide World

America's best-selling baby name book by Bruce and Vicki Lansky. More names, more up-to-date, more helpful, more entertaining, more gifty than any other baby name book! — *over 10,000 boys' and girls' names . . . more than any other book — how to name your baby: 15 rules — name psychology and stereotypes.* **Only $3.75 ppd.**

My First Years

A beautiful baby record book to save your precious memories from arrival day to kindergarten! The colorful padded cover is reproduced from an original cross-stitch design of the *My First Friends* animals, with a delicate framing border. There are 32 pages of popular subjects like the family tree, a growth record, medical history, the first birthday, favorite photos, and many more. It is also gift boxed to be the perfect shower or new-arrival gift. **Only $11.75 ppd.**

Our Baby's First Year

A colorful Baby Record Calendar that hangs on the nursery wall for handy use! OUR BABY'S FIRST YEAR is a "universal date" calendar plus a record book: 13 complete months for recording the "big events" of baby's first year as they happen. The day-by-day write-in spaces are undated, so OUR BABY'S FIRST YEAR starts whenever the baby arrives and lasts 13 months—a complete first year! For added convenience and color you can use the "baby's-firsts" stickers to mark the important milestones. Each month features a colorful baby animal nursery character to decorate the room, plus month-by-month development and baby care tips for quick reference. There's even a family tree and birth record form! A colorful and practical baby gift. **Only $9.50 ppd.**

ORDER FORM

Name _____

Address _____

City _____ State _____ Zip _____

Charge ☐ Visa ☐ Mastercharge Acct # _____ Expiration Date _____

Signature _____

Check or money order payable to Meadowbrook

Qty.	Title	Cost Per Book	Amount
			Total

We do not ship C.O.D. Postage and handling included in all prices.

18318 Minnetonka Boulevard • Deephaven, Minnesota 55391